HAPPY
CRUELTY
DAY!

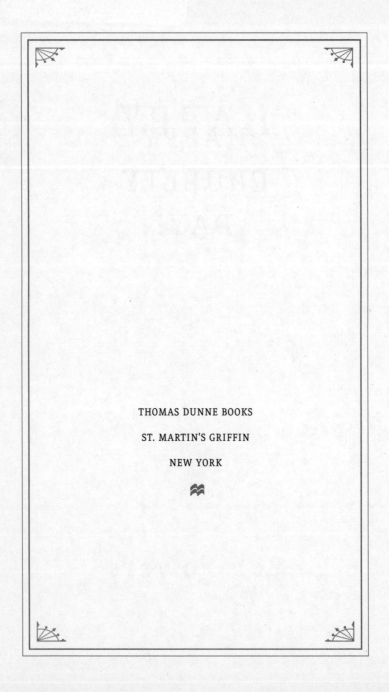

THOMAS DUNNE BOOKS

ST. MARTIN'S GRIFFIN

NEW YORK

HAPPY CRUELTY DAY!

Daily Celebrations of
Quiet Desperation

Bob Powers

THOMAS DUNNE BOOKS.

An imprint of St. Martin's Press.

Image on page x: 1916. Robert Dennis Collection of Stereoscopic Views, Photography Collection, Miriam & Ira D. Wallach Division of Art, Prints & Photographs, the New York Public Library [reproduction number: NYPG91-F81 005F]. Image on page 2: Gondola on the Grand Canal, Venice, Italy. ca. 1900–1910. Library of Congress, Prints and Photographs Division, Detroit Publishing Company Collection [reproduction number: LC-D4-42808 DLC]. Image on page 38: Delano, Jack. On the Ferris wheel at the Vermont state fair, Rutland. 1941. Library of Congress, Prints and Photographs Division, FSA-OWI Collection [reproduction number: LC-DIG-fsac-1a33918 DLC]. Image on page 66: Horydczak, Theodor. ca. 1920–1950. Library of Congress, Prints and Photographs Division, Theodor Horydczak Collection [reproduction number: LC-H814-T-2241-074-A DLC]. Image on page 100: 1918. *Chicago Daily News* negatives collection, SDN-061584. Courtesy of the Chicago Historical Society. Image on page 134: Bonn, Philip. 1943. Library of Congress, Prints and Photographs Division, FSA-OWI Collection [reproduction number: LC-USW3-033418-EDLC]. Image on page 170: USS *Saratoga*, aircraft carrier. ca. 1940–1946. Library of Congress, Prints and Photographs Division, FSA-OWI Collection [reproduction number: LC-USE6-D-008669 DLC]. Image on page 206: Palmer, Alfred T. 1942. Library of Congress, Prints and Photographs Division, FSA-OWI Collection [reproduction number: LC-USE6-D-007927 DLC]. Image on page 244: © Photographer: Rebecca Abell, Agency: Dreamstime.com. Image on page 276: Horydczak, Theodor. ca. 1920–1950. Library of Congress, Prints and Photographs Division, Theodor Horydczak Collection [reproduction number: LC-H812-T-C09-004 DLC]. Image on page 304: Delano, Jack. Daniel Field, Georgia. Air Service Command. A Weight-Lifting Class. 1943. Library of Congress, Prints and Photographs Division, FSA-OWI Collection [reproduction number: LC-USW3-034913-DDLC]. Image on page 336: In Need of a Heart.© 2005 Whiting, Joshua. Flickr.com. Image on page 370: Horydczak, Theodor. 1935. Library of Congress, Prints and Photographs Division, Theodor Horydczak Collection [reproduction number: LC-H813-C06-016 DLC].

www.thomasdunnebooks.com

www.stmartins.com

Book design by Susan Walsh

Library of Congress Cataloging-in-Publication Data

Powers, Bob, 1973–
    Happy cruelty day! : daily celebrations of quiet desperation / Bob Powers.—1st ed.
        p. cm.
    ISBN-13: 978-0-312-35952-2
    ISBN-10: 0-312-35952-7
    1. Holidays—Humor.

PN6231.H547 P69 2007
818'.607—dc22

2006034536

10 9 8 7 6 5 4 3 2

For Amanda:

Ignore that knock

CONTENTS

INTRODUCTION

Popular legend has it that many years ago a teenage boy and his mother were digging a grave in which to bury the boy's father, his mother's husband. It was said that the boy's father, his mother's husband, "done got what he deserved and deserved what he done got."

While digging, the boy discovered in the dirt a book of handwritten pages bound together with string. It had apparently been buried just a foot underneath the grass. The boy's mother told him to hold on to the book, in case they might be able to sell it later. They needed to hang on to things that they could sell.

The boy later discovered that the book contained a calendar of holidays spanning an unspecified year. He cherished the book while he was alive, which was not very long. The boy did his best to observe the holidays detailed in the book, an effort that soon brought about his swift, painful, and very embarrassing accidental death.

Over the years, the book passed in and out of different hands, and was rescued from this antique shop and that hospital's burn bin, until it fell into the possession of Bob Powers. Bob took those scribbled pages and employed a great deal of editorial license to compile those old writings into this book, *Happy Cruelty Day!*

Bob claims that the writing in this book is his. It is not. But until this fact can be proven, Bob will continue to reap profit from those scribbled pages that a teenage boy found in his father's shallow grave so many years ago.

A NOTE OF CAUTION

This is a book of holidays offering instruction and inspiration for how each day of the year is to be lived and celebrated. It is to be disregarded. Actually adhering to the instructions contained within this book is very dangerous to yourself and those close to you.

Only a handful of people are known to have attempted to follow the instructions of *Happy Cruelty Day!* and they have met with various tragic fates. One woman in Vancouver, British Columbia, got pregnant out of wedlock immediately before being arrested for treason as a direct result of her devotion to the writings in this book. The woman was eventually hanged and her son is being raised by the state. He will seek vengeance.

Another man in Gainesville, Florida, followed the book for just six days before he got stuck inside a refrigerator. And after going missing for several weeks, an entire Dutch family of six was found dead in a tunnel dug underneath their home that had apparently caved in and trapped them there. A dog-eared and underlined copy of *Happy Cruelty Day!* was found with them.

Not only is this book not to be followed, it should be actively ignored. Even those who adopt a much more casual devotion to the book's guidance can only follow it for so long before contracting rabies when they try to place a birthday hat on a raccoon. The purpose of *Happy Cruelty Day!* is not to provide strict, step-by-step instructions for your life. *Happy Cruelty Day!* merely offers a sketch of the life that could and should be yours, were you to devote yourself to a life of passion, vengeance, and heartbreak. It is recommended that you read this book only as an amusing entertainment, a fanciful diversion as you continue to walk a careful path through your chilling and loveless journey to the grave.

JANUARY

DON'T LET THEM GO.

TELL A STRANGER AT A BAR YOUR
STORY DAY!

Pick the spot at the bar where it seems like no matter how crowded and
rowdy and young it gets all around you, your little section of stools is as
solemn as a confessional. Someone is going to approach you with a half-
hearted pickup line, but you'll know by her tone that she has no interest in
getting inside your pants. She'll approach you because she can tell by the
way you're sipping that scotch that you've got one hell of a story in your
belly. Whether you respond to her line or not, she'll climb up onto the stool
next to yours and wait. You might be suspicious at first, but you know
you've got only one choice.

Tell your story tonight, or it dies with you.

No one's saying what your story should be about, but people enjoy hearing about fires being set to things for insurance money. Unfaithful spouses
and hitchhiking ghosts on highways can be quite intriguing as well. If your
story involves important details like "Pilates class enrollment forms" or
the words "math camp," embellish. Just make sure you get it all out before
the bartender says, "Last call."

After you tell the story, you should take your audience back to your
place and make urgent love. Assuming, of course, that you don't die by your
own hand in the rest room first.

Happy Tell a Stranger at a Bar Your Story Day!

JANUARY 2   JILL THE SEXY EXTERMINATOR DAY!

When Jill the Sexy Exterminator knocks on your door, you'll be trying to drag a drug dealer's corpse into the bathroom so that you can begin sawing him apart in the tub.

"Am I interrupting something?" Jill the Sexy Exterminator will ask coquettishly.

Say, "It's not what you think."

Jill the Sexy Exterminator will shut the door behind her and say, "What I think is that a very handsome man has a dead body to dispose of and he's so frazzled he might not even have time to make love to his exterminator."

Let the drug dealer's body drop to the floor and say, "I'll make time." Then make love to Jill the Sexy Exterminator.

When you're done making love, go back into the bathroom and start sawing the drug dealer's body apart while Jill the Sexy Exterminator sprays your baseboards and behind the fridge with insecticide.

Happy Jill the Sexy Exterminator Day!

JANUARY 3   GONDOLA RIDE DAY!

When a young boy and girl in love solicit you for a ride in your gondola, tell them with a sigh that they are on. When they ask you how much the ride will cost, tell them that today, money cannot buy them a gondola ride. Today, if they simply allow their gondola conductor to ask them three questions over the course of the ride, and they answer these questions sincerely, their fare will be paid. Some couples will refuse and go to another gondola because their love depends upon certain questions never being asked. Others will agree to the arrangement, because they are low on money.

At the start of the ride, the couple will be afraid to start making out because their anticipation of the first question will be too great. Put them at ease by posing a very simple question right away. Ask them, "Where did the two of you meet?" in an Italian accent.

They will excitedly recount the interminable tale of a mutual friend's birthday party. Both will say that they didn't like each other very much at first but agreed to a date anyway and before they knew it, the world was new. Just pretend to listen while craning your neck to look up skirts as you pass under footbridges.

Once they finish their story, tell them, "The next question will come in time. Enjoy the ride," in an Italian accent. The boy and the girl will begin making out furiously as the gondola passes through the city. Watch them.

After about ten minutes, their desire will have reached a fever pitch. That's when you should stab your oar into the bed of the canal. The couple will be flung forward from their seats, facedown into the belly of the gondola. Say, "Next question!" in an Italian accent.

The boy will help the girl into her seat and they will wait, annoyed. Employing an Italian accent, ask them how each would like to mourn the other, should the other die. The boy will react with indignation, but the girl will look startled, as if you've revealed a secret. The boy will protest that he would never think such a horrible thought. And the girl will say, "I'd like to disappear."

Silenced, the boy will wait for the girl to continue. She'll say to the boy, "I think about you dying every day. Not like I'm hoping for it. But not with dread either. Just to think about an event. A time when everyone is watching me, everyone is worrying about how I'm holding up. And if I disappear, which I'd like to do, a time when everyone will wonder where I am. When everyone will hope that I'll come home."

For the rest of the ride, the boy and the girl will look off away from each other at the walls of the canal. Avert your eyes from them. Simply pull the craft through the water with gentle strokes of your oar.

After a while, the boy will ask for the final question, saying that he would like to return to their hotel. Tell him, "The final question will come in time. Enjoy the ride," in an Italian accent. The boy will complain of fatigue and request to be brought to land. Using the Italian accent, say, "But I have not asked, and you have not answered, three questions. Therefore you have not paid. If you try to flee from my gondola without paying your fare, I will call the police." The boy will become irate, but don't ask him anything.

Don't let them go.

Happy Gondola Ride Day!

| JANUARY 4 | GIVE UP DAY! |

We're all tryin' to climb that wall, aren't we? And sometimes we take on projects that can be a bit challenging. Well today's the day to look challenge in the eye and say, *"Fuck this!"* Whether it be an unwieldy draft of a screenplay, a savings account, or efforts toward seminal fertilization, just rip one item off your to-do list and throw it in the trash can. You'll feel quite a weight lift off your shoulders, let me tell you, boy.

Happy Give Up Day!

| JANUARY 5 | THE WAY MAIL CARRIERS HAVE SEX DAY! |

Today, after you sign for an express mail package, you'll wander through the living room and spot your twelve-year-old daughter leaning on the windowsill, peeking through the glass.

"Whatcha doin' there, pumpkin?" you'll say to her.

You'll peek over her shoulder and see her staring at the mail carrier sorting through his mailbag. You'll know what's coming next.

"Daddy, how do they . . ."

They gave her the special health class a month ago, and ever since then she's been brimming over with questions.

"How do mail carriers have sex?" you'll ask.

You daughter will turn her beautiful and still babyish eyes up at you and nod.

"Let's sit down on the couch and stop staring, okay?"

Take your daughter away from the window and sit her on your knee. She's almost too big for that now. She's growing up so fast.

"From what I understand," tell her, "sex between mail carriers is born from a place of extreme anger. The old joke goes that whenever you see two mail carriers having sex, you don't have to beat your kids that night. I guess that's supposed to mean that their coupling usurps the anger from everyone within the vicinity of their clenched-fisted love."

"But you've never beaten me, Daddy," your daughter will say.

"No, I never have." Give her a kiss on the top of her head. "And I never will."

"Does that mean you watch mail carriers have sex with each other every day?"

"I wish!" say. "If there was a club like that it'd never go out of business."

You'll laugh at your own joke, but your daughter won't.

Say, "All joking aside, mail carriers get into lots of hair pulling and slapping at each other. To the point where it can go too far."

Your daughter will ask, "But why are they so angry?"

"When I was growing up most of them had just gotten back from Vietnam and they were pissed off at how no one ever gave them a parade. Nowadays, they're mostly cheesed that we can't seem to wean ourselves off of the big sweet tits of Arab oil."

Just then you'll hear a ruckus outside. You and your daughter will go to the window just in time to spy a girl mail carrier run up the sidewalk and smack the boy mail carrier in the face with a wad of Valpaks. They'll wrestle a little before the boy mail carrier throws the girl mail carrier into the back of his mail truck and climbs in after her. The truck will begin to shake.

Pull the shade down on the window. "Let's give those two some privacy, shall we?"

Your daughter will giggle and she'll make the hand gesture for intercourse by touching her index finger and thumb together and then sticking her other index finger through the hole it makes. You'll wish your wife were still alive to see this.

Happy the Way Mail Carriers Have Sex Day!

JANUARY 6	DANCE TO NOTHING DAY!

Today, alcohol and nudity will be a big help. Privacy is a plus as well. You can dance as long as you like, with only one condition. You have to dance boisterously and erotically (if you can muster it) to absolutely nothing. Close the windows and the blinds, unplug the stereo and even the phone, because that ring can provide a rhythm. Just get in front of a mirror and undulate like you want nothing more than to sway with your reflection until the earth caves under. Look at your nipples as your arms fly up into the silence. You're pretty when you dance and that look on your face tells me I did not have to point that out to you.

Happy Dance to Nothing Day!

JANUARY 7	JOIN A COMMUNITY CRIME WATCH
	PROGRAM IN AN EFFORT TO MAKE
	FRIENDS DAY!

What have you got to lose? If you go to their weekly meeting at least you can say you only spend six nights a week alone in your apartment reading. Just go and try to fit in.

Someone at the meeting (if a man, he will have a beard; if a woman, she will wear a tight-fitting black turtleneck to reveal breasts of a decidedly aggressive shape and lift) will shout with indignation, "Let's show those bastards whose neighborhood this is!" Make sure that when you shout, "Yeah!" you gesture with your upper body broadly enough that people might notice you, but not so broadly that they can tell you've felt so very alone for as long as you can remember. At the end of the meeting, reach out to others with questions like, "What kind of batteries should I buy for my flashlight?" or, "You ever see any shit go down, man?"

Near the end of your third meeting, following the announcements about privately run self-defense classes and requests for increased coffee and donut donations, when everyone's getting into their coats, just shout out, "Hey, anyone up for getting a beer?" If people say, "Maybe next time," then it's cool. Come back next week. But if no one responds, as if they're pretending you didn't even speak, that'll let you know that you blew it again. They don't like you. And it's safe to assume that they've already planned on getting a beer together, and they will make such a concerted effort to exclude you as to walk off in separate directions and then double back to meet at O'Flannagan's Pub once enough time has passed to ensure that you've already gone home to your apartment.

It's all part of the fun on Join a Community Crime Watch Program in an Effort to Make Friends Day!

| JANUARY 8 | ARMY MEN DAY!

You've been seeing a lot more army men walking through the main square of your town in full fatigues, armed to the hilt and looking at everything with that Thousand-Yard Stare™ thing. Sometimes they'll just be waiting in line at the Dairy Queen to get a canteen filled up with water. Other times, they'll be lying flat on their bellies in the middle of the sidewalk, making bird noises at each other. And still other times, they'll open fire on anything that moves.

The next time you see one who doesn't appear to be too involved in any sort of skirmish, go up to him and tug on the ammo belt he wears around his shoulder. When he looks down at you, ask, "Are you all ghosts?"

Happy Army Men Day!

| JANUARY 9 | YOUR PARENTS ARE AN
                 INTERRACIAL COUPLE DAY!

It's been a long while since you congratulated them for their bravery.

Tonight, when you've all finished dinner, and your dad says to your mom, "Black lady, nice food," and your mom says, "Only the best, white mother-fucker," say to the both of them, "I hope you've saved some room for dessert."

Then give them the cake you spent all day cooking from scratch.

They'll read the writing on the cake in unison: "Courage?"

Say, "I made it in honor of you guys not being the same race but falling in love anyway. It's a strawberry shortcake."

Your mom will burst into tears. "I didn't think you'd noticed."

"That you guys aren't the same race? Sure I did. That's what everyone's always spray-painting our house about, right?"

Now you'll see that your dad is crying. "No," he'll say. "How hard it was to pull this off. We thought you didn't care. I mean it was really, really hard."

"I know," you'll say. You're going to start getting a little annoyed now. "That's why I made you the cake? Hello?"

Your mom will get ahold of herself. "It's just kind of like that movie about that guy. The one who struggled."

Your dad will smash his fist into the table and say that that movie sucked. They'll start fighting again and you'll run from the table and hide in your room. The fighting will turn them both on and they'll go upstairs and make forbidden love. When you come downstairs in the morning, they won't have touched the cake. But they will have conceived your future baby sister.

Happy Your Parents Are an Interracial Couple Day!

| JANUARY 10 | TIE A MASK AROUND YOUR EYES DAY! |

You feel pretty awful starting work as a paperboy at the age of thirty-three. But there's no reason why you can't make something fun out of it. And tying a mask around your eyes is a perfect way to do that. This way, when kids on their way to school see you pushing your shopping cart full of papers and they ask, "You're the paperboy?!" you can respond, "I am the Masked Paperboy! Every morning I shall bring the news to my fellow townsfolk, anonymously feeding people's hearts and minds with objective facts."

"Do you write what's in the paper?" the kids will ask.

Lie. "Yes!"

The kids will walk away giggling. One will say, "I didn't know Donny's brother was retarded."

You're Donny's brother.

Happy Tie a Mask Around Your Eyes Day!

| JANUARY 11 | FOURTEEN WAYS TO TELL A CAJUN |
| | CHEF TO GO FUCK HIMSELF DAY! |

Today at the upscale food court the guy stirring the pots at the "Gumbo Galore" counter is going to piss you off royally when he brings up your dead wife.

He'll be shouting at passersby stuff like, "Git on up and git some gumbo, I guar-on-tee!" With some potential customers he'll offer up a personal pitch. Stuff like, "Man wears a tie that ugly he won't mind spillin' a little bit of this city's finest Cajun gumbo all over that [garbled]." When you walk past, with no desire to eat any Cajun food because, frankly, you think it blows, the chef will shout out, "What's with the sour face, *mon frère*? Only way a man could frown like that is if he was in week two of mourning over his tragically lost young wife, I guar-on-tee!"

Yes, he's very perceptive, and maybe you are wearing your loss on your sleeve a little bit, but that doesn't mean you shouldn't tell him to go fuck himself. Here's how!

First, say, "What'd you say? As a matter of fact my wife did die recently. Why don't you go fuck yourself?"

The Cajun chef will apologize for hitting a nerve and will suggest you wash away your pain with a bowl of some gumbo.

Say, "How 'bout you shove that gumbo up your flabby ass, you hear me, Mardi Gras?"

The Cajun chef will ask if you'd perhaps care for a nice shrimp po' boy.

Say, "Listen, James Carville, your food's stupid, your accent's stupid, and to top it all off you work in a food court. Even with all that against you, I still say you should go fuck yourself."

The Cajun chef will ask if you'd like some jambalaya.

Say, "No, I don't want some jambalaya. I want my wife back. She back there? No? Oh, I forgot, she's in the ground. Then how 'bout you go fuck yourself instead."

The Cajun chef will say that the conversation you and he are having is the closest he's come to a friendship since grade school. He'll tell you that his father was in the army and that he switched schools a lot.

Say, "If you were at a school for five minutes I bet the whole school would meet for an assembly so that they'd all be sure to tell you to go fuck yourself before you moved to the next base. Go fuck yourself, Ellen Barkin in *The Big Easy*."

The Cajun chef will shout entreaties for other customers to come to his counter.

Say to the other customers, "Stay away from this food. It's being prepared by a chef who is about to go fuck himself."

The Cajun chef will throw his ladle on the ground in frustration. Then he will hand you a card for a grief counselor that he knows. He'll say, "This guy can help you. Maybe you should just go."

Rip the card up and throw it on the ground. Say, "Go fuck yourself, Anne Rice."

The Cajun chef will say, "You can tell me to fuck myself all you want, but I'm only going to respond by trying to make amends. And by trying to get you to taste my delicious muffaletta sandwich."

Smack the sandwich out of his hand and say, "I miss her so much I can't even breathe. I can't sleep in our bed because I wake up panting. Aw God. Go fuck yourself, Buckwheat Zydeco."

The Cajun chef will ask his manager if he can go on break. He'll lead you out to his car and open up the trunk. "Take a look in there," he'll say.

Say, "Go fuck yourself, Creole." Then look inside the trunk. There will be a picnic basket.

The Cajun chef will say, "There are no perishables in there. Just some drinks, plates and utensils, and sealed snacks. But I can fill this basket within five minutes and we can have ourselves a picnic. What do you say?"

Say, "Go fuck yourself." Then get in his car and wait for him to fill up the basket with Cajun deliciousness.

At the park, the Cajun chef will pull out a Frisbee. He'll say, "You throw?"

Say, "I'll throw so hard you'll have no choice but to fuck yourself with that thing." Then cavort about the field with him until the guilt overwhelms you.

The Cajun chef will see you doubled over with tears and he'll shout, "I'll come over there and hold you if you let me! I guar-on-tee!"

Shout back, "Go fuck yourself, Decatur Street!"

The Cajun chef will begin walking toward you. "She'd want you to move on," he'll shout.

Scream back at him, "Goddammit, you didn't know this woman! The world should have stopped when she left. Asking me to go on is like asking me to commit a crime against nature!" Cry a little into the back of your hand, then add, "Go fuck yourself, cayenne pepper."

The Cajun chef will be standing before you. He'll put his arms around you. Just give up and fall into his embrace. He'll say, "Just let me carry the load. Just for a minute."

Let his compassion seep in and course through your veins. Let it disarm you. You'll feel so tired you won't have any choice but to stay there in his arms and let him hold you up. Say, "This doesn't change anything. You should still go fuck yourself. Guar-on-tee?"

The Cajun chef will pat your back. "Guar-on-tee," he'll say. "Shhh. I guar-on-tee."

Happy Fourteen Ways to Tell a Cajun Chef to Go Fuck Himself Day!

| JANUARY 12 | TELL YOUR DAD YOU'RE IN LOVE |
| | WITH A GIRL DAY! |

Sit down on the couch to the right of him in his easy chair.

"I met a girl, Dad," say.

Your dad will say, "Get ready for some pain."

"I don't think so, Dad," say. "She loves me and I love her. And I can feel it in my bones, we're never going to do anything but make each other happy."

Your dad will laugh so hard he'll die. You'll bring your girlfriend to the funeral. During the priest's eulogy at the burial, she'll sneak off and cheat on you behind a tree.

Happy Tell Your Dad You're in Love with a Girl Day!

| JANUARY 13 | **WHEN YOU OVERTURN THE HYUNDAI AT TONIGHT'S RACE RIOT, MAKE SURE CHICKS ARE WATCHING DAY!** |

Shall we call you "Mr. Big Strong Tough Guy with the Rage of an Entire Oppressed Ancestry Stirring in His Belly"? Or would a more appropriate name be "Jeff Lonely"?

There, there, we all know how hard it is to find that special lady. Especially when you're so busy trying to tear down over three hundred years of imperialist infrastructure one caved-in cop's head at a time. Who has the patience for dating?!

Well I think we both know where there's gonna be some pretty white college girls who share your interests and would do anything for you if you would only tell them they're absolutely right about how ignorant their parents are. At tonight's race riot, that's where!

They're going to be watching you because they're not really sure what they should be chanting and when (the only one they know is "No Justice, No Peace," which they saw an angry mob chanting on MTV when they were eleven).

No one's suggesting that you exploit the cause. All that's being suggested is when you rock the Hyundai back and forth on its axle until it flips over to its side and finally tips over onto the roof, just put a little swagger in it.

Chicks dig confidence, and showboats get laid (FACT!). Just hop up on the car's underbelly and start taunting the riot police from on high, getting all the other rioters to cheer you on. If you get a blackjack to the neck, any one of those recently matriculated suburbanites is yours for the choosing. And remember, the jail cells are gonna be mighty crowded tonight and they might be forced to go coed. Those cots are wider than you think.

Just consider it. You might save yourself thirty-five bucks for an online personals profile.

Happy When You Overturn the Hyundai at Tonight's Race Riot, Make Sure Chicks Are Watching Day!

| JANUARY 14 | S.W.A.T. AT FIRST SIGHT DAY!

Today, while rappelling thirty-eight stories down the side of a high-rise in anticipation of crashing through the windows of a known drug-running operation, you'll spy a pair of eyes possessed of such tenderness that you'll fear you might fill your night vision goggles with a torrent of tears.

You'll stop still and stare through the glass. She'll be on her couch, a remote control in her hand, her elegant gaze holding you hostage.

Lift your night vision goggles to your forehead and place your hand flat on the pane of glass. She'll rise and walk to the window. Her legs will be bare, but she'll be wearing a long men's dress shirt over her underwear.

A men's dress shirt. She has a lover. Perhaps she's a visitor to this apartment.

Or perhaps she has a husband.

When she places her bare palm against the silhouette of your black-gloved hand on the glass, you'll feel as if you've both tumbled naked onto a honeymoon suite mattress. Whatever her situation might be in regards to that men's dress shirt, it's just been changed irrevocably.

The swirling wind around you will carry the shouts of "Go! Go! Go!" belted out from your fellow team members below. There'll be a crash of glass. You'll smile at her and she'll smile back. Let yourself free-fall the remaining nine floors. And when you crash through the glass and release the contents of your AK-47 into as many chests as you can hold in your rifle sight, you won't hear a thing except for what's singing through your head.

Seventeenth floor. She's on the seventeenth floor. Just up there. On the seventeenth floor.

Happy S.W.A.T. at First Sight Day!

JANUARY 15　　KURT COBAIN DAY!

A lot of people think they can observe Kurt Cobain Day simply by wearing a cardigan sweater to work. When those people die they are going to go to hell. Solemn and heartful observance of Kurt Cobain Day involves three brief, measured rituals.

First, make some French toast. If Kurt Cobain's ghost comes by while you're eating French toast, he'll probably lick his pretty pink lips and say, "Man, I sure wish I could eat some French toast." Then he'll probably just hover over your table and look really jealous. When you're finished with your breakfast, look up at Kurt Cobain's ghost and say, "Shouldn't have killed yourself, Cobain. Fame might be a bitch, but French toast is still delicious."

Second, push your thumbs into your eyeballs until you rip narrow caverns into them and they spew forth with gelatinous eye goo. If Kurt Cobain's ghost shows up he'll probably say, "Oh Jesus! Why'd you do that?" Tell him that he robbed the world of his beautiful blue eyes and so you decided to blind yourself for some reason. When he says, "Ew!" tell him it's pussy-ass reactions like that that kept him from being able to deal with stress and that's why he blew his own head off. Then call him a faggot.

Third, hug somebody who's attractive when Kurt Cobain's ghost is watching. From over the shoulder of the attractive person, give Cobain's ghost a look that says, "Kinda wish you could have yourself a little squeeze of this, don'tcha, baby boy? You probably could've. If you hadn't swallowed a shotgun in your garage, that is. By the way, next office party, I'ma fuck this. You wanna bet?" Kurt Cobain's ghost won't make a bet because he knows you probably will make that shit happen, especially if the two of you have had a lot to drink. Kurt Cobain's ghost will be real jealous though, because even in death he still remembers that intercourse was lots of fun.

Happy Kurt Cobain Day!

| JANUARY 16 | TELL PEOPLE YOU TOOK A FRIEND FOR AN ABORTION DAY! |

When someone asks you how your day's been going, tell him or her that it's been rough because you had to take a friend to an abortion clinic this morning. If they ask if they know the "friend," only say, "I really shouldn't be talking about this."

Happy Tell People You Took a Friend for an Abortion Day!

| JANUARY 17 | TELL THE TOW TRUCK DRIVER WHERE TO TAKE YOU DAY! |

Tell him how when you walked out the door with your suitcase, your girlfriend told you you wouldn't get far. Tell him how angry you are that she'll be proven right yet again, and all because your car crapped out on you. Tell him how hard it's going to be to walk back into that house and crawl into bed next to her, but you know how to do it. You're used to it. You just crawl in next to her and lie with your back to her back. She doesn't say a word. She doesn't roll over to tell you she's glad you're back, or even to say that she told you so. She just stays still as the dead.

"You don't even talk about it?" the tow truck driver will ask.

Tell him that she never speaks to you until you apologize for getting angry and trying to leave. That she once stayed silent for six whole days before you told her you were sorry. Then she starts to gloat. She tells you you're too careful. That you're too afraid of something going wrong to really do something drastic. Tell him that just once you'd like for her to be the one to apologize. To get far enough away and stay there long enough to make her beg you to come back.

"She didn't want me to renew my AAA membership. She said if our car breaks down, we can hitch. It's ironic that my being careful is what's allowing me to be towed safe and sound right back to her."

You and the tow truck driver will climb into the cab and the tow truck driver will tell you that you were wise to be careful.

"Your AAA membership buys you a hundred-mile tow anywhere you wanna be. Now lucky for you, one hundred miles can get you all the way across the state line. Is leaving the state far enough away to make her pay attention?"

Tell him yes, and you have a friend who lives across the state line. He'll let you crash.

Your tow truck driver will say, "Thank you for using AAA, my friend." Then he'll peel out, letting the squeal from his tires scream the good-bye you never could scream yourself.

Happy Tell the Tow Truck Driver Where to Take You Day!

| JANUARY 18 | IMPRESS YOUR MOM DAY! |

Moms want to know that their little girls and boys have grown into big, strong women and men who can drink a shitload. So go and pay your mom a surprise visit.

When she greets you at the door, she'll say, "My goodness! What are you doing here?!" Or maybe, "To what do I owe this honor?" if your mom is hilarious. Put your hands on her shoulders and say, "Take a seat, Momma. I want to show you how good I am at drinking now."

She'll have anticipation twinkling in her eyes as she watches you fish through your backpack. Pull the can of Budweiser from your bag with a broad flourish. Then hold it out to your mom and say, "Would you like to inspect the can for any hidden wires?" She'll either laugh or she won't, it doesn't fucking matter.

Take her hand and say, "Momma, when I was younger, I wasn't very good at drinking beer. Looking back at the person I once was, I find that person laughable. Youth was no excuse. I should've been better at drinking. You and Father must have been so disappointed in me.

"I flew out here today to show you that you were a good mother to me, and I wanted to give you a chance to see all that you have to be proud of before you die soon."

Then hold the can in position to be popped open, take a deep breath, look your mother in the eye, and say, "Check this shit, y'all." Then pop the can open and slam that shit down your throat like it's gonna stop a car crash. When the can's empty, slap it into your skull until it's a disc, and then fling it like a Frisbee at your aged cat. Then say, "Aw fuck yes!"

Your mother will rise slowly and extend her arms to you, her lips quivering with joyful sobs. Take her to you and hold her. She is your mother and she is proud of you. Not just for what you can do, but because you want her to be proud of what you can do. This, ultimately, is the real evidence that she was a good mother to you.

Happy Impress Your Mom Day!

DO LAUNDRY UNTIL YOU GET
FUCKED DAY!

Based on pretend surveys that were never conducted ever, the Laundromat is one of the most ideal places to find yourself suddenly engaged in casual sex with a complete stranger. The following is a step-by-step guide for how to have sex with something while washing your pants.

First, get in the mood. Remember that hardly anyone in the place is wearing underwear. And the ones that are underwear-clad are wearing such a rank pair that they can smell their genitals waft up to their noses every time they take a step. While sex may not be in the air, genitals, at least, most decidedly are.

Second, bring something to read that isn't fucking retarded. You want someone to be able to say, "Hey, I read that too," and no one's going to do that if you're reading *How to Be a Working Actor*. Bring *The Corrections* or *The Unbearable Lightness of Being*. Even people who can't read have tried to read those, and they won't be afraid to ask you about them.

Third, while folding, sway just so.

Fourth, if you spot someone trying to fold a blanket alone, offer your help. Folding a blanket with a stranger in a Laundromat is the only situation wherein you and a stranger can open your arms wide and walk toward each other until your noses might touch. Wanna get your point across? Touch noses. If that works, rub your front up against him/her. He/she diggin' it? Then kiss. He/she still not shying away? Start fucking. Right then and there. Aw man.

Fifth, if you're a guy, pick up a girl's underwear and say, "You must look so fucking hot in these." If you're a girl, pick up your underwear and say to some guy, "Dude, you wouldn't believe how totally fuckable I look in these fucking panties." Then ask each other about each other's reading materials.

Sixth, always carry a box of dryer sheets with only one dryer sheet left in the box. You can start a conversation by offering the dryer sheet to the person you want to fuck with the line, "I used up all my dryer sheets because you've been making me so motherfucking wet. You want this last one so I don't have to carry around the box all night?"

Seventh, men, let him or her know you're in the mood by slamming the dryer door shut with your erect cock.

Eighth, if you wanna do laundry until you get fucked but you live at home with your mom and dad and they have a washer and dryer in the house, go to a Laundromat anyway. I know it's a haul, but don't fuck your mom and dad.

Ninth, and most importantly, I know it's laundry day and I know you don't have any clean clothes left, but please don't wear that IT'S A CHILD, NOT A CHOICE! T-shirt. It's a real drain on your pool of potentials.

Happy Do Laundry Until You Get Fucked Day!

| JANUARY 20 | MODEL TRAIN ENTHUSIAST DAY!

Today, you'll bury Meredith, your kitten. Meredith jumped in front of a model train.

She started chasing after it as it rolled along the track. And since you were trying out a new connector that you hadn't even fully soldered yet, various spots on the track had an open current. Meredith went for the engine head-on. The current held her paw to the track and baked her into a twitching mess. The engine crashed into her forehead and tumbled to its side.

It was then that you learned just where your enthusiasm had taken you. When you saw Meredith catch the current and stop still, you knew she would die there. And all you could consider was the safety of your engine. Even now, as you realign the wheels and trucks and paint over where the current turned the paint black, you curse that kitten under your breath. You've decided that you'll not try to extend your love to another living thing again. A kitten can now die in your presence and you'll feel nothing for it.

The trains have taken you.

Happy Model Train Enthusiast Day!

JANUARY 21   CLAUSTROPHOBIA CLINT DAY!

Today the building you work in will catch fire and many will be killed. When the fire reaches its peak, the elevator you're riding will fail to drop directly to the lobby as it is supposed to do. Instead it will stop between the twenty-second and twenty-third floors. You will bang at the buttons and sound the alarm, but to no avail. The car will fill with smoke and you will drop to the ground and think of pretty faces you're never going to see again. Then you will hear something.

"Take my hand!"

From the escape hatch in the roof of the car, an arm will wriggle down toward you. The arm of Claustrophobia Clint, a mythical urban hero who is overcome with severe panic anytime he finds himself in small, enclosed spaces, but who for some annoying reason seems to always have to save people caught in small, enclosed spaces.

"I can't reach you!" You'll jump and fling your hand toward his but you'll never get closer than a foot below. "Come down and help me!"

"Fuck no! Jump higher!" Claustrophobia Clint will shout.

The smoke pouring in from the escape hatch will have completely filled your lungs. Your vision will grow faint, and you'll fall to the corner with a cough that might never end.

"Oh fuck! I fucking hate this! Every fucking time!"

Claustrophobia Clint, who has tried behavioral therapy but never felt like he was making any progress, will shimmy through the hatch and drop to the floor of the elevator. He'll grab your spastic frame and sling you atop his shoulder, and then with one quick squat and a bounce the two of you will launch through the hatch and land on the roof of the car (he's a hero who can jump real high).

"Jesus, that was terrible," Claustrophobia Clint will say. "It really felt like the walls were closing in on me. God! Fuck! Fucking hell, that was horrible."

Claustrophobia Clint will pry open the doors to the twenty-third floor above you, and you will both climb out and find a stairwell to take you down to the ground. You will die on the ninth floor, but Claustrophobia Clint will make it all the way to the ground and he'll live to keep on rescuing people from small, enclosed spaces.

Happy Claustrophobia Clint Day!

| JANUARY 22 | "MY CHEATING HUSBAND'S VOLVO" DAY! |

Your wife found out about you and your secretary a month ago, and she reacted the way any betrayed woman of virtue would react. She entered your Volvo V50 sportswagon in a demolition derby. And she won.

And she's been winning. Every week since she stopped speaking to you she's been heading to the dirt bike track out by the airport and smashing up triumph after triumph. She's turned into a sensation among the regulars. When she pulls into the ring with those four words spray-painted onto the hood, MY CHEATING HUSBAND'S VOLVO, the crowd stirs itself into a frenzy. They revel in the joy of some foolish husband's car about to be destroyed by his woman scorned. But when she starts to win (after all it is a Volvo), there is no limit to how hard that crowd wants to cheer her on. The derby commissioner says he's never seen a derby star break out so fast.

Tonight's the division championship. If she wins tonight, she takes your wagon out to Cleveland for a shot at a $50,000 cash prize. If you wanna make amends with her, you can send her fan base reeling by getting on a bus and taking yourself out to that track.

You had thought your wife had driven the Volvo into a lake to punish you for your infidelity. So when you first see your car pull into the track, you'll want to scream. But when you see what she can do, when you see what art she can make from her rage and her defensive driving skills, you'll fall in love with her like never before.

You don't want to let her know you're there ahead of time. Just buy your ticket and cheer her on with the rest of the civilians. Wait until she wins. When she's standing in the center of the track and is being handed her trophy, interrupt the ceremony by climbing down and walking halfway to her.

Your wife and the commissioner will both stop the ceremony to see what you're up to. The crowd will read in your wife's body language that it was your Volvo all this time. They'll immediately start booing you and pegging you in the head with beer and batteries. Just stand there about twenty feet from your wife with your arms held out from your sides, waiting. The tension will be thick enough to stop up a blown muffler. When she finally drops her trophy and runs into your arms, the crowd will roil itself into such a fever pitch you'll think we finally figured out how to win that Iraq thing over there.

Stand by her side as she finishes the ceremony, and then go to your Volvo and climb into the driver's seat. Pull away slowly, letting your wife hang out the passenger side window so she can wave good-bye to every last one of her fans. They'll all wish her the best, but they'll be worried that her having made up with you will stamp out her rage and pull her out of the demolition game forever. You'll be wondering too. Guess you'll find out for sure next month when you're in the stands in Cleveland, screaming your head off while your wife busts the shit out of a big mess of chrome with her cheating husband's Volvo.

Happy "My Cheating Husband's Volvo" Day!

JANUARY 23   CHECK THE RIGHT BREAST
POCKET OF THAT VINTAGE
SHIRT FOR AN OLD, FADED
TO-DO LIST DAY!

Most days, when you go to your local Used Clothing Emporium, you know before you even leave the house that the size tags on the pants will all be off by three inches and all the sweaters will have a faint water stain on the belly that you won't notice until you're waiting on line to pay. But on those special days, the minute you get your first breath of mothballs you are certain you're gonna find a new and treasured addition to your wardrobe.

And then there's a day like today, when your trip to your local Used Clothing Emporium doesn't just feel lucky, but downright fated.

So you sift through rack after mile-long rack of deep color plaids and bowling shirts that used to belong to someone named Ray, but you're not so much browsing as you are hunting down something lost, like you would a pair of keys or hope. The funny thing is, you're patient. You know it's here, even though you don't know what it is yet. The feeling of certainty excites you. You haven't felt certain about anything in about six years, right? Yeah, it was six years ago.

A few more screeches of bent-steel shirt hangers along the peeling silver painted pipe and there it is: a red and navy plaid western-style shirt with ivory snaps for buttons. It kind of looks like the shirt you're wearing right now, but like the color scheme was directly inverted.

Without a doubt it's the one. Everything around you kind of goes silent and blurry and still, just like when you saw that face at that party six years ago.

Go try it on. Fits perfect right? Now check the right breast pocket and see if there's an old, faded to-do list in there.

Well whaddaya know!

grapes for fruit salad
eggs
money order—$372
mom's b-day gift
call futon place
Emily maybe (stupid???)
firewood

Kind of wacky when you find stuff like that in used clothes or used books, huh? Even wackier, and this might explain why your hands are starting to shake real bad, check the right breast pocket of the shirt you put on this morning for a brand-new to-do list that you scribbled out just before leaving the house.

Well waddaya know!

grapes for fruit salad
eggs
money order—$372
mom's b-day gift
call futon place
Emily maybe (stupid???)
firewood

Same handwriting even. You should buy the shirt and then go and visit loved ones to see if they still exist.

Happy Check the Right Breast Pocket of That Vintage Shirt for an Old, Faded To-Do List Day! By the way, who's Emily?

JANUARY 24 | YOUR HIGH SCHOOL GIRLFRIEND IS NOW AN ASS MODEL DAY!

Write to her via Popshot Posters, the poster publishing company that prints and distributes the poster in which you found her. Something like . . .

Dear Popshot Posters,

I've recently noticed that an old acquaintance of mine is featured in one of your posters. The poster I am speaking of features four women in thong bikinis bent over like animals who've spotted prey with their rear ends raised and perched atop the closed gate of a bright yellow flatbed truck. Two bearded, obese gentlemen are hanging out of the truck's driver and passenger side doors. The caption to the poster reads, "Fatso's Butt Truck. Free Delivery. Fort Lauderdale." The model with whom I am acquainted is the third from the left, in the blue thong bikini. Her name is Tamara Hull. We had a thing.

I haven't seen her since prom and I was hoping you'd be able to forward this note along to her. Let her know that I said, "It's Dave! Dave Jesser! I'm good. I'm good. Congratulations on the whole poster thing. That's so great. That's so great. That's so, so great."

Let Tamara know that I'm still in Township Falls and I see her parents around a lot. I never visit Fort Lauderdale but I've always meant to. If Tammy ever wants to get together and catch up (I'd love to hear about the modeling and what it's like to ride in a truck!), she should send me along her contact info and I'll be in touch. I'm single and my brother died this year.

Thanks, Popshot Posters!

Happy Your High School Girlfriend Is Now an Ass Model Day!

JANUARY 25 POLICE CHASE PAST YOUR GIRLFRIEND'S HOUSE DAY!

Every freeway chase has to end, and yours will be no different. When it does end, you can expect to be spending quite a long time in prison, considering how many innocent people were murdered during that sad excuse for a liquor store holdup you botched this afternoon (death toll: one mother and all seven of her sons, ages two, three, five, six, eleven, twelve, and fifteen).

The police are ordered not to try and stop you, so as to avoid an avoidable accident leading to even more loss of life. So they're just going to follow you and keep you in their sight until you either pull over, run out of gas, or crash into something or, God forbid, someone.

They can't understand why you keep getting off the freeway just to get back on and double back in the opposite direction. What they don't know is you have more on your mind than crossing into Mexico. They don't know that the past six months have been the happiest of your life because they've been spent in the arms of a girl. Like anyone on the run from the police, you'd like to put as much distance as possible between you and those black-and-whites. But the farther you get from your Sarah, the more she draws you back into town.

You're going to have to find a way to say good-bye. Get off the freeway and lead all nine cruisers to her apartment building on the west side. Remember, they can't try to block your way. All they can do is follow your lead.

You won't be able to pull over, so just circle her block. She'll be watching you on the TV, so she won't know you're out there until the first run around the block when she hears all the sirens on your tail. She won't come to the window right away since she'll first have to hide all of your hand-guns and all of her cocaine. By the third or fourth turn around the block, you can bet she'll be leaning out her window to catch a glimpse of you. It's time to send her a kiss.

Roll down all your windows and turn your speakers up full volume. Then drop the CD in the player, the one with the first song that you kissed her to. Or the first song that you and she danced to. Or the song that you both just keep playing for each other, the one that makes you share a smile every time it comes on, for whatever reason. Play that song.

She won't hear it over the sirens, but the first car behind you will. This won't be his first police chase, and he'll know what you're up to.

"Kill the sirens," he'll shout into his radio. "Flashers only."

When you're halfway round the block the wailing will stop. When you come back to her apartment building your song will whip out from your car window and float up into her apartment and she'll lean on her sill like she was the audience to a serenade. The flashers on the cop cars will bounce like strobe lights and everyone in the neighborhood will nod along to the song that was written just for you and your girl. Once, twice, eight times you'll circle the block before the song fades. Once more around and you'll toss your St. Christopher necklace out the window for her to collect and hold on to.

By the time you head back to the freeway the face of every cop on your tail will be wet with tears. They'll gasp along with everyone watching from their windows when you come to that turn at the corner but you keep going straight. At that point the whole city will turn off their TVs and go find someone to hold tight. It won't matter whether you get caught or run free. The only life you wanted was up there in that window, and you'll have already said good-bye.

Happy Police Chase Past Your Girlfriend's House Day!

JANUARY 26

MAKE A MOVE ON THE LADY IN FRONT OF YOU WAITING IN LINE FOR MILK DAY!

So it's day three in the milk line for you. Your wife and kids have come to visit you a couple of times a day to bring you a bucket to defecate in. Your mother stopped by yesterday to tell you that your father had passed away that morning (he needed milk). And people near the front of the line have been getting shot at intermittently.

But hold the phone. Who's the refugee with the pretty blue eyes? She showed up a few hours ago to take her brother's place in line after he slipped into a coma. You didn't notice her at first because she's covered in so many cloaks and a big part of her head is wrapped in bloody bandages. But just now she turned and wept in your direction. Looks like she digs the goods.

You only have a couple more days to make your move. Less, if rumors of an airlift are true. What are you waiting for? She's right there sobbing into her hands, waiting for you to take the hint. Are you gonna let this one slip away?

"You know," you should say, "the warlords are coming back. There's no time to waste."

If you want, you can do it without leaving your places in line. Everyone's watching that woman deliver her baby about ten feet behind you. Turn that gravel under your feet into *The Sands of Pleasure*.

Happy Make a Move on the Lady in Front of You Waiting in Line for Milk Day!

JANUARY 27   CROWD CONTROL DAY!

Today, a crowd of angry people will surround you demanding refunds. You'll try to explain that you don't sell products, but they'll tell you that they were told you were the one to sign off on this. When you ask them what product they're trying to return, they'll all start shouting at once and you won't understand them. When you revert back to, "But I don't sell products," they'll grow fiery and ask you why you asked them which product they're unhappy with if you don't sell products. Suddenly, they'll all take out their receipts and read from the return policy on the back in unison. It will sound beautiful. Occasionally, they'll fall silent and allow one little boy with an angelic voice to sing important passages solo, like, "If the item is not in its original packaging . . ." Once the recitation ends, they will all begin pummeling you with the products they wish to return. At first, this will be hilarious, since they will all be trying to return a plush toy frog that "Rib-its" when you squeeze it. But it won't be long before they stuff one of the frogs into your mouth and hold your nostrils closed. The name of the plush toy frog product is "Wally Warts."

Happy Crowd Control Day!

JANUARY 28   CRUELTY DAY!

Lie to him. When you lie with him, tell him a lie. Tell him you had Chinese for lunch, when, truthfully, you had a pizza.

Steal from him. A postage stamp. One first-class stamp. Steal it from his day planner while he showers.

Humiliate him. Secure a plastic bucket of confetti above the front door so that when he walks in, the confetti showers over his head and his shirt.

When he's standing there with little pieces of paper all over his body, point at him and laugh and say, "You look like such an asshole."

Make him shit when he doesn't want to. Fix him a sundae full of chopped-up laxatives right before he leaves for choir practice. He'll sing off-key, and his fellow choir singers will find him disgusting and shun him. He will be too embarrassed to explain that it was only because he had to take such a mean shit. He'll drive home crying.

Move him around while he's sleeping. If he's on the bed, put him on the couch. Don't leave a note.

Blindfold him and spin him around and swing a bat at his face.

Frustrate him. The next time he approaches you, say, "Do we know each other?" He'll spend days trying to convince you that he is the man you've loved for three years now. Don't let on that you know. Just keep saying, "Um, I think I'd remember something like that. I'm calling the fuzz."

Frame him for a crime he did not commit. Such as vandalism or espionage.

Take him out to a karaoke bar, encourage him to get up and sing, and when he does, stand on your chair and boo him as loudly as you can. Lead the rest of the bar in a chorus of boos and heckles until the karaoke DJ is forced to take his microphone away from him in order to get on with the show. Sneak out of the bar so that when he comes back to the table to ask you why you would do something so cruel, you won't be there. He'll look all around the bar but he won't find you. He'll be alone.

Happy Cruelty Day!

| JANUARY 29 | HOLD IT ALL IN DAY! |

Boss treating you unfairly? Deli counter guy put mayo on your pastrami again? Relatively certain your spouse is cheating on you? Well today's the day to hold it all in!

You know what you should say, and you know there's nothing worth saying until it all gets said. But hey, why make waves? Besides, that knot of frustration in your belly has been with you so long it's practically your best and possibly only friend. Why not give it a name, like Ben, and tell Ben your troubles until Ben turns into a malignant tumor? Or you could continue to have imaginary arguments while alone in your car. You always win those!

No one likes a complainer. So, whether your boyfriend didn't come to your birthday party or your roommate used up all your insulin, just let it fester.

Because today's Hold It All In Day!

JANUARY 30   SHE'S IN THE HOSPITAL DAY!

You walk through the hospital with urgency. If there are any doors on hinges, you march toward them and fling them open with a loud clap. Everyone looks your way as you run to your ex's bedside.

You don't carry flowers or a teddy bear. Of fucking course not. Everyone else believes her story about getting dizzy from antihistamines while gardening on the roof, but you know damn well it was an attempted suicide and you're furious. You don't hear from her for a month and a half, and then you get a call that she tried to off herself. The walk to the hospital room seems to be taking forever and you hope that by the time you get there your urge to slap her in the eyes has cooled down a bit.

Crowding into the room are her husband of one year and his miserable mom and dad. They're at every occasion. How she can keep from releasing a single never-ending yawn is beyond you.

She's in the middle of smiling her way through a story when you burst in. She spots you, and her face turns solemn. She mutters through the remainder of the story, and then everyone turns to acknowledge you.

Her torso is in a body cast. "You look like a fucking idiot," you say.

She shakes her head, closes her eyes. "Tom, take Beth and Martin out to the vending machines for a bit." Tom is her dull-as-ducklings husband and he knows his place. He obeys.

"You wanna talk about this, you talk to me about it," she says after they've gone. "These people are sweet."

"You just referred to the man you married as 'these people.'"

"They love and care for me," she says. "And they accept the fact that I accidentally fell from the roof. Because they would never want me to be so unhappy that I might want to jump. Don't upset them with the truth."

"I wouldn't care if your in-laws were tied to burning posts. I care about you."

"You care about yourself."

"I do. And if you take your life I swear to God I'll destroy this world."

She can tell you mean it, but she says, "You wouldn't." Perhaps to get you to say it again.

"You fucking know I would, you terrible woman."

Her husband pokes his head through the door. "Honey, can I get you some tea or a snack?"

"Run out to the store, sweetie? And pick me up some magazines to read."

Her husband says sure thing. She says, "Lock that door."

You do. She says, "Climb atop my body cast."

You do. She turns her head on its side on the pillow. You rest your lips on her cheek. You keep them there.

She says, "We have about ten minutes before he comes back."

For about ten minutes, your lips sleep upon her cheek. Your legs straddle her body cast.

Happy She's in the Hospital Day!

| JANUARY 31 | IT'S DRINKIN' TUESDAY!

Call in sick. And from the minute you wake up to the minute you pass out, just never stop drinkin'. However, and this is essential, everyone must perform this annual ritual alone, in your respective apartments, sitting in a tense posture on the edge of your beds.

Happy It's Drinkin' Tuesday!

FEBRUARY

WAY UP THERE AT THE TOP, A
CHEERLEADER RENEGES ON YOU.

HANG ON TO YOUR WIDE-EYED INNOCENCE DAY!

Even though it's getting colder and you're getting hungrier and things aren't working out the way they're supposed to, hang on to your wide-eyed innocence. Don't ask what's buzzing behind all those glassy eyes you see floating by on the sidewalk. You'll make them forget their answer. They all think that the game is rigged, and they think that you should have been broken by now. Keep your head down and wear a sweater. Don't catch a cold. Don't lose hope. I bet you don't even know it's yours to lose, do you?

Happy Hang On to Your Wide-Eyed Innocence Day!

TRY TO MAKE SHIT HAPPEN WITH YOUR MIND DAY!

Want that bag of chips but don't feel like getting off the couch? Maybe you're telekinetic. It's been a while since you spent some time trying to find out (at least a week!), and you do have a few hours to kill. Go on. Try to move shit with your mind.

You know you have a lot of untapped potential in various areas (ability to play a musical instrument, hold down a job, love another) and you just need to buckle down and put in the required effort. Well isn't it possible that you could also be able to make shit happen with your mind but you just haven't gotten around to it? Like that guy you see on your bus that you've been fantasizing about. If you put in the hours to refine your unholy power to control people's thoughts, I'm betting you could get him to believe he shares those feelings of emotionally void sexual attraction you've been harboring for him all these years.

You just need to practice. And there's no better time to start than tonight if no one's up for going out drinking!

In observance of Try to Make Shit Happen with Your Mind Day, children under the age of twelve are encouraged to swear.

Happy Try to Make Shit Happen with Your Mind Day!

FEBRUARY 3   GO AND LIVE IN THE WOODS DAY!

Don't just quit, quit big! What are you gonna do, leave your current data analysis position just so you can sit around for a couple of weeks before you go and take the data analysis position at the marketing firm across the street?

Fuck that. Go into the woods and live in the hollow of a tree until you learn to bind wood into a cabin. Stop speaking any and all established languages as well. Develop your own language. You'll find the dictionary in your bones. In case you can't, though, lemme get you started:

The word for "pussy" is now "kana hooo!"

There, now you have the foundation for a new society. Go kill some animals.

Happy Go and Live in the Woods Day!

| FEBRUARY 4 | HERE'S HOW YOU'RE GONNA DIE DAY! |

So here's how you're gonna die:

Garbageman Stan has been inseparable from his best friend, Trashman Tony, ever since the first week Tony joined the waste management force and Garbageman Stan was assigned as his probationary period supervisor. Garbageman Stan showed Trashman Tony how to make the best of this life on the dirty curbs, and Trashman Tony repaid him with the devotion and loyalty of a sibling.

A great bond can be destroyed only with the most spectacular of explosions.

A month and a half ago, Trashman Tony's mom, Mrs. Tony, died in the night in her bed in Tony's home. Trashman Tony stopped by Garbageman Stan's house for some comfort. He found that Garbageman Stan had run off on a payday bender, but not before marring the beautiful Mrs. Garbageman Stan's face with a shiner to her eye. Trashman Tony took Mrs. Garbageman Stan to the couch and laid her down with a piece of meat over her face. Trashman Tony listened to her complaints about Garbageman Stan, then told her about his mom. And that's when she kissed him. They would conduct their affair for three whole weeks, over eight separate encounters, before Garbageman Stan caught them together.

Garbageman Stan challenged Trashman Tony to a duel, as is dictated in the waste management force's code of honor. They would divert their trucks from their routes and meet at either end of a ten-block stretch of road at dawn. When the streetlights flickered off, both gentlemen would start their engines and accelerate full speed toward each other to collide at the peak of their engines' prowess.

The way you're gonna die is you're gonna wake up just before dawn today and start jogging because you'll have decided that it's about time you tried to get into shape and turn your life around. All stretched out in your brand-new sneaks with your favorite song on your headphones, you'll jog three hopeful steps into the street when those two trash trucks grab hold of you tight at sixty-five miles per hour and flatten you right smack-dab in the middle of their grilles. When they pull the trucks apart, you'll have been reduced to something like a kind of paste, with hardly a bone not ground down and all of your skin and tissue melted in the heat of that burning mountain of iron and waste.

Garbageman Stan will be dead, too. Tony won't walk again. And Mrs. Garbageman Stan is gonna remarry.

Happy Here's How You're Gonna Die Day!

| FEBRUARY 5 | ADEQUATE RESPECT FOR THE PRETTY DRESS DAY! |

"If you have adequate respect for the pretty dress, when you get to watch one be removed from a body, you feel a twinge of sadness."

—Some guy in prison

No matter your sexual orientation, today is the day to celebrate the existence of pretty dresses. They beautify the landscape. They make you look all that much better when you stand next to them. And yes, they make the bodies inside them look like a stick of butter melted on top of a cookie. So if you see a woman or a transgender male wearing a pretty dress, shake her or his hand and say, "Thanks for wearing that dress, yo. You prettied up the ATM line for all of us."

Happy Adequate Respect for the Pretty Dress Day! Quit cryin'.

FEBRUARY 6 | DRIVE-THRU DAY!

You should have spent the night before getting real drunk and filling up a lot of water balloons with your piss. Today, when you're finished sleeping it off, get drunk enough to drive through some fast-food drive-thrus without getting "the blindnesses." Place a giant order at each drive-thru. Ten items minimum. When you pull up to the window, your food won't be ready, so shout into the window, "Let's go! I'm sittin' here with my dick in my hand! Let's go! Let's go!" When the kid behind the window finally hands you all your food and asks for some money, say, "You're about to meet my insides, baby." Then slam the kid in the face with your balloon full of piss.

Drive off without paying and repeat at the next drive-thru. Before long, you're going to be chased by policemen. You will either get away, crash your car and die, or go to jail for drunk driving, assault, and theft.

Happy Drive-Thru Day!

FEBRUARY 7 | WRITE THE POEM THAT MAKES HIGH SCHOOL BOYS FISTFIGHT IN LOCKER ROOMS DAY!

People don't become poets because they love words. People become poets because they love to watch adolescent boys in bath towels get into fistfights in locker room shower alcoves.

As far as you're concerned, your life will have been worth nothing if you fail to write a poem that makes a damp-chested boy between the ages of thirteen and seventeen, wearing only a white bath towel, throw a sloppy punch at the face of another boy who is wearing just as little, whose skin is just as damp, who is just as blind to what a paradise his high school gymnasium locker room can become when a moment of violence erupts inside of it.

You've already tried several different poems that you've scribbled inside the doors of various lockers. One made a boy blush, another made a boy quickly cover it over with a Magic Marker before anyone else saw what was written there, and another made a boy dress hastily and rush out of the locker room (you always hide in one of the neighboring lockers to watch your readers' reactions). But none of them have managed to incite a half-naked fistfight amid a thick cloud of steam.

Yet.

The poem you've spent the last eight months composing has got to be the one. It's called "Mud Lips" and it's about what happens when a child who was kept hidden in a dark basement for twelve years is sent to summer camp. It's about awakenings, is what it's about, and there's a lot of blood in it. It's 8,200 words long so you're going to have to write small with a thin-tipped Sharpie. It's going to take all night, but it'll be worth it tomorrow when you watch through the slats of a locker as a boy reads your poem word by word. You'll be able to see the artery in his neck pulse a little faster as he gets closer and closer to the end. And you'll see him close his locker door, walk to the shower alcove with his fists clenching and unclenching by his sides. He'll walk directly to his best friend underneath the third showerhead on the left. He'll turn him around and he'll land one punch solid on the cheekbone and send his friend's head to crack against the tiled wall. And he won't even know why.

A fistfight will have begun. Like your poem pulled the trigger on a starter's pistol, the half-naked boys will be fighting right before your eyes. Finally your poetry will be given the recognition it has always deserved.

Happy Write the Poem That Makes High School Boys Fistfight in Locker Rooms Day!

| FEBRUARY 8 | NOT ROSH HASHANAH DAY! |

Remember, today is not Rosh Hashanah. Better luck next time!

| FEBRUARY 9 | SET STUFF ON FIRE DAY! |

Burning photographs of friends and lovers who've betrayed you is quite the cliché, but it only became a cliché because it just works so fucking well. What else are you gonna burn? A credit card bill? Ooooh!!! You're a real hellion, aren't you?

If you have evidence of a murder you committed, yeah, that'll work. But you had to burn that anyway. It's like you're doing chores. You need to burn something that represents a first step down a dangerous and self-destructive path. Like a letter begging for your forgiveness. Or . . . *a fucking photograph of a guy or girl wrapped up happily in your arms!*

Granted, burning a memento from the past could also signal your first step down a healthy path of spiritual renewal and self-discovery, which is really great for you but we don't wanna hear about it, okay? We're all sitting at our desks one mouse-click away from checking to see if farmpics.com has a free tour so let's keep things naughty. Thanks.

As to the act of incineration itself, sitting cross-legged in the middle of the living room floor is nice. Blinds closed, door locked, lights off, lovely. Kind of let your eyes glaze over as the flames dance in their reflection, as if something's just been resolved in the blood-drenched caverns of your mind. And let the fire burn just a little bit longer than you're comfortable with, till you're unsure that you can put it out. Whether you put it out or you let it burn and walk calmly to the street as if you're unaware that you're just a silhouette against the raging fireball that used to be your home is up to you on Set Stuff on Fire Day!

Happy Set Stuff on Fire Day!

FEBRUARY 10 | OPENLY WEEP TO AVOID INVITES TO HAPPY HOUR DAY!

Guess what? It's Friday. That means around 4:00 P.M. you should expect a visit from Enormously Large Evelyn, the records receptionist in HR. She's going to invite you to join the rest of the team at Yeasty's! for happy hour.

Run to the bathroom? She'll only leave a Post-it on your monitor. The best way to say no is to cut the invite off at the knees. When Evelyn peeks over your cubicle wall, make sure she sees a coworker sending an anguished peal of sobs into the phone. You might have to cry into an empty receiver until 5:30, but no one will ask if you're okay until Monday.

Happy Openly Weep to Avoid Invites to Happy Hour Day!

FEBRUARY 11 | SHE AGREED TO TOUCH YOUR THING AT THE TOP OF THE FERRIS WHEEL DAY!

She's a beautiful cheerleader who's failing English. You're a lonely nerd who is ugly and smart. She came to you last week and asked you to write her term paper for her.

"If I don't get a B on that term paper, I'll repeat the whole year," she said. "I'll do anything in return. I'll even take you shopping to buy cool clothes so that you can be accepted by the cool kids. Maybe you'll even find out that you were cool all along and you just needed to be invited to the cool party. I'll even pretend to be your girlfriend if you want," she said.

"Touch my thing," say to her. "On the top of the Ferris wheel at the carnival. Just like all the girls do."

Her face will scrunch up in disgust. "I've never touched a boy's thing on a Ferris wheel," she'll say. "I've never even been to the carnival."

Say, "You want to pass English?!"

She handed the paper in on Friday and she'll get her B+ back today. Which means tonight, she has to ride the Ferris wheel with you and touch your thing when your car reaches the top.

At the beginning of the second revolution, when they start pausing the cars in place, you'll pull your thing out and be ready to go. This way she won't have to waste time fumbling with your zipper. Once the car stops at the top, you'll look over at her. She'll have her eyes closed. She'll lift her hand and move it toward you. She'll lower it just inches above your thing before she yanks her hand back and wraps it around herself.

"I can't do it!" she'll say. "It's just too gross."

Zip up. "That's okay."

She'll say, "Really?"

"I mean, I was really hoping to finally have my thing touched," tell her. "But I can't make you do what you don't want to do."

She'll say, "But you wrote my paper for me."

"I like writing papers," tell her. "If you don't like touching boys' things, it's not a fair deal."

She'll say, "To be honest, I do kind of like touching boys' things. But not as currency. I don't want to have to touch someone's thing just because I'm doing poorly at school."

Say, "You shouldn't have to. You're right. But not everyone is as forgiving as me out there in the real world. For example, if you are ever given a high-paying job in exchange for promising to touch the job interviewer's thing, and you try to back out of it, not only will he take back the job but he could break your thumbs. As if to say, 'Don't wanna touch my thing, eh? Then I'm gonna make it so you won't be able to touch anybody's thing.'"

She'll say, "That really happens?"

Tell her, "It could. If you bite off more than you can chew."

The ride will come to a stop and the carny will open the gate on your car. But before you can get off, she'll plant a long wet kiss on your lips. "That's for being so nice to me," she'll say.

You'll be on cloud nine, until you step off the ride and start getting beaten up by the football team who all saw her kiss you. The football team doesn't like it when their cheerleaders kiss people who aren't on the football team. Though your lips will be swollen and you'll have to have your jaw wired shut, you'll still feel that kiss on your lips. You'll feel it all the way home from the hospital.

Happy She Agreed to Touch Your Thing at the Top of the Ferris Wheel Day!

| FEBRUARY 12 | POP OPEN A BOTTLE OF CHAMPAGNE DAY! |

There are so many little moments in your life that are worthy of celebration. Don't let them pass you by. Anytime something happens today that is worth celebrating, whether you win an Oscar or you remove a Band-Aid to find that a cut has scabbed over, pop open a bottle of champagne and start filling up glasses.

You're going to need a pretty large cooler with wheels so you can keep all of the bottles chilled. And it would be a good idea to keep near shopping districts and more built-up areas because you'll have to make a lot of liquor store stops when you run out of bottles. Additionally, eat some bread to absorb some of the alcohol because you're going to be ingesting approximately 750 milliliters of champagne every twenty minutes or so.

You'll be surprised at how many opportunities there are to pop open some champagne. It can start as early as breakfast, when your wife cracks open an egg without getting any shells in the bowl. Then at work, if someone manages to print out a document without the printer jamming even once, break out the bubbly!

You don't even have to drink the champagne to celebrate with it. What if you buy yourself a new tie today? Are you really going to just wrap that tie around your neck without christening it first? Hells no! Just stretch that baby out on the sidewalk and smash a bottle of champagne over it. Then take it to get it cleaned.

You should be careful when you're driving, however. If you start making a lot of green lights, you'll have no choice but to celebrate. Unfortunately, it's illegal to even open a bottle of champagne while driving, so make sure to open it when none of the other motorists is looking at you. The same with drinking it.

At various times during the day people will ask you why you just popped open some champagne, such as when you pop open some champagne because you're on a crowded elevator that doesn't stop until it hits your floor, or when you find a lingerie catalog in your mailbox. Explain to anyone who asks that your priest was bitching at you for not appreciating the little moments in life, and you wanted to show him he's full of crap.

Happy Pop Open a Bottle of Champagne Day!

FEBRUARY 13 — HOW 'BOUT NOBODY GATHER 'ROUND A FIRE AND SING A BUNCH OF QUEER-ASS SONGS DAY!

This one's also known as "Let's Not and Say We Did Day." It's about refusing to participate in a warm, unifying evening of old and new friends joining together in the woods to pretend that singing "Row, Row, Row Your Boat" is gonna change the fact that some people's dads come into their rooms late at night. Kumbaya, my Lord?

No.

Look, this isn't *Meatballs*. Chris Makepeace is not going to win any races today and Bill Murray is not going to get back together with one of the butchest love interests ever put to celluloid. The only thing any of us has in common is the fact that none of us should ever gather round in a circle to do anything ever. We're just wrong for each other. We're not in a "Gather Round a Fire and Sing Some Songs" place right now. The harder you try to force it, the more plaintive our disgust for each other will become. Oh and way to break out the acoustic guitar on How 'Bout Nobody Gather Round a Fire and Sing a Bunch of Queer-Ass Songs Day. Good planning. (*Just like when you booked the trip to Denver during Denver Blows Week last year.*)

From now on, you don't get to plan any more of our group vacations. From now on, Dave gets to plan all of our group vacations.

Happy How 'Bout Nobody Gather 'Round a Fire and Sing a Bunch of Queer-Ass Songs Day! Don't fuck this up, Dave.

FEBRUARY 14	TELL YOUR DEAD ROOMMATE'S MOST RECENT EX THAT HE'S DEAD DAY!

"Hey." You'll start off with that when you see her at the bar tonight. You'll have spotted her hanging on a guy with far more affection than you ever saw between her and Lee in the three months they spent together.

"Hey you!" She's going to say that back to you.

"How've you been?" She's been fine.

"How's Lee?" Lee's dead. So are his parents and older sister. They were all four of them in a chartered plane flying over to a wedding on an island off the coast of Florida. Lee's dad was worth a million or two, not a huge shitload, but he of course consorted with the type of folks who charter planes for the delivery of wedding guests to islands off the coast of Florida. Sometimes, even though rich people pay for them, chartered planes crash.

"I thought about calling and telling you when it happened, but—" No you didn't.

"I understand. I mean . . . God. Lee. That's so sad."

"Yeah."

You should then walk away from each other and maybe never see each other again. Try to go back to enjoying your evening. That will probably involve you returning to your table and telling everyone there about how you "just had to tell that chick about Lee, my roommate who died. She's his ex. They only went out for a couple months, but man. That was weird." And she will most likely return to her table and tell everyone there, "I just found out this guy I dated for a little while last year died in a plane crash." People at her table will say, "Holy shit."

Happy Tell Your Dead Roommate's Most Recent Ex That He's Dead Day!

FEBRUARY 15   LIE TO YOUR CATS ABOUT THE CRUCIFIXION OF JESUS CHRIST DAY!

Your new wall-mounted crucifix kicks ass. It's way gorier than your previous wall-mounted crucifix, which made it look like Jesus was just kind of hanging out on some wood for a little while. Just another hippie with his arms spread open like he was waiting for some free love. You wanted to replace it with something more accurately depicting the gruesome and bloody murder that the Lord endured for his children, but your wife wouldn't let you so you had to wait until she divorced you first.

You moved into your new apartment today, and the first thing you did was hang above your mantel the most revolting wall-mounted crucifix you could buy. It is truly a marvel of religious iconography. A crucifix so gory and graphic that people will want to put a cakepan underneath it to collect the blood that is sure to drip from Jesus' feet.

It wasn't long after you hung the crucifix that you were distracted by the sound of animals growling.

You turned around and saw Frodo and Morpheus, your pet cats, approaching with their backs arched, ready for war. They stared up at the cross and released a litany of hisses and moans. Then Morpheus turned on

Frodo and swatted at his face. They started fighting like never before. It became clear that your new crucufix is so realistic and so bloody that your cats assumed a predator must be in the house. They couldn't be sure of what could have caused such carnage, so they turned on each other. You had to act quickly to try and calm them down.

First, you tried to convince them that it wasn't Jesus' blood. "He just helped someone in a car wreck," you told them. It pained you to speak falsely of the crucifixion, but you only did so for the sake of peace. Your cats didn't buy it anyway since they don't speak English. The fighting grew more vicious.

Next, you took out your drawing pad and sketched a picture of Jesus conspiring with some birds and some mice in a basement meeting room. You made it look like they were hovering over some blueprints. You hoped that your cats would see the drawing and that they would decide that Jesus had gotten what he deserved for consorting with their enemies. But you couldn't hold them still long enough for them to take in the drawing. The fighting grew worse and now you fear that one of them is really going to kill the other.

Pray to that crucifix on your wall, asking Jesus to forgive you for making light of his brutal murder, and to guide your next move. "I want to keep the reminder of all that you went through on my wall," say. "But I can't do that until my cats believe that they are safe in the apartment. They're such simple creatures and the only thing that can appease them is trickery."

And that's when you'll find the answer, as plain as the light reflected off of Jesus' upturned eyeballs. The icon on your wall will seem to speak. "Make the necessary sacrifice," it will tell you.

Finally, it will become clear that if your cats believe a predator is loose in the house, you are going to have to deliver them their predator before they will trust each other again. In order to keep that magnificent crucifix on your wall, you are going to have to wrestle and kill a wolf before their eyes.

Getting your hands on a live wolf will be the easy part since you live near a prairie and you're handy with a tranquilizer gun. Stash the sedated wolf in the hallway closet and wait.

After several hours, you'll hear a rustling from behind the closet door. The cats will hear it too. They'll approach the door and growl at whatever might be waiting behind it. In a whirlwind, the wolf will burst through the door and send the cats running. It will bound straight at you where you are sitting in your easy chair. As you had hoped, the sedative will be lingering and the wolf will be far from agile when it lunges at your neck. Whipping the fishing knife in front of you and slicing open the wolf's throat will be easier than you'd feared. The wolf will collapse in your lap and the blood will drain from his body and down your legs to puddle on the floor.

The cats will come out of hiding and sniff at the carcass. They'll be growling, but no longer at each other. The trust that Morpheus and Frodo had spent so many years building will be restored. The predator that killed the man on the wall will have been slain.

Murdering that wolf will allow you to sit alongside your cats and marvel up at your crucifix for as long as you desire. Your cats will join you in your reverence. You may see the son of God, the man who gave of himself for the good of all mankind. But they'll see the tiny little human that was ripped apart and strung up by the wolf who had invaded their home. It could have been them up there on that wall. Neither of your cats can ever forget that. And as long as they can look upon the little man bleeding on the wall, forget it, they never will.

Happy Lie to Your Cats About the Crucifixion of Jesus Christ Day!

FEBRUARY 16   DANCE FOR SOMEONE WHO
IS SHOOTING A GUN AT YOUR
FEET DAY!

When you step off the subway this evening, you'll hear a gunshot and the ground near your toes will burst. You'll look up and see before you a man in a black trench coat and ski mask pointing a revolver at your feet.

"Dance!" he'll shout. "Dance like the earth underneath your shoes is on fire."

Do not run. He wants to see you dance. If he wanted to see you run, he'd have told you to run. Do not run or he'll shoot you in the back.

What you need to do is look deep within yourself and let the part of your soul that you despise the most guide your movements. This man wants to watch you move. With honesty.

Purveyors of dance have armed themselves and are taking to the streets shooting at the feet of nimble-looking pedestrians hoping that the threat of homicide might bring about some inspired movement. The pickings have been so slim this season that lovers of dance are starting to feel betrayed by the dance community. Most of the productions mounted this fall have been lifeless, derivative, or just plain dull. It was thought that there might be a resurgence of experimentation once 9/11 was far enough in the past and companies no longer felt required to address the Towers. But choreographers with their backs up against the wall shrugged their shoulders and trotted out the same old flailing-in-a-body-stocking crap and prayed that nobody noticed. Their prayers were not answered.

Now no one is safe. But if you are true to your heart and your body, the worst that will happen to you is you will be briefly inconvenienced. When the dance lover shoots at your feet, simply move so as to confess. Once he drops to his knees in tears, you may bring your dance to its conclusion and continue on your way. If you're unsure of how to conclude the dance, just drop to a split and throw out some jazz hands.

Happy Dance for Someone Who Is Shooting a Gun at Your Feet Day!

FEBRUARY 17 | YOUR SUPERVISOR SUFFERS FROM PYROMANIA DAY!

It hits her every day around 3:30, when everyone else is getting ready for a group yawn. She slams her door shut and draws all the blinds, and then you see her phone line light up. You thought she was just making plans to see whomever she's cheating on her husband with. But she's not, she's very faithful, she's just calling her sponsor.

"I can see the flames flicker, Harold. I can see them, Harold. They're just so motherfucking beautiful, Harold."

"Breathe."

Around 4:05 her phone line blinks off. And at 4:15, she comes back out and asks you to reprint the memo you typed up earlier in the day. She's very calm then.

"Do you have any corrections?"

"It was fine. I just . . . must have misplaced it."

You can sometimes smell the smoke underneath the sudden gust of air freshener wafting from her office.

While you fetch the memo from your hard drive, she goes to the window and takes sleek breaths, like she's smoking an imaginary cigarette.

She stays at the window until five, when you ask her if she needs anything else and she dismisses you with a shake of the back of her head. As far as you know, she stays there all night. She did once.

Some nights, she stays until as late as nine or ten, when she's certain everyone has gone and the cleaners have finished their shift. She moves a copier from its spot on the floor and builds a small pyre from cardboard paper clip boxes and plastic report covers and a scarf or glove or some other item she might have worn to work that day, and she lights a tiny blaze. Tall enough to get her blood into her ears, but small enough to stamp out after just a few moments before the smoke detectors sound. Then she sweeps the remains and the ash into a small trash bag that she'll toss into a Dumpster on her walk home, and she slides the copier back over the scarred carpet. The next day she'll know what's under there.

Wreckage. She did that.

Happy Your Supervisor Suffers from Pyromania Day!

FEBRUARY 18   CASHIERS ARE WAY HORNY DAY!

Today's the day when you and your friends will walk up to the counter at the Rite Aid with a big cart full of Tequiza and Smirnoff Ice and Jell-O shooter molds and prescription roofies and whatnot and the cashier is gonna say, "Wow, looks like you guys like to party."

And if you and your friends don't respond, she'll say, "You know, I like to party."

And if you and your friends just kind of nod absently and continue pooling your money, she'll be like, "When I say I like to party, I mean I like to have sex."

And if you and your friends are like, "Yeah, whatever, lady," and then you go back to arguing over why Bob never has any cash to chip in, she'll add, "With guys. I mean I like to have sex with guys."

And if you and your friends still haven't caught on and you just jam the wad of money into her hand, she'll just give up on the hints and say, "Look, can I have sex with you guys?"

Then all you and your friends have to do is vote on it!

Happy Cashiers Are Way Horny Day!

FEBRUARY 19	ASK THE BUS DRIVER DAY!

Ask the bus driver whether you should run away from your parents to Hollywood to become a movie star, and he might say yes because he always wanted to do that but never got the chance. Now he'd like to see you go in his stead. Bus drivers always want something better for their passengers.

Happy Ask the Bus Driver Day!

FEBRUARY 20	I AM THE CHIEF OF POLICE DAY!

Today, if you are in an office, whenever you see someone with a blue tie, the first person who shouts "I am the chief of police!" gets to be the chief of police. And he can walk around and demand that everyone give him a dollar, pretending that he's getting a cut of their weekly take. And he can also demand a little bit of everyone's cocaine. This will continue until someone jumps up and shouts, "I am the wife of the chief of police!" before breaking down in tears and signing some divorce papers because she can't take all the cheating anymore.

Happy I Am the Chief of Police Day!

| FEBRUARY 21 | IT'S TIME YOU HAD "THE TALK"
DAY!

You'd hoped your temp assignment might have ended before this came to pass. Fact is, Roger Leventhal, Esq., the attorney whose secretary you've been filling in for these past few days, has been giving you the desk instructions that only a man in love would give.

"I'll be on my conference call. But if Martha calls, interrupt me," he'll say. And how about when he asked you, "What sort of flowers say that I've abandoned all my usual defenses and safeguards against getting too close, and that even if I get chewed up and spit out into the sewer, I'll celebrate every patch of flesh that you might deign to rip from my body with your bared and frothing fangs?"

You said chrysanthemums. And then you began to worry.

He's just like a little boy lately, calling his divorce attorney and telling him to give his soon-to-be-ex-wife whatever she asks just as long as it gets things finalized as soon as possible. This guy is head-over-heels in love and being head-over-heels in love means throwing caution to the wind. But if Roger Leventhal, Esq., isn't able to consider the possible consequences of reckless behavior, his temp's going to have to do it for him.

Bottom line, it's time you talked to the attorney whose secretary you've been filling in for these past few days about sex.

Explain to him that it's only natural for a forty-seven-year-old, recently separated, seven-figure-salaried attorney (who happens to be quite liquid, thank you very much) to start having some confusing feelings about girls. But you have to warn him that some girls might take advantage of those feelings just to get him to marry them because they're scared of dying poor. Tell him there's only one way to be sure if this Martha person is really in love with him. This is delicate, so use these words and you should get through it okay:

Mr. Leventhal, I'm sure Martha is a lovely woman, but don't have sex with her unless she really likes to watch you ejaculate. Say to her, "I wanna masturbate in front of you and I want you to sit in this chair and watch me come all over my own belly. I'm gonna sit cross-legged on the floor here. Will you watch me make myself come, Martha?" If she agrees and she looks like she's way into it, she really does love you and you shouldn't even bother with the prenup. But if she acts like she doesn't dig it, she's a cop.

Phew, you'd think after temping as long as you have, this wouldn't be such a big deal. But the squirm factor seems to get worse every time, doesn't it?

Happy It's Time You Had "The Talk" Day!

| FEBRUARY 22 | BRING A PRESENT TO A FUNERAL DAY! |

Hallmark hasn't quite figured it out yet, so how 'bout you start a gift-giving tradition by wrapping up a kitschy little overpriced knickknack and just leaving it on the foyer table at the reception for your friend's dad's funeral. Imagine how she'll feel when she finally has everyone out of the house and she gets to plop down on the couch and open up the only gift anyone thought to bring.

"Jenny bought me a pack of *South Park* refrigerator magnets for my dad's funeral!" she'll think. "Man oh man, am I lucky to have such a thoughtful friend that she remembered my appreciation for the subversive animated program *South Park* on the day my dad was lowered into his grave. He died at fifty-six of cancer, by the way."

Whatever you do, don't call your friend until she calls you to thank you for the gift. Even if you never hear from her again. She needs to be taught some common courtesy.

Happy Bring a Present to a Funeral Day!

| FEBRUARY 23 | YOU ARE FEELING SLEEEEEEPY DAY! |

You're harboring a secret that grows more burdensome with every hour. If you hold it in any longer you feel like you might explode. You could never in your right mind confess because confessing will be the end of you. The truth will have to come out by accident or in that rare moment when your guard is down. That's why tonight you should go and volunteer to be hypnotized by a dinner theater hypnotist in the hopes that while in a hypnotic state you will accidentally confess to setting the fire that killed your spouse and three children.

You've gone to such great lengths just so you can be angled unawares into shouting once and for all, "I did it! I rigged the pilot light to go out that night! I killed my little babies and I really apologize big time!" You've tried drinking a lot with old friends, hoping for that 4:00 A.M. conversation where drunks who've been drinking together for hours start unloading all the secrets they've been dying to throw to the tabletop. You've holed up in a motel room for days with a wizened prostitute, grasping for that kind of intimacy that only comes when you're talking to someone who plans to wash all evidence of you from her body as soon as you run out of money. You've even become an international spy and allowed yourself to get caught by hostile governments, praying to be administered a hypodermic full of truth serum. But no dice. As far as anyone knows, the fire inspector's report still stands, and that fire was caused by a faulty gas trigger.

So tonight, go see the Amazing D'Agostino and volunteer to be hypnotized. It's not guaranteed to work out, because the Amazing D'Agostino is a pro. He knows everyone in the audience is just dying to get hypnotized and confess to their extramarital affairs and sister lust and other crippling guilts. That's why the Amazing D'Agostino only makes his volunteers cluck like a chicken and steers clear of asking any leading questions that might cause someone to spill their guts. To quote the Amazing D'Agostino, "This is dinner theater, kid. It ain't church. Make 'em smile and peddle the veal."

But maybe you'll get lucky. Maybe you are so brimming over with the need to confess that the truth will spill forth as soon as that golden amulet starts to swing from the Amazing D'Agostino's fingertips.

Happy You Are Feeling Sleeeeeepy Day!

FEBRUARY 24 | STARZ "SEEING WHAT FITS UP YOUR ASS" DAY!

Today, for twenty-four hours, there's a Starz channel called Starz "Seeing What Fits Up Your Ass," which is a twenty-four-hour live feed of you walking around the house and checking to see what items you can put inside your ass.

It's not clear that it's really you. Or rather, it's definitely you, but it's not clear how "you" it is. You look sort of hypnotized, or at least real focused on putting things inside your ass to see if they fit. You can probably watch the channel too. Sometimes, people just sort of show up on a live video feed of them walking around the house seeing what they can fit up their asses. Even though they were at work all day and they have witnesses.

At around 11:00 A.M., it was weird. You had just shoved a high school crew trophy up your ass and it went in real easy too. Then you tried to stuff this enormous bowl of fruit up your ass. The bowl must have been three feet in diameter, and there were oranges and pears and bananas piled high. You'd just kind of squatted over it, then lowered yourself down real slow, as if you were afraid of scaring the fruit away. When one of the pieces of fruit would inevitably tumble from the bowl, you'd get up and put it back in its place with great care and deliberation. Then you'd get in position to lower your asshole over the bowl of fruit for another try. It took you like forty-five minutes to give up, and when you did you didn't seem disappointed at all. In fact, you looked really at peace the whole time.

Right now you're trying to shove the living room wall up your ass.

Happy Starz "Seeing What Fits Up Your Ass" Day!

| FEBRUARY 25 | TAKE A POTTERY CLASS IN THE HOPES THAT YOUR REAL FATHER WILL BE THE INSTRUCTOR DAY! |

You'll be his star pupil. He'll find in your ashtrays and keychain caddies the seeds of a master potter. He'll devote more attention to you than to the rest of the class, largely because he thinks your pot-making is awesome. But something in his bones will tell him there's more to it than that. He'll need to be near you, and if you're of the gender he likes to fist, he might mistake the need for a sexual one. You'll run crying from the classroom when he makes a move but you'll leave behind a clue to the fact that he's your real dad. Like a surveillance photo of him dropping you off at an orphanage or DNA test results you obtained by slicing off a piece of his elbow when he showed up to class wasted and passed out on his desk (have you ever *been* to the Learning Annex?).

After you skip your next class he'll probably show up at your job (you either wait tables at a diner or are a senator) and he'll say, "I could tell by the way you pottered that you had the blood of a master potter flowing through your veins. I just never imagined it was mine." Then he'll give you his sob story about being too young to raise a kid. Don't cut him any slack. Tell him you have customers to take dinner orders from or bills to vote on and that he can wait for you to make time for him.

He will. He's your father.

If the guy teaching your pottery class isn't your real father or is a woman or if you already know who your real father is, pipe down and make a shitty ashtray.

Happy Take a Pottery Class in the Hopes That Your Real Father Will Be the Instructor Day!

FEBRUARY 26   COMMIT TREASON DAY!

You have $8,000 in credit card debt that you're trying to pay off. Luckily, you also know the secret launch codes for all the nuclear weapons in America. Sell your secret codes and you can kiss that debt good-bye. Ask for ten grand to give the buyer (the entire Middle East) room to bargain you down to eight. After you pay off your debt, you'll be hanged.

Happy Commit Treason Day!

FEBRUARY 27   SKINNYDIP (BUT ALONE) (AND QUIETLY) DAY!

Today is that special summer day when everyone has to swim naked and alone just like when we weren't born yet. No splashing or rope swinging (excuse the pun) either. Just nice even strokes out into the middle of the pond, tread a bit, then back again. You can stay out there all you want. I hope you're not looking for some romance. Unfortunately, this is a very sacred holiday in most parts of the United States. Even if someone saw you out there and was just bursting with the need to shout, "Mind if I join you?" or, "If I swim out there to you will you have sex with me?" he or she will more often than not respect the holiday and your right to celebrate it by leaving you be.

Happy Skinnydip (but Alone) (and Quietly) Day!

| FEBRUARY 28 |

POLICEWOMEN ARE AMAZING IN BED DAY!

The awesome thing is, and a lot of people don't know this, but policewomen are in fact allowed to have sex with people who aren't policemen. They can have sex with strip club owners and restaurateurs and ex-husbands, even battered women who need a place to sleep after the shelter's already closed for the night! And underneath a policewoman's hat is this unbelievable head of long brown hair wrapped up in a bun that she'll let cascade down her back when she's up for some.

But be careful. If you're not good at having sex and you have sex with a policewoman, she might plant heroin on you.

Happy Policewomen Are Amazing in Bed Day!

MARCH

THEY WILL LOOK UPON YOUR BODY AND THEY WILL PRAY.

| MARCH 1 | SIT IN ABJECT TERROR DAY!

"Nothing ever happens to me," says the whiny little baby. "I sure wish I could be involved in something intriguing and momentous, replete with brief erotic interludes preceding moments of sheer terror."

Did someone say terror? Well you're in luck. Because today's Sit in Abject Terror Day!

That's right, couch potatoes. For all of you who gave up hope of ever finding some small jostle of excitement to disturb your otherwise flat, static lives, today's the day to go fucking batshit with fear! And I'm not talking about that pussy anxiety crap you sob to your couples counselor about until he prescribes you a vial of anti-sissy medication. I'm talking barricade yourself in a closet because They're coming. I'm talking smother your pets now because at least by your hand they'll die a humane death. I'm talking motherfuckers in capes!

"But— But— But—" says the little baby girly-girl, "But how can I sit in abject terror if I can't think of any reason why anyone would even know I'm alive, let alone want me dead?"

Let's just say you're a pawn in a game you didn't know was being played, and no one can make the next move until you're eliminated. Or fuck that, let's just say they're coming. Duck, motherfucker.

So pull that afghan up just below your bugged-out eyes and tremble your clenched fists as you watch the doorknob jiggle with increasing violence because today's Sit in Abject Terror Day.

Happy Sit in Abject Terror Day!

| MARCH 2 |

YOUR MASSEUSE IS AT THE
DOOR DAY!

"I'm being chased," she'll say.

"Greta, meet my wife. Pauline, this is Greta, my masseuse."

Greta and Pauline will shake hands. Pauline will fix Greta a drink.

"I left my boyfriend last week," Greta will tell you. "He's a real sleaze-ball. He got some guys to follow me today. Lucky I remembered where you live. I don't have many clients in this neighborhood."

Pauline will tell Greta, "My husband just raves about you."

Over dinner, you will be excited to have Greta and Pauline at the same table, as you've spent many hours imagining having sex with the both of them at once.

"So, Greta," Pauline will ask, "do you ever get disgusted by the state of a client's skin?"

Greta will have to take a moment to chew all of the food she had shoveled into her mouth. "No," she'll say. "If it's really gross, with open sores or loose moles, I refuse to do the job because I could cause damage by doing a rubdown on skin like that. But really, it's just the job."

After dinner, Pauline will invite Greta to spend the night.

"Only if you let me give you a rub," Greta will say.

After her rubdown, Pauline will fix up Greta's bed for her, then she'll join you in bed.

"She's going to get back together with her ex-boyfriend," Pauline will say to you. "She told me as much during the rubdown."

"That thug?" you'll ask.

Pauline will say, "You know, that rubdown wasn't that good."

Demand that Pauline take back what she said about Greta's rubdown or else you'll leave her.

Happy Your Masseuse Is at the Door Day!

| MARCH 3 |

STEAL A CHERRY PIE FROM REBECCA DE MORNAY'S WINDOWSILL DAY!

When you walk home from the fishing hole today, you're going to be intoxicated by the delicious scent of a freshly baked cherry pie. You'll close your eyes and allow the scent to lead you down the row of identical ranch-style homes lining the road. When you finally open your eyes, you'll be just twenty feet away from where that golden brown pie is resting on an open windowsill to cool.

You'll drop your fishing gear by the picket fence and crouch low to the ground to avoid being seen by whoever might be inside. There won't be any truck in the driveway, which means it's probably just a housewife home alone. No angry farmer with a shotgun to chase you away from his dessert for the evening. You'll scurry to the window and just as you're about to grab that pie plate into your hands, Rebecca De Mornay will appear out of nowhere with a schoolmarm's smile on her face.

"Rebecca De Mornay!" you'll exclaim.

"I hope you ate your veggies seeing as you're so eager for dessert," Rebecca De Mornay will say.

You were prepared to make a run for it if you got caught. But you weren't prepared to get caught by Rebecca De Mornay. Better think of something fast.

"Hey, you were great in *Risky Business*," tell her.

"That was over twenty years ago," she'll say. "And here I thought you were a fan sneaking around for souvenirs. Turns out you just wanted to steal my cherry pie the way these young actresses are stealing all the plum roles away from me."

Rebecca De Mornay will start to cry. Tell her she's still got a lot of years ahead of her.

"The only parts I'm offered are moms and schoolteachers," she'll say. She'll really be crying hard.

Tell her that she should just go back to doing theater. She'll say that

that's a good idea and she'll scold herself for indulging in self-pity. That's when you should throw some dirt in her eyes, grab the pie off the sill, and book it.

Happy Steal a Cherry Pie from Rebecca De Mornay's Windowsill Day!

| MARCH 4 | THE KISSINGS DAY!

Today there will be a rash outbreak of kissings, starting with . . .

7:32 A.M.—the home of Jeffrey and Wilma Craig, Milford, Wisconsin. Mr. Craig will awake to the sound of his morning news radio station. He will roll over and kiss his wife, Wilma, of eleven years. He will go to the bathroom and wash.

9:41 A.M.—Theodore Roosevelt Elementary School, Wilmington, Delaware. Assistant principal Laura Marcus will lead third grade language arts teacher David Willis to the Xerox room under the pretense of needing assistance with a toner change. Once the door is closed, Marcus will place her closed lips upon his slightly parted lips. It will have been a long time coming.

3:59 P.M.—La Brea Jiffy Lube, Los Angeles, California. Waiting to get his car serviced, Jacob Reed will take his new kitten out of the cardboard carrier provided to him by the shelter, and he will kiss it three times between the ears and once on the spine. Jacob will put the kitten back in its carrier and he will believe that today is the start of a better time.

8:20 P.M.—Rich People's Attics, a New York City antique shop owned by Johnson Crane. In the back office Johnson Crane will make love to Charles Evans, his boyfriend of eleven months. This will involve many kisses.

11:04 P.M.—O'Hare Airport, Terminal D. JetBlue flight 86 will arrive at gate 21 and release the round smiling face of Lisa Cohen. Waiting for her, impatient to find out the decision Lisa said she would make while visiting her parents in Sacramento, will be Tobias Hutch. When Lisa sees Tobias, her smile will expand by 13 percent. She will walk to him and lift her lips up to be kissed. Tobias will comply. In the kiss, her decision will be plain. Tobias will take her bag and they will walk to short-term parking.

Happy the Kissings Day!

MARCH 5

INADVERTENTLY STEAL FROM A DRUG KINGPIN DAY!

What the hell else is there to do in this one-lesbian town? Nothin', that's what!

So when you and your friend decide to rob a stranger in town who looks like he's got some spare cash on his person, pick a stranger who is actually a bagman for a very dangerous drug lord and who is in town to exchange several million dollars in cash for several briefcases full of an exciting new synthetic drug that feels better than cocaine but doesn't make anybody die. But you, of course, can't know that the stranger was about to make a drug deal. You can't realize what you've done until you're in the passenger seat of a car and you open up the stranger's bag and find $2.4 million. Your friend will pull the car over and you'll figure out what to do by the side of the road.

You'll decide to confront the drug lord and you will, of course, end up killing him and taking over the cartel. Congratulations, and I love you.

Happy Inadvertently Steal from a Drug Kingpin Day!

| MARCH 6 |

SHE'S LOCKED IN THE MEAT
LOCKER DAY!

If you're wondering where your girlfriend is, she's locked in that meat locker over there with the guy everyone thinks she should be with because there's no chemistry between the two of you. I'm sure nothing's going on inside there. He's just her "will they–won't they" guy. I'm sure it's so "won't they" in there.

Sure, they probably have to kind of cuddle together to keep warm, but it probably means nothing to her. She's only doing it because she has no choice. You have nothing to worry about. You've heard her tell you she loves you over and over again with that adorable distant look in her eyes. She could stay inside that meat locker with the guy everyone (even you, if you look deep down inside) thinks is the right guy for her forever and it wouldn't make any difference. Your love is strong enough to conquer her undeniable need for the one she's supposed to be with.

Anyway, two strong guys are gonna hold your arms and make you stand there staring at the locked meat locker door for a couple hours. Your girlfriend and the guy she's supposed to be with are locked up inside there.

Happy She's Locked in the Meat Locker Day!

| MARCH 7 |

THE KID WHO SELLS YOU YOUR
CHINESE TAKEOUT DOESN'T CARE
HOW RETARDED YOU ARE DAY!

All day long you go from being coddled and doted upon at the hands of shopkeepers and mailmen to being ridiculed by everyone from schoolchildren to female mail carriers.

You'll go up to the deli to buy your grandmother's cold cuts and damn if old Mr. Nathanson doesn't just cradle you in his arms and sing you a lull-aby, you're so retarded. Your cold cuts in hand, you barely get two steps out the door of the deli before you get slammed in the face with a snowball and surrounded by middle school students who try to make you eat yellow snow. So you eat the snow and get a big laugh and then it's off to the 7-Eleven to buy your brother's lotto ticket, where Ahmed welcomes you to as many Big Gulp refills as you can stomach.

Such an emotional roller coaster. No one but the retarded can watch a day go from good to bad and potentially back to good again with every turn of the corner.

It's hard to be retarded.

But there is one place you can go where you're just another $4.35 who doesn't pay attention to board of health violations. Down the block at Mandarin Palace, when you order your "sesame chicken with NOOO BROC-COLI!!!" in that really loud, retarded way, all the kid behind the counter wants to know is "whiteriefrierie?" You'll put a little extra tard in it when you answer, "I hate broccoli!" but he just writes "white rice" on the order slip and goes back to bagging fortune cookies and soy sauce packets. The kid who sells you your Chinese takeout doesn't care how retarded you are, just like you don't care that he's Chinese and has orange hair.

Go ahead, show him your new gloves. He won't even look at them. He'll just nod his head a bit as he continues to sketch on the back of a menu possible flyer designs for his upcoming DJ gig. To him you're no different than the drunk waiting in line behind you to order from that fried chicken part of the menu. Or the dipshit on the phone complaining that he didn't want any snow peas in his Hunan beef. Even when you go full-on retard and show him how good you are at karate kicks, he doesn't so much as blink an eye. He just bags up your order, shouts out, "Sesamechicken!!" and shoves the bag into the hand you just used to send a pulled karate chop into the pile of unfolded menus.

This is one of the few destinations on your schedule where you're no less normal than anybody else. You'll get no derision from the kid who sells you your Chinese takeout. And you won't be getting any handouts beyond the free fortune cookie wrapped up with your fork and your napkin. Just like it says on the sign outside, the only thing you can expect from Mandarin Palace Takeout is a nice hot plate of "Epicurean Elegance." You pay now.

Happy the Kid Who Sells You Your Chinese Takeout Doesn't Care How Retarded You Are Day!

| MARCH 8 | YOU HAVE A CAN-DO ENTREPRENEURIAL SPIRIT AND YOU SHOULD RUN WITH THAT HARDCORE PORNOGRAPHIC PLACEMATS IDEA DAY! |

Americans, or at least the Americans you'll allow your kids to consort with, love two things above all else:

1. Photographs of penises in mouths. The more the better!
2. Lifting up their plates of food to see what's underneath!

Well what'll happen when Joe Six-Pack and Jane Supporting-Joe-Six-Pack sit down at the table with their rugrats and they all lift up their plates to check for spiders or angels like they always do, and what will they see but the most glorious color photographs of human mouths full to the brim with knob?

They'll wanna kick a pay phone they'll be so hooked, that's what! You're gonna be rich! Now go buy some land.

Happy You Have a Can-Do Entrepreneurial Spirit and You Should Run with That Hardcore Pornographic Placemats Idea Day!

MARCH 9

PRETEND YOUR APARTMENT IS A FORT AND INVITE FRIENDS OVER SO YOU CAN PRETEND THEY'RE MONSTERS TRYING TO GET IN AND EAT YOU DAY!

Pile up all your pillows and couch cushions in a kind of circle and hunker down with your cordless phone and some chicken. Then call up your friends and tell them to come on over and bring some beer. When they buzz your apartment and ask to come up, tell them you know that they're monsters and they're just trying to get in so they can eat you and everyone else in the building. When your friend says, "What?" repeat yourself. Your friend might say something like, "Quit being a fucker. It's me, Ed. C'mon, it's chilly out here." That's when you should tell your friend that you know that monsters have the ability to mimic their prey, and you can assume that Ed is dead and that the monster should leave because you're vengeful. Eventually all of the friends you invited over will get pissed off and go away. Then you'll be alone.

Happy Pretend Your Apartment Is a Fort and Invite Friends Over So You Can Pretend They're Monsters Trying to Get In and Eat You Day!

MARCH 10

IT'S REMAIN CLOTHED WHILE IN PUBLIC DAY!

Happy hour is an exciting time for fans of jalapeño poppers all over the country. But before you make your functional alcoholic's sprint toward the local theme restaurant, remember to keep an eye out for people who will demand that you remove your clothing in public.

Ladies, how many times have you been stopped at a light on your drive to

Chili's when the balding man with an "I'm impotent" goatee in the '91 Tercel across the intersection starts flashing his headlights at you and miming the act of lifting up his shirt? Suddenly, you're in a quandary. "Does he just want me to show him my breasts in their bra, or is he hoping to see my bare nipples? This bra is difficult to refasten once undone. And how long should I remain topless in order to satisfy him? Oh, cursed debacle!"

No need to fret. For today is that one day of the year that you are to remain fully clothed while in public, even if someone demands that you expose your naked body!

So let's say you're walking down the street and a crowd of, say, one hundred men start shouting, "SHOW US YOUR TITS!!! HURRY UP AND SHOW US YOUR FUCKING TITS!!!" All you have to do is smile and take out your pocket calendar and point to March 10, shaking your head as if to say, "Sorry, fellas." Once they remember the date they'll unhand you and help you look for some of the buttons they ripped off of your blouse. They might even offer some Polysporin to help scab some of the cuts on your face and neck. Then, they'll start kicking over trash cans.

It's a fine day of relaxation for men and women alike. The corporate sector used to be a man's kingdom. But lately, no matter what he's the VP of, a man can't even walk outside to a sandwich cart without windows flying open and women bellowing out from their offices, "WHIP OUT YOUR FUCKING COCK AND WAGGLE IT AT ME, SHITFUCKER!!!" And sure, he'll pull his penis from his pants and kind of shake it at them or slap it back and forth against his upper thighs to make a kind of clap-clap sound, but the modern ladies of today's corporate world are not easily satisfied. "NO, FUCKDICK! ERECT! MAKE IT HARD, LIKE YOU'RE READY TO FUCK US BLIND!!! OR YOU'RE DEAD!!! YOU HEAR US?! YOU'RE FUCKING DEAD!!!" So there he is, today's captain of industry reduced to masturbating on the sidewalk under the watchful eyes of scores of judgmental colleagues, doing all he can to achieve an erection and waggle it at the surrounding expanse of offices just so he can go and have his lunch in peace.

But not tonight. There truly will be a happy hour this evening, because tonight you can stride with the confidence of someone who doesn't have to disrobe in public at a stranger's demand.

Happy It's Remain Clothed While in Public Day! Now, who wants to go halvesies on a quesadilla?

MARCH 11	FILL YOUR POCKETS WITH GLITTER AND CONFETTI AND THEN STEP IN FRONT OF A SPEEDING BUS DAY!

Your coat and pants pockets should be overflowing with glitter, and you should also have big handfuls bunched up in your fists and wads of confetti stuffed in your shoes and socks. This way, when the bus smacks into you, the glitter will burst in a fat twinkling cloud enveloping the entire bus in the shiny rainbow-colored beauty. The bus will roll right over you and then come to a stop. The door will open and the driver and some passengers will file out to the street.

They won't be looking at you. They'll be looking up at the sky, at the granules of rainbow and all that confetti showering down upon the street as if someone just won a war. They'll watch it all fall down, turning the street where you died into something magical.

"It looks like a fairy tale," the bus driver will say.

The driver and the handful of passengers following him will approach you to find out whose death it was that brought such enchantment upon the world. They'll look at you in your ripped and bloodied Gap jacket and your Levi's jeans and Nike sneakers, one foot wrenched backward, and they'll be silent. The angel looks just like them. The angel is out of shape even. The angel that God just summoned back to heaven still has a Philadelphia Phillies hat on his head. Glitter will continue to hover in the air, and all of the passengers still on the bus will have their gaping mouths pasted against the windows, watching you as if a yellow light is going to shine down and carry you up to God. One of the passengers will push her way out the exit of the bus and fall to her knees on the street. She'll pray in Spanish.

Happy Fill Your Pockets with Glitter and Confetti and Then Step in Front of a Speeding Bus Day!

MARCH 12 — SIT ON A ROOF AT DUSK, BUT DON'T BRING YOUR RIFLE DAY!

I don't know about your neck of the woods and I don't really care all that much, but from where I'm sitting it's gonna be a pretty nice evening. That's why around 6:30 I'm going to climb out onto my rooftop and just kinda soak in the twilight. Join me? We can watch the folks in their cars ease down on the clutch as they get closer to their families. We can chuckle at the Rorschach-inspired shapes of the bald spots of the boyfriends on the sidewalks, and we can wander down the cleavage of the girlfriends on the sidewalks from our bird's-eye view. We can bring beverages, like a cran-apple drink or some vodka. We can smoke marijuana. We can just lay back and get heavy-petted by the breeze and if you want to kiss, I don't know. Maybe.

We can talk some stuff out that we can't talk about at a lower altitude, and we can spit on things or confess to crushes we have on mutual friends. And I promise not to bring my rifle this time. That was a bad idea, I'll admit it. That was my bad, yo. But how the hell does a newspaper get to print a headline like RUSH-HOUR SNIPER CAPTURED BEFORE FIRST SHOT FIRED when they have no idea whether I was going to shoot anybody? As far as I know, it's legal to own a rifle and according to my lease, I have roof access. Is this Russia?

Happy Sit on a Roof at Dusk, but Don't Bring Your Rifle Day!

MARCH 13	GO STARE DEEP INTO THE REST ROOM MIRROR AND SORT SOME SHIT OUT DAY!

Lay your palms flat on the sink and just lean in real close, never blinking your eyes, like if you blink once you might miss it when your reflection begins to fade and fill in with gray. Kind of shake your head a little. Like, "No . . . Can't be . . . no . . ."

Your coworkers will come and go, patting you on the back as they pass, using the sink next to yours and asking if you watched a particular sitcom the night prior and whether you thought a certain misunderstanding was as hilarious as they did. Say nothing. Hold your eyes directly ahead as if you're waiting for God to finish a joke.

On the occasions when the rest room is empty save for your slack form, start sorting this shit out. Say it out loud:

"Who'd respect you? Why?"

Wipe your hands with a paper towel, crumple the towel, and beam it into the wastebasket with all the fury you can salvage from your bile-drowned spirit. Then lay your palms flat on the sink again, the filthy germ-crawling Formica, and stare into those frightened eyes until they're bloodshot bright red. Say it out loud:

"You're gonna let it all slip away. In the end, you'll have meant nothing."

Breathe deep. Now close your eyes. Keep 'em closed until it's time. The rest room is gonna be someplace else when you open them again. Keep 'em closed.

Open. Say it out loud:

"Can't . . ."

Happy Go Stare Deep into the Rest Room Mirror and Sort Some Shit Out Day!

MARCH 14

EXPRESS DISAPPROVAL OVER THE EXISTENCE OF YOUR REDHEADED STEPCHILD DAY!

Whether you married her for love or just because she collects bigtime disability and doesn't mind that you turned her kitchen into a meth lab, marriage is marriage. And marriage means warts and all.

But no one likes to be reminded that his best gal was once involved with someone who had red hair. Which is why it turns your stomach to see the progeny of that relationship walking past the TV with a stack of Oreos in his freckled little hands. It's like the sun-stained little urchin's very existence is sending raspberries into your face with chants of *My mommy fucked a redhead so hard their coarse thrusting resulted in all seventy-five pounds of unholy me that stands before you drinking a cup of grape juice. Look at my red hair! No one would ever mistake me for your child! I am proof that your lover had sex with someone else in the past, at least once. Though she probably did it lots of times, because you have to have sex with millions of people before you finally look at someone with red hair and say to yourself, "What the heck. Might make for a funny story at least."*

Well then, why not let your redheaded stepchild know you would prefer that he had never been born. Hitting works. But locking the beast in the closet can really send a message as well. Though if you do that often enough the Damien will be expecting it so he'll start stashing some toys in there to play with the next time. Oh, that's a good one too, breaking the little monster's favorite toy, I mean. You do drink, don't you?

Happy Express Disapproval over the Existence of Your Redheaded Stepchild Day!

| MARCH 15 | OUTLET SHOPPING DAY!

Today is about brand-name bargains! So, why not head out to the farthest outskirts of the state and drop by a seven-mile expanse of outlet shopping strip mall. You might just be able to pick up a plaid American Eagle shirt for five dollars cheaper than you would normally pay for a plaid American Eagle shirt. Also, there are socks!

Happy Outlet Shopping Day!

| MARCH 16 | GO TO A DINNER THEATER FEATURING A MAGIC ACT AND ASK THE MAGICIAN, "IF YOU'RE SO FUCKING MAGICAL, WHY HAVEN'T YOU TAKEN OVER THE WORLD YET?" DAY!

He claims to have unholy powers that can make small birds materialize from shirt cuffs and large-breasted assistants disappear into another dimension. But if he's so fucking magical, why has he not yet tapped his wand to manipulate a lotto drawing to his favor, yielding him vast riches? Why does he refuse to exert his hellish talent to bring into being a giant pony, eighteen feet tall, and then charge young girls admission to look upon the awesomely adorable steed in captivity? Why has he not waggled his fingers to conjure a massive army of half-human killing machines and stormed the seats of government across the free world? In short, if he's so fucking magical, why is he doing dinner theater at a motor lodge that brags about being located just a half mile away from an interstate off-ramp?

Ask him tonight. After he saws his assistant in two and she turns out to be all right (make sure she's all right before you say anything), shout

out, "Hey, if you're so fucking magical, why haven't you taken over the world yet?"

The magician will stop the show and explain that he could use his terrifying powers to mold the world into a realm of his own design and take control of the minds of men so that all and sundry will be subject to his will. But then his power would no longer be magic, it would be law. He would cease to be a magician so that he might be a God. And no one likes God.

"But everyone loves magicians!" he'll shout, and then he'll make roses burst from his shirt, eliciting a standing ovation from the crowd.

"So it's because you want to be liked?" you'll shout over the roar of the crowd. "It's because you want the applause?"

The magician will shout back, "God can have his massive flock. I've got all the sheep I want right here." Then he'll continue with his grand finale (making an overweight audience volunteer levitate in his chair). Shut your mouth and let the magic happen.

Happy Go to a Dinner Theater Featuring a Magic Act and Ask the Magician, "If You're So Fucking Magical, Why Haven't You Taken Over the World Yet?" Day!

| MARCH 17 | EVERYONE'S ALL ALONE, BUT YOU MOST OF ALL (SHIT) DAY! |

Anyone who is lonely believes that everyone else in the world is happier and has more love in their lives than he does. In the lonely man's mind, everyone is laughing at his pain in between trading body oil applications with each other. But in reality, when someone is happily in love or surrounded by trusting friends and family, the only people who are on his mind are the ones he cares about. He might remember when he was alone and he might give thanks for what he has. But people who are not in his life really don't concern him.

Except for you of course.

It's true, for most people the feeling of being the joke of society is all a head game played to elevate self-pity. But unfortunately, people really do laugh about you. Not in a "that's so hilarious" kind of way. But in a "holy shit, this is one of those horribly tragic situations where all I can do is offer a little laugh to keep from crying" kind of way. And yeah, there are a lot of people out there who are pretty lonely. But when you come to mind, it perks those people up a bit. "Least I'm not that bad off," they say before turning everything around for themselves.

And no, Captain Paranoia, no one's been watching any surveillance tapes of you writhing on your bathroom floor and moaning. But we can tell you do it a lot. Not by your eyes so much as by the way you wear your skin.

Happy Everyone's All Alone, but You Most of All (Shit) Day!

| MARCH 18 | PICNIC DAY! |

Tell your friend Steve, "It's your job to bring the Frisbee. If you don't bring the Frisbee, you're fucking dead!"

Tell your friend Anna, "You're responsible for the Cokes. If I don't have a can of Coke in my hand within five minutes of my ass touching soil, I swear to God you'll feel a big fucking boot up your ass!"

Tell your kids, "Don't forget the bug candles. Unless you want me to start drinking again. I think we both remember how many times you nearly died when I used to get real loaded and slam your heads against the bedpost. Shit, you probably remember better than me, being as you were the sober ones back then. I still say that was all your fault. Least I never tried and fucked yas. Not my type I guess. Anyway, I get bit by one mosquito and you're gonna wish it ate me whole. I love you both, by the way. Just sayin'."

Tell your spouse, "Make sandwiches. NOW!"

Tell your coworker, who just recently got a divorce so all of a sudden he has to be invited out everywhere and the whole fucking city is supposed to try to get him laid as some kind of payoff for having let his family disintegrate, "Just bring yourself. I'll take care of everything. Including the ass I'm supposed to set you up with."

Tell your grandmom, "I SAID MOOOOVE, BITCH!!!"

Look into the mirror and tell yourself, "Even if someone screws up and you have to beat the living shit out of them, it's ultimately your fault. The universe will repay you in misery. Now go get some fresh air."

Happy Picnic Day!

| MARCH 19 | ANYBODY REMEMBER TO CUT HIMSELF A PIECE OF "I'M A FILTHY WHORE" CAKE DAY! |

Carvel might not have these on display. But trust me, they sell 'em.

Now come on, for God's sake. You work hard all day pawning away all those pieces of yourself into which you might have invested just a little bit of pride. You run the hustle and you skim the till. You lie and you scam and in the end you'd partake in a haggle over the asking price for your baby's asthma pump. When you walk past a church, nuns shout, "There he is!" and then they run out to the sidewalk to kick you in the genitals. Whether you're selling the land out from under an assisted-living facility to make way for a parking lot or you're in the truck stop ladies' room from 10:00 P.M. till 2:00 A.M. performing oral sex for crystal meth, you're a filthy whore and you're way fucking good at it. It's time you got some goddamn cake.

Sorry, but I'm sick of this shit. My dad was given a cake last September just because he turned sixty-eight. And here you are sanding away at every characteristic of your person that might designate you a member of the human race as opposed to, well, a "cunt," and do you get a cake? Sure, the

Guide Dogs for the Blind Association was good enough to put your face on a poster that reads: GOD MAY HAVE TAKEN OUR VISION, SO FUCK GOD. BUT THIS GUY MADE IT SO WE CAN'T BRING OUR DOGS INTO GROCERY STORES, SO DOUBLE-MOTHERFUCK THIS GUY! But did they give you a cake? The blind don't know how to party.

Happy Anybody Remember to Cut Himself a Piece of "I'm a Filthy Whore" Cake Day! Now get your hand outta my pocket, shitbag.

| MARCH 20 | THE SWIMMING DRUNK DILEMMA DAY! |

You wanna go swimming and you wanna be drunk as hell when you do it, right? But ever since you were a little baby your dad told you to never drink on an empty stomach. So you'd better get some chicken and some crazy bread (THAT BREAD'S CRAZY!) in your belly before you hit the bar, unless you wanna get all squiggly in the knees like last night.

But ever since you were twenty-seven years old your mom's been telling you never to swim on a full stomach. So if you eat the chicken and crazy bread (THAT BREAD'S FUCKING NUTS!), you won't be able to swim for an hour!

So then, you could either skip the chicken and the crazy bread (IT'S UNHINGED) and be pickled with gin and soaking in the deep end within ten minutes. Or you could eat some chicken and some crazy bread (DEAR GOD, THE BREAD IS OUT OF ITS FUCKING MIND! RUN!), then get started on the drinking. But before you can swim you'll have to wait an hour to digest the chicken and the crazy bread (IT'S GOT A GUN!), thereby running the risk of falling asleep or in love before you ever even make it to the pool.

Kinda wigs you out, doesn't it? Now you understand why the Swimming Drunk Dilemma is the subject of so many Philosophy 101 term papers.

Happy the Swimming Drunk Dilemma Day!

| MARCH 21 |

**SET THE GENIE FREE FROM THE
MAGIC LAMP DAY!**

When the little green genie appears from the puff of smoke, he will thank you for setting him free.

"I am now duty-bound to grant you three wishes. Anything that you desire is yours. Your worst troubles and greatest calamities will disappear. All that you have to do is speak it so that I can hear, and it shall be done!"

Don't say anything. Just stare at the genie for a second, then go back to looking out the window.

"Any wish you wish, it is yours," the genie will say.

Ignore him.

"Hey, did you hear what I said?"

"I heard you," say to him. Don't bother looking at him.

The genie will float up near your shoulder to look out the window with you.

"What are you looking at?" the genie will say.

"So much gray," say, less to him and more to the miserable world you see stretching on into infinity outside your window. "Such ghastly gray. It's so cold and bleak."

The genie will look at the unseasonably sunny day outside. He'll think to correct you, but instead he'll try to just get the wishes over with so that he can go out into the world.

"Ahem. Once again, if there is something troubling you, simply wish that it be gone and you'll never have to think on it again."

Tell the genie, "You can't help."

The genie will say, "But I can do anything. Anything at all."

"Can you make the gray go away?"

The genie will again look out the window.

"I . . . I could. If I could see any gray."

Just nod. "You can't help. No one can help."

The genie will sit by you for a moment, unsure what to do. "Have you tried talking to somebody?" he'll ask.

"Shrinks," tell him. "They give me pills and they tell me to cheer up."

"I don't normally do this," the genie will say. "But I'll let you wish for unlimited wishes if you'd like."

"I just want to be left alone," say.

The genie will say, "I can grant you that. But that is only one wish. If you wish for me to go, you must say that you release me from my debt to you for having set me free."

Say, "Fine, I release you. Now get the fuck out of here. Just leave me alone."

The genie will begin to thank you, but he'll fear another outburst. He'll float to the door, and he'll stop just before leaving. He'll turn to you and say, "Feel better."

Don't acknowledge him. Just let him go.

Happy Set the Genie Free from the Magic Lamp Day!

MARCH 22	DOOR-TO-DOOR BIKINI
	SALESWOMAN DAY!

Getting laid off has been hard enough on your marriage. But when the door-to-door bikini saleswoman comes by, the temptation will be so great that you might as well just go ahead and fill out some divorce papers before you even offer her a sandwich.

"I've got so many wonderful bikinis to offer this season, there is no way I'm leaving this house without having sold you two," she'll say with a tickle of her long red fingernail down the bridge of your nose.

"Fine!" you'll shout. "Just hand over whichever two you want me to buy and go."

The door-to-door bikini saleswoman will start to cry. "Everyone thinks I'm just out to make a buck," she'll sniffle. "But that's not it. I sell these bikinis because it's important to me. Outfitting the community in the perfect sun- and swimwear is what I feel like I was meant to do. Ever since I was fifteen I just knew."

"I'm sorry," you'll say. "How old are you now anyway?"

"Seventeen," she'll say.

"Go on, my seventeen-year-old true believer. Sell me some bikinis."

She'll bound from her seat and shout, "Where can I change? I know! How about behind this four-foot-tall recliner! No peeking."

And so you'll spend the afternoon with the door-to-door bikini saleswoman modeling bikini after bikini for you in your living room. Occasionally, they'll come untied and she'll have to do what she can to keep herself covered up while giggling. When she complains of the heat, you'll offer her a large soapy sponge to squeeze some cold water down her chest and belly. When she gets thirsty, you'll give her an ice cube to suck on.

After four hours of slipping in and out of bikinis while trying to crouch her five-foot-five-inch frame behind the four-foot-tall recliner, the door-to-door bikini saleswoman will leave very happy, having met her quota of selling $600 worth of bikinis with just one house visit. But she won't stay happy, because the check you'll have written her is gonna bounce like a Superball.

Happy Door-to-Door Bikini Saleswoman Day!

| MARCH 23 |

REMEMBER WHEN YOU STILL KNEW WHY YOU WERE CRYING DAY!

Seems like a long time ago, doesn't it? Believe it or not, your sobs once had a direct cause-and-effect relationship with experiences in your life. Even more surprising, you used to be able to tell when the crying started and stopped. Why not use today to make a list of all those moments in your life when you can remember there being an obvious impetus for your blubbering? How could you forget all of those cathartic crying jags brought on by things as obvious as a skinned knee, or a funeral, or the movie *Terms of Endearment* starring Debra Winger and Shirley MacLaine. The list will fill out with the more blurred but still empirically obvious sources of pain, like that time you confessed to the authorship of a secret admirer letter and they all pointed and they all laughed. Or that three-month period when you seemed to see garbage and hunger everywhere you looked. Or that time you watched a snowfall through a noose.

Wherever the list stops, draw a line. That's the line between the ability to dream and the feeling that no one ever listens to anyone ever.

Happy Remember When You Still Knew Why You Were Crying Day!

| MARCH 24 |

BEFRIEND A RUNAWAY, *BUT DON'T PUSH!!!* DAY!

Runaways run away because they get molested so much they have to cut school to make time for it. So when they finally steal their stepdad's crank revenue and get on a bus, they take it to Hollywood usually, to become famous. If they're rich and famous then everyone will listen when they say no. Some might go to New York if they dig musical theater, but most will go to Hollywood. (Note: Just because everyone in musical theater has been molested, it does not follow that everyone who has been molested digs musical theater.)

Your job is to befriend one of them and try to keep her from becoming a hooker. It's difficult convincing them that you're not another molester or a pimp. The only people who talk to runaways are pimps offering free soup. Sure, some pimps just like to give runaways free soup. But other pimps want to convince the runaways to have sex with strangers for money. (IT'S THE FUCKING TRUTH!!!) You have to show the runaway that there are people out there who are just as nice as pimps. Show her that there are more options open to her than being forced to have sex with strangers for money in gratitude for free soup.

Prove to her that you're different than the pimps. Instead of soup, offer your runaway a bowl of your "world-famous chili." Make it clear that you expect nothing in return. You just offer chili to everyone you meet because you're so proud of the fact that you know how to cook wet beef. This way the runaway won't think you're trying to manipulate her at all. She'll think that you're just an annoying person with few talents.

The important thing is not to push. Runaways are kind of snobby in that they think everyone wants to have sex with them. So don't offer to let her crash at your place. Instead, give directions to a shelter. Or leave little Postit notes on her blanket of newspapers that say, "You're special and no one can take that away from you." This way, if she ever writes a book about life on the streets you'll see your name on the dedication page. If you don't have a book dedicated to you before you die, your life will have been for nothing.

Happy Befriend a Runaway, *BUT DON'T PUSH!!!* Day!

| MARCH 25 | GO TO A PARK AND SEEK WISDOM FROM THE STATUE OF SOME GUY YOU'VE NEVER HEARD OF DAY! |

If you lived in Philadelphia you could go and ponder the statue of Rocky until you were imbued with the courage to reveal the secret love you've been harboring for your secretary these forty-six years. "Help me, Stallion," you'd say to the shiny, chiseled titan. "Knock down my fears of rejection like so many Clubber Langs." But sadly, we can't all live in Philadelphia.

"But what if I were to commute from Cherry Hill, New Jersey?" you might ask. Be quiet for a second. The point is, no matter where you live, there's probably a park with a statue in it. No matter what kind of shit-storm you've gotten yourself mixed up in, it's worth a shot to try to get some inspiration from that statue of the guy who invented the bike rack before you use up all your vacation days for the trek to Mount Rushmore.

So head on down to the park, real casual like, find your statue, and let it all out. Just make sure no one's watching. Best to rub your upper lip to cover your mouth when you talk. Teenage gangs hang out in parks, and if they think you're talking to yourself they might beat you to death.

Happy Go to a Park and Seek Wisdom from the Statue of Some Guy You've Never Heard Of Day!

| MARCH 26 | HAVE SEX WITH THE FARMER'S DAUGHTER DAY! |

When you started working for the farmer, he warned you not to have sex with his daughter. "If you know what's good for ya," he said.

You figured he was just making an empty threat, so today you're going to have sex with her.

The sex will be great because the farmer's daughter is very buxom and giving, much like the fertile soil on which the barn where you'll have sex with her is built. You'll sneak out of the barn afterward, expecting to see the farmer pointing a shotgun at your head.

The farmer will in fact be watching you sneak away with your overalls undone. He'll watch from his kitchen window, and he'll shake his head in dismay.

Over the next few days, the farmer's daughter will call you to the barn to have sex with her every afternoon. With each interlude, she'll seem to grow a little bit sadder and a little more desperate for your attention. She'll cry afterward, on occasion. And she'll make an effort to refer to you as her boyfriend when you converse. She'll say things like, "You're the best boyfriend ever." You'll never respond to that. Whenever you get up to leave, her mood will turn solemn. Occasionally she'll trip and cut open her hand all of a sudden, forcing you to stay long enough to tend to her wound.

After a week or two, your interest in her will have waned. One day, she'll barely be able to breathe when she asks you to join her in the barn. You'll ask her why her breath is so short and she'll say, "I haven't been able to sleep because I feel like you're going to break it off with me. I'm terrified."

You'll tell her that she's right. You do think the two of you should stop seeing each other. "Look what it's doing to you. This can't be a good relationship if it makes one of us unable to sleep or breathe."

She'll tell you that it doesn't need to be serious, that you don't have to be boyfriend and girlfriend, but you'll insist it has to end. Her breath will come back once she accepts that you're not going to join her in the barn anymore. She'll seem relieved that the hammer has finally dropped, but when she walks away she'll cut the saddest figure you've ever seen. And a farm is no stranger to sad figures.

That night at dinner it will just be you and the farmer.

"My daughter is up in her room crying," he'll say. "I guess it finally ended between you two."

"You knew?" you'll ask.

"You're all she's talked about," he'll say.

"It was hard to end it," you'll say.

The farmer will throw down his napkin. "I warned you to stay away from my daughter, didn't I? The girl is clingy. She has real low self-esteem and she's in no shape to get into an emotional relationship with somebody. Every time she sleeps with a boy she treats him like he's the love of her life."

Don't say anything except, "I wouldn't have if I had known."

The farmer will bark, "Oh the hell you wouldn't have. The girl's so pretty she'd coax a dead man from the grave."

He'll take a bite of his biscuit, then he'll say, "If only I could have raised her to think she was worth more than what a two-bit drifter like you might want her for."

Happy Have Sex with the Farmer's Daughter Day!

| MARCH 27 | **EMPTY THE BIGGEST ROOM IN YOUR HOUSE OF ALL FURNITURE AND DECORATION, THEN YOU AND YOUR MATE STRIP NAKED AND SCOWL AT EACH OTHER DAY!** |

Sorry, this one's only for couples who've lived together for three years or longer. Not that those who've lived together for less than three years blow. It's just that for today you do not matter and neither does your intimacy. Wait outside. There's a truck that sells tacos outside.

Now then, for those who've stayed, I hope you've found the room you wish to use. It should have white walls and wood floors and in one of the longer walls there should be two windows that pour in the soft gray light of the late afternoon dim. Remove all furniture, pictures, paintings, and extension cords. Make it look the way it looked when you first saw the place and decided to call it home. Then strip.

Don't sweep the floor. You want to feel the dirt and debris that gathers against baseboards attach itself to the skin of your ass and thighs. Even though you've never done this before, I'm sure you both will choose the wall you wish to sit against without any discussion.

Now just sprawl your legs out in front of you and curve your back up in a slouch so that there's enough room between you and the wall for a cat to squiggle behind each of you. The thing about this posture is no matter how much you exercise, your bellies are still going to fold in on themselves and you will look fat.

Let all muscles go loose, not with peace of mind, but with exhaustion. Like atrophy can be effortful. Now look at each other. You know that body. You know those creases of skin and those breasts and those toes and legs and testicles. You've pressed your lips against every inch. That body is yours because you say so.

Now let a scowl bloom from your lips. For whatever reason, just put it there and let it settle there. Look at that face way over there across the room. There's a scowl on that face that's meant just for you. It's not a bad thing. You're simply glaring at each other because sometimes faces fall ugly.

Hold it there. Just there. Keep it just there. After about fourteen hours, put on your clothes and go find food.

Happy Empty the Biggest Room in Your House of All Furniture and Decoration, Then You and Your Mate Strip Naked and Scowl at Each Other Day!

MARCH 28 | **THINGS YOU DID NOT WIN WHILE YOU WERE SLEEPING DAY!**

You did not win a brand-new bicycle, and neither did you win a Vespa built from items found around the home, such as a portable electric radiator and whirlpool jets. You won no all-expenses paid vacation to Tahiti because you have no one to take with you, and if you were to ask to receive the cash equivalent of the prize, everyone would understand why when they saw the shallow purple valleys just underneath your eyes. And the prizegiver did not want to be engaged in such an unhappy interaction.

About the prizegiver. You have made inquiries as to his identity. Please desist, for your own safety.

The respect of a friend you hold too dear was not a prize that you were awarded while you slept last night. And you did not win the love of the little fool that would end up breaking you into shards if he or she ever got a grip on you. Your friend believes that you don't have "conversations" so much as "presentations." The little fool was celebrating a birthday at a bar and not enjoying herself all that much. But she got a little drunk and, without it being suggested, suddenly found herself being helped to a slow dance in somebody's arms. And from those arms there seemed to float in the air between them a kind of enchanting snowy chill, and they woke up together this morning and couldn't wait to start making phone calls to mutual friends.

You did not win a free small fries or soda, and neither did you win a cigarette boat. And sadly, neither one million dollars nor two hundred and fifty dollars was awarded to you. The big pink bear too. You didn't win the big pink bear because you didn't knock down the milk bottles. You were sleeping.

Also, you were unable to win a smile from the small child held in the arms of the woman in line in front of you at the grocery store. And you did not win the suspicion of that woman even.

Perhaps tonight you might have better luck. Happy Things You Did Not Win While You Were Sleeping Day! Try again.

| MARCH 29 |

YOUR MARIJUANA-ADDICTED EX
WOKE UP THIS AFTERNOON AND
WROTE A SHITTY SONG ABOUT
YOU WHILE SITTING IN BED
NEXT TO A NAKED MUTUAL
ACQUAINTANCE OF YOURS DAY!

The phone company won't be able to change your phone number until at least late Monday morning. So it would be best if you ripped the phone out of the wall. The dim little fool plans to call you and sing into the phone, so rip the phone from the wall if you don't want to be reminded of the person who used to sit naked in the wicker basket chair in your bedroom, strumming a bass while you filled out continuing education registration forms on the bed.

There's a line in the song where rain is rhymed with pain. It's so good you got out of town last year. Everyone's ending up exactly where you would've guessed. The song is called "A Song for You." Fucking Christ.

That mutual acquaintance he's with is Jennifer, by the way. She's the girl who used to sell shitty ecstasy while waiting tables at the bar you tended. Guess what? The ecstasy-dealing gig fell through due to a rather severe assault at the hands of a dissatisfied customer. But the waiting-tables gig is really coming along.

Anyway, if his phone call gets through to you, I don't know. Jesus.

Happy Your Marijuana-Addicted Ex Woke Up This Afternoon and Wrote a Shitty Song About You While Sitting in Bed Next to a Naked Mutual Acquaintance of Yours Day!

| MARCH 30 | GO TO AN EMERGENCY ROOM WAITING AREA AND PACE DAY! |

You like strangers to wonder about you but you don't like them to talk to you and you adore Spanish language soap operas, yes? Then you need to head on down to your nearest hospital's emergency room waiting area and pace.

You should wear brown penny loafers and a docile-patterned plaid shirt tucked into your Dockers. Don't bring a jacket so that when you first walk in it looks like you were probably there the whole time but just stepped out for a smoke or a lotto ticket. All other parties present will be near-entire families waiting to find out whether their eleven-year-old daughter/sister survived the hit and run. You'll be the only one alone. No enormous father still wearing his phone company hard hat to hold you in his gargantuan arms. Just you pacing back and forth, sipping from cold cup of coffee after cold cup of coffee (bring a lot of change for the coffee machine because you have to get change from the desk otherwise, and you don't want to draw too much attention from the girls back there if you want to stay for the whole afternoon). Those families won't take their eyes off you. They'll be glad to see someone else suffering. They'll hope that you hear bad news so that maybe their news will be good.

Just for fun, but this can be risky, whenever a surgeon steps through the swinging doors into the waiting area, get up and look in her eyes anxiously. The surgeon will register you, then she'll quickly look away and shout out a last name to avoid having to tell you she doesn't know anything about your loved one. After a while, on maybe the sixth time you've jumped out of your chair hoping for good news, she'll get fed up and you can be sure that while she's operating on the next patient, she'll start asking around the table, "Hey, anyone know who that one guy out there is waiting for? He's bumming me out." You should split before you're asked to leave, though.

If you want to make a scene before you go, keep it contained. Just pick up an empty chair and slam it to the ground a few times shouting, "Why?! Why?! Why?!" Then head out for some hot dogs and go home and go to bed.

Oh, and how about you lay off shaking your fist up at God this time, okay, Mr. Heston?

Happy Go to an Emergency Room Waiting Area and Pace Day!

| MARCH 31 | GO TO A FIRING RANGE DAY!

Today's the day to go over to the firing range and as the paper target with the silhouette of the guy comes closer and closer to you, shoot rubber bands at it. If when you try to buy another target they tell you that you can't shoot rubber bands at it, tell the counter person that's cool. This time, when the paper man comes rolling toward you, yell at it. Then when it gets close enough, dive forward and rip it to shreds with your bare hands like a real man.

If when you try to buy your next paper target you're told that you can't fight your target hand-to-hand and that you'll have to use a gun, tell the salesperson everything's cool and you'll use a gun. Go get your rifle out of your trunk and bring it into the range, showing it off to the counterperson as you pass. As the paper target rolls toward you, take the rifle by the barrel and lift it up over your head like an executioner with his ax. Then when the target gets within reach, bring the rifle butt down and smash the shit out of it, swinging over and over until the target's just a wad of ripped-up construction paper all over your rifle butt. Even though everyone reading this assumes it'll end with the counterperson telling you to leave the firing range and you responding by shooting a round into his chest, do it anyway.

Happy Go to a Firing Range Day!

APRIL

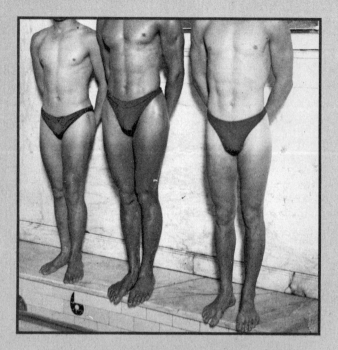

TOWEL EACH OTHER AFTER EVERY PRACTICE,
AND DURING MEETS, AFTER EVERY DIVE.

| APRIL 1 | YOUR POT DEALER HAS
A DAUGHTER IN THE GIRL
SCOUTS DAY!

She has some cookies that need to be sold.

"Hey man, if I worked in an office it'd be no sweat," he says. "I'd just post the sign-up sheet on my cubicle, just like the rest of the dads, and in one day she'd meet her quota for the camping trip."

He hasn't even sold you your pot yet. You and he are sitting on your bed going over the options in the color brochure spread out across your comforter. He smells terrible.

"A lot of people like the Samoas," he says. "But I fucking hate the Samoas."

"Do any Girl Scouts sell their own cookies anymore?" you ask.

"Are you crazy, man? It's too dangerous," he says, while scratching underneath his shirt. He complained to you once that his gun holster itches.

"So I figured," he says, "who wants cookies more than all the potheads who smoke my shit? You guys are all stoned out of your gourds with the munchies, and then in I walk with a chance for you to binge on some snacks and support the futures of a whole lot of little girls."

You say, "But you haven't let me buy my pot yet."

He points to the Thin Mints. "These are fuckin' primo shit. Buy six boxes."

You buy six boxes.

Happy Your Pot Dealer Has a Daughter in the Girl Scouts Day!

| APRIL 2 | VISIT WITH YOUR ASSASSIN FRIEND DAY! |

"Thanks for making time for me," Jenny will say, pouting.

She's always been this way. Back when she was working those late hours as an editor at MSNBC, she'd berate anyone who dared schedule a birthday party when they knew she'd be at work. And now that she's an assassin and she has to disappear to another continent for four to eight months at a time, everyone is supposed to drop everything for this long series of "Good-bye Jenny" events.

"I guess now I know how little you'll be missing me when I'm gone."

Tell her, "You act like you were sentenced to go into this line of work. You get paid $75,000 for pulling a trigger on a gun. And we're all supposed to feel sad because you have to go and live in Morocco for a while?"

"How'd you know I'm going to Morocco?" she'll ask.

Point to the plane ticket she's holding in her hand.

"Fuck!" She'll rip up the ticket and log onto Orbitz.

"So are we getting drinks or what?"

"Just let me change my itinerary, okay? Or were you hoping to be the one they would torture until you give up my location?"

Go and wait outside on the stoop. She'll get weepy after a Cosmo, and it'll be nice to say good-bye to her. Until she has that Cosmo, though, just bite your tongue.

Happy Visit with Your Assassin Friend Day!

| APRIL 3 | TOWEL EACH OTHER OFF DAY! |

You and your fellow college diving teammates don't quite have it together this season, and it's because you're all still afraid to really care for each other. You turn out for practice every morning. You all cheer each other on at the meets, and it can't be said that any one of you cares more about himself than about the team's success as a whole. But you all treat the diving team as if it's something outside of your lives. You've built a wall so that what happens inside the confines of that natatorium can't touch your *real* lives, the lives you lead in your dorm rooms and classrooms.

What you have to do to solidify your diving team is you have to open the doors to the natatorium so life can walk in and go for a swim with you boys. Your teammates share a goal with you, they stand side-by-side with you as you all push yourselves to the limits of your physical ability. Day after day you watch each other strive to create a momentary flash of grace. Acknowledge all that you share, and the ragged incongruities that make you all beautiful to each other will show themselves in contrast.

And most importantly, you should all towel each other off after every practice, and during meets, after every dive. You all have nice, toned bodies and we want to see you towel each other's wet bodies dry. We want to imagine that back in the locker rooms you're peeling off your Speedos and gently padding each other's groins with the towels, so do that too and tell us about it. You want to win your division, don't you? You want to make your fathers proud?

Happy Towel Each Other Off Day!

| APRIL 4 | THE ALLEGORY OF THE PASTA MAKER DAY! |

There was once a couple aflame. In the throes of divorce, a man and his wife directed the whole sum of their bitterness and rage into a single dispute over the custody of their jointly purchased pasta maker.

It began when the husband was carrying boxes out to his Nissan. Settled precariously atop the last of the boxes was the pasta maker. As the husband made for the door, his wife reached out and snatched the pasta maker into her embrace.

"You're not taking the *PastaMatic*," she said.

The husband defended his rightful possession. "The fuck I ain't," he said. After much shouting, it was in a huff he left, and the pasta maker was returned to its home on their kitchen counter. But it was not plugged into the wall socket, and neither would it ever be again.

In the ensuing months, the husband fetishized that dusty countertop appliance as if it were the key to a secret door of escape from his feelings of loss and resentment. The pot came to a boil when in the middle of his fifth sleepless night in a row he broke into his former home, grabbed the pasta maker from the kitchen counter (noting that he didn't have to unplug it from the wall), and climbed upstairs to stand at the foot of his old bed and wake his wife and her new boyfriend from their sleep with a whisper of her name.

"I'm taking the *PastaMaestro* now," he said.

She saw the flames in his eyes and decided to stoke the fire. "Walk out that door with the *PastaMucho!* and my lawyers will have you working for me by the time this divorce is final."

Her new boyfriend concocted a plan to bring the matter to a close. The husband appeared not even to have noticed the boyfriend until he finally spoke.

"Why not let an outside party decide who gets the *PastaMarksman*?" he said. The wife thought that was a good idea. And for some reason, perhaps just to get to the end of this story, the husband agreed as well.

So some old and wise person, probably a town elder or a cop, he showed up in the bedroom and said, "I'll cut the *Pastameliorator* in half so's both y'all get a piece."

The wife was into it but the husband said, "No, let her have it. I'd rather give up the *Pasta (and I mean) Lotsa!* than see it destroyed." The wife went, "Score!" and grabbed for the appliance but the old guy yanked it out of her reach. He said, "No way, little baby ho. Your husband clearly loves the *Pastamerica (USA!) (USA!)* most for whatever reason. He probably fucks it. But anyway, I'm giving him dibs."

That's when the wife killed everyone in the room using magical powers.

Happy the Allegory of the Pasta Maker Day!

APRIL 5	YOU ARE AN UGLY PERSON DAY!

Walk tall, beast! A call has been sounded to the harelipped, the hunch-backed, the overly ruddy complexioned. Rise up, unroll that turtleneck from atop your nose, and let your offensive visage feel the sun's grin.

You are not unattractive. Your brother's wife is "unattractive." You have the power to actually piss people off just by sitting down at a neighboring table in a restaurant. Salesmen don't even want to sell you their wares, you're so ugly. And since it is not legal to have you thrown in prison for being as ugly as you are, everyone hates the Constitution of the United States.

But today you are recognized for being as important a minority as the beautiful, the wealthy, the people who have telekinesis. Today is the day to remind the world of your presence. When you talk to strangers, touch them on their biceps. When you pull over to help someone change a flat on the freeway and they tell you they'd rather wait for AAA, get out and change the flat anyway. When you sneeze in the office and the chick in the neighboring cubicle doesn't say, "God bless you," go to the cubicle and lean in real close to her ear and shout, "Um, *ahhh chooo?* Fuckin' douchebag!" Then grab her by the wrist and slap your balled-up snotty tissue into her palm, clenching her fist shut around the tissue before you return to your seat. Also, don't forget to mail out framed 5×7 photographs of yourself to everyone for whom you have an address. Include no note of explanation.

Happy You Are an Ugly Person Day! See you at the parade!

| APRIL 6 |

CALL A TRUCE IN YOUR WAR OF WITS SO THAT YOU AND YOUR ARCHENEMY CAN FUCK DAY!

You might want to get a handle on that premature ejaculation problem first. You're mad geniuses in a never-ending battle for world domination, after all. When the begrudging respect you hold for each other turns to an erotic longing so palpable that you're both willing to postpone death ray construction to find out whether your coupling will make the winters boil and the summers freeze, the whole bang-bang shouldn't dribble away after a few minutes when you mutter, "Oh . . . uh . . . oops. I'll get a washcloth."

You guys should fuck on top of a mountain. In fact, you guys should fuck each other *with* a mountain. The moaning should be mistaken for a summer storm's thunder. If you get bored or sore with one particular position you should go into villages and steal some village elders and fuck each other with them.

Don't come yet.

Now stay genitally conjoined but start beating the living shit out of each other. Spit fire on each other and start talking really breathy and potty-mouthed. God that's hot. Your minions are engaged in battle at the mountain's base and they're almost all dead, just so you know. Now, one of you should ask what the other is thinking about, and the other should lie to spare feelings. Then go at it again but lazier this time. Be playful. You have all day before you have to return to your respective secret headquarters underneath their respective riverbeds, so why not make the most of this bed? Say what you feel. There's nothing sexier than communication, you know. It's almost as sexy as searing runes into your lover's thigh with your prosthetic pinky laser.

Remember, eye contact.

Happy Call a Truce in Your War of Wits So That You and Your Archenemy Can Fuck Day!

| APRIL 7 |

BUY A TOWN AND NAME IT AFTER YOUR EX-BOYFRIEND DAY!

Now that you're worth billions, you can start engaging in the kind of behavior that you should be ashamed of. For starters, you can buy a town and name it after a particularly unforgettable ex-boyfriend. Then you can manipulate an entire population of people accordingly.

For example, let's say your ex-boyfriend's name is Leo and your relationship with Leo was so turbulent and emotionally damaging that you hope he is being tortured in a nameless prison somewhere in Eastern Europe. Why not name your town "Leoville" and then run it into the ground until every last resident is penniless and homeless and all of the buildings are left empty to rot like so many forgotten skeletons of the life that once flourished there? Perhaps once you've destroyed a local economy and the populace that relied on it, all in the name of the pain a boy once made you feel, you might decide your spurning has been avenged.

Or, what if you have an ex-boyfriend named Patrick and though he's been gone for many years, your love for him hasn't dissipated in the slightest since the day that you first met? In that case, you could name the town Patrick Gardens and you could nurture and legislate the town until it is the portrait of prosperity. Then, if your name is Melissa, you could make the town's slogan: "Patrick Gardens: Founded by Melissa, Who Wishes She Hadn't Been So Preoccupied When Her Career Took Off. She Built a Whole Town for You, Patrick. That Town Is Here, Waiting for You, If You're Willing to Give Her Another Chance." It won't fit on a license plate, but it will fit on a billboard. Have a lot of billboards put up on all the highways that pass nearby. He might see one and he might pass through out of curiosity, just to see what you're capable of when you let your love control the checkbook.

Happy Buy a Town and Name It After Your Ex-Boyfriend Day!

APRIL 8   SHOOT THE MAN IN THE MOON
            DAY!

The police came and took your stepdad off to jail on a warrant for writing bad checks in Arkansas, something he did before he met your mom. You came up to his and your mom's walk-in closet because you like to go in and sit there whenever you get nervous. As soon as you walked in you saw the padlock on your stepdad's gunbox was released and dangling from the latch. You lifted the lid and there was the handgun, resting out of place as if he had taken it from the box but dropped it back in. You checked and saw that it's loaded. Who knows? Maybe he went in and loaded it when he heard the police at the door, then he changed his mind and came out with his hands up.

Your mom is at the police station and she said she'll wait there all night. She didn't make any plans for your supervision. You're eleven now, but this is the first time that you've been left to spend the entire night in the house completely alone. Take the handgun from its case, go up to the roof, and shoot the man in the moon.

This might be the only chance you'll have to use his handgun. When he gets back, he's sure to lock it up again. Ever since you can remember you've been dying to find out what the man in the moon will do if he gets hurt. You always thought you'd have to wait for a space shuttle to crash into it. But maybe not.

Climb out on the roof late tonight, aim the gun at his splotchy gray face, and fire once. Then wait a while. It can take a long time for a bullet to travel that far into space. Maybe even all night long. Just lie on the roof and watch the moon for an expression of sharp pain or anguish. Or maybe just a small twitch. If you don't see any change, you either missed or the bullet didn't get there in time to beat the sunrise. In which case you should shoot him again tomorrow night, but earlier. And make sure to only shoot one time every night. Shoot more than once and the police will come and get you just like they got your stepdad.

Happy Shoot the Man in the Moon Day!

| APRIL 9 | YOUR NAME IS GREG AND YOU CLEAN UP AFTER ORGIES DAY! |

Your name is Greg and you clean up after orgies. You get paid $70 to show up every Sunday morning at 11:00 A.M. and clean the floor of all of the spilled wine, cubed cheese, and *other*. You've never seen one of the orgies in person, but you used to know somebody who went to a few.

"That was when I was involved with a particularly offbeat older lady by the name of Grace," said your former girlfriend's Uncle Leland. "I have to say that it was interesting. But not everything that is interesting is necessarily something that I'd ever want to experience again."

Kimmy, your girlfriend at the time, got excited to finally hear the inside scoop. She was intrigued by your job and was always excited when you told her about a particularly hard-to-explain puddle or when you showed her trinkets like cufflinks and compacts that you found during your morning sweep. "Were the girls pretty, Uncle Leland?" she asked, nearly bouncing on her couch cushion.

"The next time you walk into town," Uncle Leland said, "take note of the first thirty-seven people that cross your path. No matter who they might be. I want you to imagine exactly those thirty-seven people scattered about a meeting hall in various states of fornication. That will give you an idea of the range of physicality that you'll find at the Modern Living Party."

That's what they call it. "The Modern Living Party."

You're not with Kimmy anymore. No girlfriend to speak of at the moment. You can't afford a girlfriend on a cleaning man's salary. Right now, sitting on your coffee table, there is a locket with a little boy's photo inside. You know the little boy, 'cause he's you. Or was, when you were six. You found it this morning cleaning underneath a bar stool. You had been planning to find new employment for about six months. Staring at the locket that used to drape from your mother's neck, you really regret not having stepped on the gas with that job hunt.

Happy Your Name Is Greg and You Clean Up After Orgies Day!

| APRIL 10 |

PLAY A DRINKING GAME CALLED "BURST INTO TEARS" DAY!

The way you play is, a player says something wonderful that's happened to him or her. Such as, "By the time I was twenty-four I had the job I always dreamed I'd have and it was even more rewarding than I'd imagined."

Everyone else has to either be happy for that player or be miserable for themselves and how sharply their own lives contrast to the life of the player who just spoke. If you're happy for the player who just spoke, you drink. If not, you burst into tears and run from the room until someone you're not attracted to comes looking for you. Then you have to take that person who came looking for you into the bedroom and make out with him or her on the coats.

Happy Play a Drinking Game Called "Burst into Tears" Day!

| APRIL 11 |

A BALLOON RIDE OVER FORT LAUDERDALE DAY!

Today, you'll soar over Fort Lauderdale in a hot air balloon. Your husband will have arranged it.

"I reserved the balloon that says, 'Show Us Your Tits,'" he'll tell you. "So we'll probably get the whole city to take off their shirts from up there."

Once in the basket and floating across the blue sky, you'll find your husband was right. It'll be like a stadium doing the wave. The earth below you will be alive with young women exposing themselves to God.

"It's glorious," you'll say to your husband.

"Happy anniversary," he'll say to you.

Kiss him. "We have a lot of work to do," you'll say. "Let's start tossing the beads."

Happy a Balloon Ride over Fort Lauderdale Day!

| APRIL 12 | YOUR JOB AS AN ORGAN PIRATE IS MAKING YOUR BOYFRIEND JEALOUS DAY! |

It's hard to sustain a love life when you make your money by drugging tourists, stealing their kidneys, and leaving them to wake up in a bathtub full of ice with a "Dial 9-1-1" note written in lipstick on the mirror. Boyfriends don't mind that you cut into strange men's bellies and steal their organs. Boyfriends mind that before you can start the bathtub surgeries, you have to seduce the men back to their hotel rooms first.

You had hoped your current boyfriend would be different. He's been a card dealer in Vegas for a long time, and he's dated all variety of stripper and showgirl. He used to say that you were a walk in the park comparatively. But tonight he's going to start asking the questions that they all ask when they start to wonder exactly what it is you do to get those men to take you home.

"How'd you get him up to his room before the sedative kicked in?"

"I'm good at my job," you'll say while undressing at the foot of the bed. He'll respond to your naked body with as much passion as if it were a floor lamp. And he'll keep on asking questions.

"Did you grab his cock?" he'll ask.

You did. You placed your hand on the crotch of his suit pants and suggested that he show you his room. He barely made it through his door before he tumbled face forward onto the king-size bed. The cutting isn't the hard part. You got used to the cutting after your first job solo. The hard part is dragging the body into the bathroom and hoisting it into the tub.

"I did what I had to do," you'll say.

He'll make the argument that always wins.

"And what if when you get back to his room the sedative hasn't kicked in yet?"

Will you then have to kiss him? Will you then have to strip for him? Will you have to do all the things that would be necessary to keep him convinced that you're just an attractive woman he met in a bar and this is his lucky night?

"The sedative always kicks in," you'll argue. But it didn't once. For three whole minutes after the door shut the guy remained conscious. And if your boyfriend knew what you had to do for those three minutes in order to keep the con alive, he'd walk out the door without packing. "And there are lines I don't cross."

"You can lose sight of those lines when there's a three-thousand-dollar kidney at stake," he'll say.

Once it's clear that he's basically calling you a whore, he'll get up from the bed and put his arms around you and he'll tell you that he's just worried about you getting hurt.

"I know," you'll say. "I'm not going to be doing this for much longer."

But there'll be questions every night when you come home now. Even if he doesn't ask them out loud, the questions will be in the air, waiting for answers, from the minute you walk through the door. Based on past experience, you've got about two more months before he sleeps with a cocktail waitress and moves out.

Happy Your Job as an Organ Pirate Is Making Your Boyfriend Jealous Day!

APRIL 13

THE ONLY THING KEEPING ME FROM SHOWING THOSE KIDS MY ASSHOLE IS YOU AND OUR BEAUTIFUL DAUGHTER DAY!

He loves you as much as he hates being a high school math teacher. Every day it's getting worse at that school. The overgrown punks just so determined to send their lives down the toilet. They ignore your husband. They laugh at your husband. Every day your husband comes closer to doing something that will kick him out of that school forever.

And every night he comes home and he sees your beautiful eyes echoed in the face of that adorable little girl under a blanket in her crib. One smile from you, one nuzzle of his daughter's cheek, and he remembers what he's doing it for. To keep his family happy.

"You listen to me go on and on, and I'm sorry," he'll say to you after dinner tonight when the baby's asleep. "But I swear to God when they start mouthing off in that classroom, sometimes I just wanna yank down my pants and spread my cheeks so the craggly brown crust of my asshole is staring them in the eyes and I'll tell him what they can mouth off into if they want. I'll tell 'em to lick it clean till it's as white as the chalk on that chalkboard up there."

Take his head to your bosom and say, "Shhh."

"I hate teaching," he'll say.

Caress his hair and say, "Shhh."

"I swear to God," he'll say. "The only thing keeping me from showing those kids my asshole is you and that little girl upstairs."

Just hold him tight. He'll feel better in a little while. Then both of you should go upstairs and watch your daughter sleep.

Happy the Only Thing Keeping Me from Showing Those Kids My Asshole Is You and Our Beautiful Daughter Day!

| APRIL 14 | SOME OF THE CATS DAY! |

Some of the cats are plotting something together. Every time you come out of your bedroom, you find a good three-quarters of your cats scattering from a kind of semicircular grouping underneath the kitchen table. The rest of the cats, all of the older ones, they look up from their naps when you come out. They give a drowsy look at the younger cats, then at you, then you swear you see them give their heads a slow mournful shake before returning to sleep.

Cats don't call meetings but for one reason. And you know what that reason is so you should go turn out the pilot light in the oven and turn on the gas. Then go back into your room, stuff the door frame with wet rags, and wait to hear the soft quiet thumps as they all fall on their sides and die.

This is what you get for letting Lentil hang out in the hallway. Apparently some outdoor cat filled Lentil's head with talk of "feline ascendance" and "shackles of domesticity" and "how to hover over a human's mouth to steal her breath when she's asleep." Kill them all now. Even the older ones. They're not innocent, they're just tired and they'd rather nap and wait for more food than use their dark talents to suck the breath of Jesus out of the shell of man.

Don't think. Take the little fuckers out right now.

Happy Some of the Cats Day!

| APRIL 15 | IF YOU START COLLECTING YOUR LOOSE CHANGE IN LITTLE JARS DAY! |

If you start collecting your loose change in little jars, you will feel that rush of adrenaline that great artists receive when they discover they've embarked on a journey toward the completion of a great work. With each jangly handful of coins tossed from your pocket to your change jar, neighbors and roommates will think they've heard a sculptor slap another fistful of clay upon his wet amorphous beast.

Some people, small-minded people, keep jars of change solely for the doing of laundry. These are the same people who think that a stone is for skipping across the lake, that paint is for houses, that garbage should not be welded together to make a statement about the state of low-income housing. These people do not have the creator's soul that burns inside of you.

In months, years, or perhaps decades, for there is no time limit for the fruition of greatness, you will one day bring your masterpiece to Coinstar. People will stare at you, in much the same way they stare at people pushing cartloads of aluminum cans (another of the great misunderstood pursuits. MUST WE ALL PUSH PAPERS ACROSS A DESKTOP?!!!). Ignore these undead ghouls, pounding upon the walls of their tombs of middle-class debt. Let your masterpiece cascade into the Coinstar. Is the sound any different from the clatter of a waterfall? That is the sound of your work being appraised.

There once was a man who had accumulated fifteen years of loose change, and he brought it to Coinstar when he decided to leave town. He walked away with over a thousand dollars. The reason he was leaving town was because his wife had taken his child and run off, only to send him divorce papers two months later. Once the divorce went through, he decided it would be best if he moved. He also decided to cash in his change, so as to not be reminded of the past fifteen years of his existence.

Happy If You Start Collecting Your Loose Change in Little Jars Day!

| APRIL 16 |

YOU JUST HAD AN APPENDECTOMY AT "THE HOSPITAL OF LOVE" DAY!

As you come to, your girlfriend will be waiting beside your bed. So will two candy stripers wearing pink uniforms with plunging necklines.

Ask your girlfriend, "Where am I?"

Your girlfriend will say, "You're at the Hospital of Love. It was the closest. This is Candy and Kitten."

Candy and Kitten will wave hello to you in a really cute way.

"They had sex with you while your appendix was taken out," your girl-friend will say.

Exclaim to your girlfriend, "Oh my God, I've cheated on you. You must feel horrible."

She'll tell you to relax. "It's part of the hospital's healing philosophy."

"What philosophy?" you'll ask. "Sexual healing?"

Kitten will say, "That's just a song, silly. Here at the Hospital of Love we have a motto: 'Come in sick. We'll have sex with you and make you all bet-ter too. Unless you're really sick and there's no hope. But we'll still have sex with you.'"

"Catchy," say. Then to your girlfriend, "So what did you do while they were having sex with me?"

"I pretended to have a seizure so that I could get some action myself," she'll say. "He was great. I never caught his name. But he was wearing blue."

A wave of grief will wash over you and you'll suddenly feel worse than before you checked in. That's when your doctor will walk in.

When your girlfriend sees your doctor she'll say, "That's him! This is the guy I had sex with!"

Your doctor will look at your girlfriend and say, "Hey! That was great earlier! Feeling better?"

Your girlfriend will say, "I feel fine. I was just faking it."

Your doctor will say to the room, "I can usually tell."

Everyone will laugh, except you. You'll just moan.

Candy will tell the doctor, "He seems worse than ever, doctor. Ever since he woke up he's been like this."

Your doctor will say, "Some people react badly to hospitals." Then he'll place his hands on your girlfriend's breasts and play with them while Candy and Kitten kiss.

Happy You Just Had an Appendectomy at "The Hospital of Love" Day!

| APRIL 17 | LET YOUR SON AND YOUR
GIRLFRIEND GET ACQUAINTED DAY! |

Your wife was a trapeze artist, and she died the way every trapeze artist hopes to die: She fell from three hundred feet onto her neck and then was trampled by startled circus elephants. You and your son used to go to every show so you saw the whole thing. It was a rough day.

It took three years before you were able to date anybody new. And after several catastrophes, you think that you've finally met someone worth introducing into your son's life.

You vowed after your wife died that you wouldn't force a new girlfriend on your son unless he felt a real bond with her on his own. But it takes a while for your son to warm up to somebody. He's kind of a dick that way. In order to guarantee that that bond will be there, you're going to have to thrust them both into a life-or-death situation so that they'll have to depend on each other for survival.

The best way to do this, of course, is to drug the two of them and throw them in a two-person raft headed downstream through dangerous rapids toward a giant waterfall. You'll have to time it so that they wake up in time to keep the raft from going over the falls. You should also slip a note into your girlfriend's life vest that says, "Don't worry. I planned the whole thing. All you have to do is save his life and we can love each other forever. Paddle!" When they come to shore, your son will have to let you date her because she'll have saved his life and those are the rules.

If a trip to the rapids is too far a trek for you, you're going to have to stage a bank robbery and take the two of them as hostages. Just keep them locked up in a basement together for around twenty to forty days. During that time, they'll calm each other's fears, they'll plot elaborate escapes, they'll even put on little puppet shows to entertain each other.

There's really no limit to how close they can grow if they are imprisoned in a basement together. Which is why you need to be careful. Your son is only sixteen and your girlfriend is thirty-seven. So it's plausible that when she finds out he's still a virgin, she'll make love to him so that he can experience sex before his death, which could come at any moment.

But if they don't screw, by the time they reach safety, they'll be so tight you'd think they were seated next to each other in homeroom.

Happy Let Your Son and Your Girlfriend Get Acquainted Day!

| APRIL 18 | DRUNK IN SEVENTEEN BUILDINGS DAY!

This could take a lot of drive time depending on where you live. But by midnight tonight, you have to have been drunk in seventeen distinct buildings. And we'll defer to your local government's zoning laws for the definition of "building."

There will be, however, a far more specific definition of "drunk." We're not just talking about whether you'd fail a Breathalyzer or hit a kid. What you have to do is, if you're still sober, write down on a piece of paper the name of the one person that you should not make out with tonight. This can be your ex-lover, your cousin, or the prosecutor who's trying to put your dad in jail. When you think you're ready to determine whether you're drunk enough, take out that piece of paper and ask yourself if you would make out with that person at that moment. If your answer is "In a heartbeat" or "Too late, and can anyone help me move my stuff back into his/her apartment this Sunday?" then yes, you are drunk enough to begin walking in and out of buildings.

Happy Drunk in Seventeen Buildings Day!

| APRIL 19 | WALTER ISN'T DEAD ANYMORE DAY!

Walter's back at work today, thirty pounds lighter, and completely free of the mysterious respiratory illness that sent him to what several doctors guaranteed was his deathbed. He's going to trot into the office like a little boy at Christmas, excited to see how you all decorated his cube and brimming to tell you about his near-death adventure.

The first woman with whom he'll come in contact is Marisol, the records administrator. He'll grab her in his arms and tell her how happy he is to see her face. She'll look up into his eyes and start screaming. When he sets her free from his embrace, Marisol will back away slowly, pointing at him and reciting prayers in Spanish. Then she'll make the sign of the cross and flee.

Walter will stay there at the door, trying to figure out what just happened. Then he'll shout out, "Hey everybody! I'm back!"

Slowly, the heads will rise above their cubicle walls, all eyes bugged wide with terror.

"Hey guys, man I sure am glad to see all of you again. What'd I miss?"

Their arms will rise and all fingers will point in Walter's direction. They'll start howling like demons until you are forced to hustle Walter into a conference room.

"We don't have much time," tell him. "They mourned you."

"But I didn't die," Walter will argue.

"You were sick for so long, the productivity came to a halt as we waited for word of your condition. As department manager, I decided it would be best that we all mourn you as if you were already gone. I told them you'd passed on."

They'll be pounding at the door to the conference room.

"So, they're under the impression that I'm . . ."

"Undead," tell him. "A zombie. Yes. Some of these people have been on this floor for thirty years. They only believe what they read in the body of a company memo."

The pounding will grow louder. You'll hear the wood around the door hinges begin to crack.

"You have to get out of here," say. "Climb up into the drop ceiling."

Both of you will get up on the table and knock a pane of the drop ceiling from its frame. The door will crack louder in the door frame. Walter will be up in the drop ceiling, his legs dangling. First, second, a third crash and the door will fly off its hinges. Walter will hold his hand down to you and pull you up with him.

In your memo to the floor, you made Walter dead. Now that he's walking, they assume that you brought him back to life. They believe you must both be destroyed before a race of walking dead is unleashed on the populace. The war between the army of the living and the army of the mistaken-for-undead has begun.

Happy Walter Isn't Dead Anymore Day!

| APRIL 20 | WORST EVER DAY!

One aspect of your day has to be the worst of its kind. It can be anything from a cheese sandwich to a dog. It just has to make you say, "That was the worst cheese sandwich ever!" or "That was the worst dog ever!" Or, if it's sex with five attractive people and you've never had sex with five attractive people before, no matter how fantastic it is, you can still say, "That was the worst sex with five attractive people ever!" Because hey, have you had better?

In case you do not yet understand the concept of today, seven additional examples are provided below.

If you die in such a way that makes you think you have never died so shitty, you should say, "That was the worst death ever." Or, drive to the supermarket and park in a parking space that in every way (distance from entrance, ability to open doors due to proximity of neighboring cars, odor) is simply the worst parking space you've ever parked in, and say, "This was the worst parking space ever!"

The remaining five examples are snack foods.

If you have a Cheeto that is the worst Cheeto you've ever had, you will say, "That was the worst Cheeto ever!" If you have a Frito that is the worst Frito you've ever had, you will say, "That was the worst Frito ever!" If you have a piece of Angry Angry Pussy that is the worst piece of Angry Angry Pussy you've ever had, you will say, "That was the worst piece of Angry Angry Pussy ever!" If you have a barbecue-flavored Frito that is the worst barbecue-flavored Frito you've ever had, you will say, "That was the worst barbecue-flavored Frito ever!" And finally, if you have a piece of barbecue-flavored Angry Angry Pussy that is the worst piece of barbecue-flavored Angry Angry Pussy you've ever had, you will say, "That was the worst piece of barbecue-flavored Angry Angry Pussy ever!"

Happy Worst Ever Day!

<hr>

| APRIL 21 | GET COMMISSIONED BY A SOUTH AMERICAN DICTATOR DAY! |

You make forty-foot-tall stone sculptures of very realistic-looking puppies. They've become very popular in America, and last year you made a fair amount of money from your work, but you still have to temp.

Today, your art dealer is going to tell you that a South American dictator would like you to create a sculpture of two giant puppies fighting over a giant rubber ball. He wants it done in two months so that it will be on display when his country celebrates the two-year anniversary of the bloody coup that put him into power. It will pay you more than you would make from three years of temping.

"But America will consider you an enemy of the state if you take the job," your dealer will say.

America expects your allegiance even while it forces you to compromise your dreams? It's a hard decision, but you should accept the commission from the dictator, if only to be able to say the following words:

"Tell the dictator he'll have his puppies."

It's not often that you get to say things like that.

Happy Get Commissioned by a South American Dictator Day!

| APRIL 22 | YOU DIVORCED THE PILOT DAY!

Your ex-wife, Grace, is a commercial airline pilot, and after the divorce you made a point of never flying United to avoid being one of her passengers. Considering how incendiary the proceedings were, had she ever discovered you in the cabin of one of her flights it's likely she would have crashed the whole jet just to take you out. It hasn't been too difficult to avoid her flights, since you're terrified of flying anyway.

Today you're flying Delta to Chicago. Unbeknownst to you, Grace left United for Delta about four months ago. She's in the cockpit and she just got a look at the manifest and saw your name.

"Finally got you to take an interest in my work," she says when she comes back to your seat.

"Hello, Grace," say to her. "You've lost weight."

"No money to eat," she'll say.

All of the other passengers will be watching or listening in. Suggest that you and she continue your conversation when the plane lands since the other passengers might not like to watch their pilot lose her temper. Grace will refuse. Try to calm her down.

"I have to say, you look better than ever," tell her.

"Are you traveling on business?" she'll ask. Suggest that perhaps it's best that the two of you not go into too much detail about each other's lives.

"What's her name?" Grace will ask. You'll see her eyes go small, the way they always did right before she threw a vase at your face. Out of the corner of your eye you'll see several passengers turn their heads in your direction.

"Smith, Beecher, and Weinhart," say. "A client of mine is being sued by a client of theirs."

Grace will ask where you're staying in Chicago and whether it would be okay for her to come and visit you tonight. She really is looking better than ever.

"We shouldn't," say. "It will end badly."

Grace will say that she understands. She'll recommend that you fasten your seat belt because she thinks the plane might be running into some turbulence pretty soon.

"Grace," say. "Don't be crazy."

She'll smile and say that she's sorry but she has no control over the force of the wind in the skies. As she walks back to the cabin, everyone in the plane will fasten their seat belts.

For the next hour and a half, you'll endure the worst, most terrifying turbulence you've ever felt. You'll throw up twice. Your neighbor will throw up three times. Several people will shout at you for not having accepted their pilot's offer. "Was your marriage so bad that it's worth risking our lives?" they'll shout.

Shout back, "It was a mess! Nothing but head games and bile!"

Up in the cockpit, Grace will just sob and jerk the controls up and down and left and right, treating the plane like a bumper car. Her copilot has seen her like this before, and she'll know not to object.

A passenger will scream at you, "Goddammit, go up there and tell her she can have some of that tonight! My wife is turning blue!"

People will start tossing their food trays and peanuts at you until you unfasten your seat belt and pull your way up the aisle, grabbing hold of each headrest as you go to steady yourself.

Knock on the cockpit door and ask Grace to see you. The copilot will open up and you'll see Grace yanking the plane left and right through the calm night sky.

"You win," tell her. "I'm at the Radisson."

Grace won't stop jerking the plane to and fro.

"Grace, I'm yours. Tonight. Come by."

Grace will continue to yank at the controls. You'll make your way back to your seat. The other passengers will grip their armrests and glare at you. The plane will continue to bump and shake.

A few minutes later, a flight attendant will approach you with a slip of paper that reads: "Can we get dinner first?" There'll be a box for yes and a box for no at the bottom of the note.

"For God's sake, hurry!" the flight attendant will shout.

Check the box for yes, and the flight attendant will clamor back to the cockpit with the note. A moment will pass, and then the plane will steady. A cheer will go up from the cabin and several people will pat you on the shoulder, talking to you about "taking one for the team." Try to forget that you'll be having a rendezvous with your ex-wife in just six hours. Instead, just close your eyes and dream of land.

Happy You Divorced the Pilot Day!

| APRIL 23 | PUPPY THE GUPPY DAY! |

You have a ten-gallon tropical fish tank, meticulously ornamented, and containing only one guppy. You've named your guppy Puppy. From now until the end of time, it's you and your friend, Puppy the guppy.

"Puppy doesn't like you. I'm afraid we can't keep seeing each other," you've told several women you've dated over the years. "I'm sorry, it's not you. It's Puppy."

Puppy is very protective of you. One might call Puppy possessive.

"He's pretty awesome to me," says Puppy. "But when I think about him giving his attention to someone else, human or fish, I just wanna go rip-shit." In a jealous rage, Puppy will often try to trash his fish tank, but he usually just ends up gently swimming into things.

"All I wanna do is make Puppy happy," you say. "But I can never do enough, it seems."

But Puppy has not been speaking to you ever since he caught you updating your Nerve Personals profile.

"I'm a man. Puppy's a fish. He's the most important living thing in my life but I just need more." You shake your head. "This isn't going to end well at all."

It really isn't.

Happy Puppy the Guppy Day!

| APRIL 24 | MASQUERADE DAY!

Rooting through your wife's handbag looking for her cocaine, you'll find an invite to a masquerade ball that occurred three weeks ago. Confront her.

"Did you find my cocaine?" she'll ask when you come back into the room.

Say, "You're out. We'll have to call Guillermo." Take the invitation out of your pocket. "Why didn't you tell me about this, Jenny?"

"I didn't think you'd be interested," she'll say.

Say, "But you love masquerade balls. I would have gone for you."

Jenny will look down at the floor.

"Wait a minute," say. "Three weeks ago I was in Cincinnati. I remember there was one night when I couldn't get you on the phone."

She'll say, "I went."

"With Beth?"

Long, boring story short: Beth is your ex-wife who hired Jenny to have you killed. While plotting the assassination, Jenny fell in love with both Beth and you, but she realized that you would provide her with the better future. So she broke it off with Beth, promised to kill her if any harm came your way, and married you. They're still friends.

"She's a lot of fun at masquerade balls," Jenny will say.

"And I'm not?" you'll ask. But you know the answer to that. You always choose a "visual pun" kind of costume that requires lots of explanation. And you always complain of itching.

Say, "I feel so inadequate."

Jenny will say, "Only when it comes to masquerade balls. In every other area, except for ski weekends, you're the best."

Go outside on the front step and smoke. You should wait until the cocaine arrives before you two discuss this further. If you're both irritable because you haven't done any cocaine yet, you might say something you regret.

Happy Masquerade Day!

| APRIL 25 | SADDEST SANDWICH DAY! |

Today you are going to enter the Saddest Sandwich contest, wherein participants compete to see whose sandwich makes the most people feel really sad. You are going to come in second with your "PB and DS's MBC" (peanut butter and dead son's MatchBox car) with the crusts cut off. The grand prize will go to "Holocaust on Wheat."

Happy Saddest Sandwich Day!

<table>
<tr><td>APRIL 26</td><td>REMEMBER THE HUE AND
TEXTURE OF AN EX-LOVER'S
SKIN DAY!</td></tr>
</table>

"It could keep the neighbors awake it seemed to glow so bright." (Edward Mangum, Seattle, WA. Pisces.)

"I wanna say her ass felt like velvet, but when you're in love with a new chick, everything feels like velvet. But I used to rest my cheek on her ass, sometimes I'd fall asleep there, and it was like I could use nighttime as a pillow for my head." (Lisa Colleti, Pittsburgh, PA. School board administrator.)

"He was this beet bright red all over except where his thighs met his crotch. That was this sick white. And he was coarse. It felt like there were several layers of skin that needed to be peeled off but he would never get around to it. Like vacuuming. His skin suited him." (Christine Eleanor, Chatsworth, CA. 1966–2000.)

"She was yellow. Like she was supposed to be beige or whatever, but her insides were made of the colour orange." (Kevin Brown, Sheffield, UK. Hobbies include painting.)

"Fucked up, yeah, but I swear his nipples were the exact same color as the surrounding skin. So, you would, I mean, I would get really weirded out because he'd just have these bumps of skin with no other disparity. It looked like the way someone would design an alien in a movie." (Chelsea Solchnikov, Plano, TX. Democrat.)

Happy Remember the Hue and Texture of an Ex-Lover's Skin Day!

| APRIL 27 |

GET INTO A FISTFIGHT DAY!

No one's saying you have to win. In fact, you should lose. After all, who wants to hang out with the asshole who just won a fistfight? It's the guy who lost, the one who probably brought it on himself, the charming prick who's saddled up on his bar stool drinking his own nosebleed with a beer chaser that you wanna talk to. Look at him. He just got the shit kicked out of him and he's laughing out loud at his girlfriend for worrying about the cut on his head.

Don't just look at him. *Be* him. Go walk in front of a dart game and get your ass kicked by someone who smells like fresh drywall.

Because today's Get into a Fistfight Day!

| APRIL 28 |

THERE'S REALLY NOTHING ALL THAT WRONG DAY!

No one's saying anything is even remotely right. But the way you woke up today, with that feeling of "I swear to God if I leave this bed today it's going to be to write a letter to the editor and that's it!" You need to settle down. You're paying bills, you haven't scared off all of your friends yet, 13 percent of the gender you desire finds you attractive, and that percentage is a few points above average. Add it all up, and your life is going pretty smoothly.

Which is exactly why you feel so fucked. You want some drama, yes? You don't just want to absently lose touch with friends and lovers. You want to cut them off and threaten them with violence if they should dare show their faces in your life again after what they did. You're not the sole target of a vast conspiracy and you want to know why for fuck's sake! What the hell does it take to get your girlfriend to cuckold you with a guy who is only working the angle to get his hands on your collection of porcelains?!

And why is it that entire years have passed since someone left a cryptic note under your windshield wiper?

Sorry to say it, but everything's pretty even keel. Perhaps you could make a few rash decisions? Or were you hoping to spend tomorrow in celebration of Yep, Same-Old Same-Old in This Cubicle and How's About You Day?

Light a match.

Happy There's Really Nothing All That Wrong Day!

APRIL 29	**YOUR WATERCOLOR OF THE VIRGIN MARY IS NOT DRAWING THOUSANDS TO KNEEL BEFORE IT DAY!**

Your press release was pretty good, yes. "Virgin Mary Appears in Seven-Year-Old's Painting of the Virgin Mary." However, the Virgin Mary Appearing on Stuff appraisers found no spirit of the special old lady in your painting. Apparently, since you intended to paint a painting of the Virgin Mary, it doesn't count. It only counts when she appears in auto grease and on bagels.

Dr. Clement Borges of the Greatest Diocese Association wrote in his report to the association's trustees, "This painting, while accurate, does not appear to be anything more than a painting of the Great Ma'am executed by a marginally gifted seven-year-old. In short, the Virgin Mary Wuz Not Here."

Marcia Tiegs of the Catholic Power Collective was much harsher in her response to your work. "There should be no suggestion that Our Wonderful Woman of the Hills might be associated with this work of filth in any way, shape, or form. Plus, too much blue. Seriously, it's like the kid ran out of every other color but blue, yet he had to finish. I hate this kid and hope he's sick."

And the *Catholic Reporter* wrote, "It's just a painting by a kid. It's not like it's an oil stain on a garage floor or some mold. Run, don't walk, away from this painting of the Virgin Mary, if you're looking for something the Virgin's appeared on, that is. By the way, saw her in my pancake syrup again this morning. That makes five sightings for me. Face!"

Your art teacher, however, gave you three gold stars. Take that to the bank, Duccio.

Happy Your Watercolor of the Virgin Mary Is Not Drawing Thousands to Kneel Before It Day!

APRIL 30   SHERIFF WALLACE WILL BE
THE LAST TO SAY GOOD-BYE DAY!

The state line will be five miles behind you when Wallace's flashing lights start to pop in your rearview. You'll pull over with a sharp brake and a veer onto the shoulder. Wallace will follow in stride, though it's certain he'll have noted the aggression.

"Lotta boxes back there. Can you see out the back with your trunk half-open like that?" Sheriff Wallace will ask.

"Saw you, didn't I?" you'll say.

Sheriff Wallace will tap his fingers on the rubber frame of your rolled-down window.

"Shirley's a handful," he'll say.

"Just like her daddy?"

Sheriff Wallace will stop tapping his fingers.

"Whyn't you step out of the car?" he'll say.

"Was I speeding, officer?"

"No," he'll say. "No, you wasn't." He'll take some steps from the window and turn his back to you, waiting, staring down the empty road back home. You'll get out of the car and face him.

"You knew this was coming," you'll say.

"I knew," Sheriff Wallace will say.

"You know there's no chance you're gonna turn me around," you'll say.

He'll breathe deep, almost like his chest is tight. "Yeah," he'll say. "Yeah, I know she sent you on your way a long time ago."

You and Sheriff Wallace will look off in different directions at all the fields of nothing stretching out from the highway.

"I tried to raise my daughter strong, but I ended up raising her mean," Sheriff Wallace will say. "She know you're gone?"

"She might know by now," you'll say. "I left a letter on the kitchen countertop. If Wilbur didn't eat it while he was waiting for his kibble, she might know by now."

Sheriff Wallace will nod. "Then you best be getting on before she comes looking for ya," he'll say. "I'll go back and see to her."

You'll hold out your hand for Sheriff Wallace to shake. It was good having him in your life. He's meaner than his daughter and based on rumors, he might just as well have pulled you over to shoot you in the face as to say good-bye to his son-in-law. But—

"I always liked you," he'll say. "I always thought my daughter was finally thinking when she got you to propose to her."

You'll let go of Sheriff Wallace's hand and climb back into your car. He'll climb back into his and turn it around to go and calm his daughter down. You'll drive north and he'll drive south.

Happy Sheriff Wallace Will Be the Last to Say Good-bye Day!

MAY

FROM WATCHING YOU, THEY LEARN DESPAIR.

| MAY 1 | ASK YOUR NAKED MAID WHAT MIGHT HAVE BEEN DAY! |

Mandy the Naked Maid has visited your apartment on the last Tuesday of every month for the past two and a half years. You first answered her ad back when your upholstery business was finally starting to bring in some cash, and the idea of a naked maid appealed to you on several levels.

First, the fact that she was offering a service that was closer to that of a stripper than a prostitute gave you some comfort. You were tickled by the thought of soliciting a woman for something illicit, but you doubted whether you could go as far as intercourse, or any physical contact, for that matter. It was a lonely time, and the illusion of being desired by a woman was important to you. You doubted the illusion could hold up during something physical. The possibility of feeling her muscles grow tense under your touch was nightmarish. Just watching, that was much safer.

Second, your place was a mess. You needed to hire somebody. Two birds, one stone.

Mandy arrived, and you knew when she first emerged from the bathroom in her high heels and see-through apron that you would not be seeking a replacement any time soon. Over the course of her visits, you learned that she entered the naked maid racket to pay her way through dental school. Over the first few months, she claimed that she had no boyfriend. Then later she admitted to living with somebody, making a point to add that she was unsure where it was heading. You felt this qualification was manufactured for your benefit, and you appreciated it.

Over the past two and a half years, you've had a couple of relationships yourself. But you continued to set aside that last Tuesday of the month to have Mandy straighten up while you followed her around masturbating.

"This is going to be my last visit," she'll tell you today.

"I thought it might be that time," say. "You're graduating soon, aren't you?"

"Graduated," she'll say. "Last week. With honors."

Say, "I wish I could have been there." Then pull the dust broom from her hand and ask her if she'd like to smoke some grass with you.

Sprawl out on the floor, leaning up against the furniture all blissed out and naked together. Just a couple of old pals sorting through the good times.

"Remember that day I masturbated while you cleaned the kitchen?" you'll say.

Mandy will laugh. "What about the time you masturbated while I cleaned the bathroom?"

"How could I forget!" you'll shout. "You were like, 'Hey what are you doing?' And I was like, 'Duh, I'm masturbating while you clean the bathroom.' And you were like, 'Makes sense.'"

After you stop giggling, Mandy will say, "Remember that snowstorm?"

It snowed one Tuesday in February about a year and a half ago. It snowed so hard Mandy was worried her train wouldn't be running and she didn't know where to stay.

"I wish you could have stayed," say.

"There had to be rules in order for this to work," she'll say. "I stay as long as you pay."

"We're human beings," say.

"No we aren't," Mandy will counter. "We stopped being human beings as soon as I walked in here and put on my see-through apron. We became characters in a fantasy from that point on."

Ask what might have happened if you had never called her ad. Would she have found you attractive if you had met her in a bar?

She'll say, "Yes."

Neither of you will say anything else. You'll both just let that "yes" rest in existence without anyone stepping forward to question it. The yes is as important to the past two and a half years as the see-through apron and the Dust-Buster. She'll look at her watch, but you'll already know what she has to say.

"You've only got eight minutes left before I go. Did you want to masturbate while I clean some more?"

Say yes. Tell her you want to watch her sweep under the refrigerator. Happy Ask Your Naked Maid What Might Have Been Day!

MAY 2	TEACH YOUR SON TO REALLY BEAT DOWN THE WIMPS DAY!

Your son is a bully who has been doing pretty well for himself in the schoolyard. He takes in about six dollars a day in lunch money, and he really has a smile on his face when he comes home after having beaten a nerd senseless. It's like beating up geeks is the only source of self-confidence for him. You've been really happy for the kid.

But today will be a bad day. Your son is going to come home crying louder than any of those wimpy nerds has ever cried. He'll have been humiliated in front of the whole school when the wimpiest nerd that ever set foot at Grover Cleveland Middle School finally stood up to him and fought back. It turns out that that nerd has been getting some free training from an ex-boxer who cleans up the movie house now. Teaching the nerd to fight has sort of given the ex-boxer a reason to get up in the morning, something he hasn't had since he lost his own son when the kid ran unsupervised in front of a car. Back during the ex-boxer's drinking days.

So your son is going to be inconsolable and bloody. It will be as if his reign at the school has been relinquished with one little bout. You're going to have to help him.

"Hey, kiddo," say to him. "Failure isn't when you fall down. It's when you don't get back up again."

Give him your brass knuckles. "You always have to be one step ahead of everybody else. If those nerds are learning to fight a fair fight, you just have to start fighting unfair. Pull out this little surprise and you're never gonna lose again."

Your son will wipe his tears and say, "Thanks, Dad." Your heart will melt. Happy Teach Your Son to Really Beat Down the Wimps Day!

| MAY 3 | IF YOUR CALLER ID SCREEN READS "THE LAST STRAW," LET THE ANSWERING MACHINE GET IT (UNLESS YOU KNOW SOMEBODY WHO WORKS AT A STRAW STORE) DAY! |

A lot of your friends have weird jobs, and you know one or two of them work at the mall. If I were gonna open a straw store at the mall, I'd call it "The Last Straw" since it has fewer letters than "The Straw That Broke the Camel's Back." When store owners get signs made, they pay by the letter.

Now, can you remember whether any of your friends ever mentioned that they could get you a discount on bendy straws? How about swirly straws? Loop-di-loop straws? If not, I wouldn't take that call if I were you.

Possible messages from "The Last Straw" follow:

"It's over. I can't try any harder. I'm going back to [insert name of better paid, less physically repulsive former lover of significant other here]. You're just so angry at the world."

"Thanks for coming in for that fourth interview, but we decided to hire This Other Guy."

"This is the cancer clinic calling. Just wanted to say our first diagnosis was wrong. You have cancer in parts of the body we didn't even know existed. Someone upstairs has it in for you. Please don't call back."

"This is the government of America. We just passed laws that make it nearly impossible for an American like you to earn an honest living. We hope this news doesn't make you go batshit or anything. This is the government calling, by the way. Did I already say that? I'm a little out of it this morn—[BEEEEP]"

"Hi, this is happiness. Is this [name that isn't yours]? It isn't, is it? Oops, wrong number."

"Honey, it's Mom. I'm about to die but I wanted to say I never really dug you all that much. Later, yo."

Ouch. I'd stay to help you get through this, but my shift at the Paper Rings That Keep Cups of Coffee from Being Too Hot store starts in twenty minutes.

Happy If Your Caller ID Screen Reads "The Last Straw," Let the Answering Machine Get It (Unless You Know Somebody Who Works at a Straw Store) Day!

| MAY 4 | ARCHERY FINALS DAY! |

It's early May, which means that taking place across the country today are the final scrimmages of various intramural archery programs. And I'm betting there's one near you. Perhaps at a small northeastern college? Get out there and root!

Happy Archery Finals Day!

> ### MAY 5

ASK YOUR BLIND DATE WHETHER HE CAN EVER HEAR THE SOUND OF BLOOD SCREAMING THROUGH HIS VEINS DAY!

The hard part is finding the right moment. The seventh lull in the conversation is always good. Right about that time when the both of you realize the date isn't going very well but you haven't even gotten your entrees yet. Just fold your napkin with about twelve sharp creases, wincing with each fold, and place it on your plate before you take his hand and say, "I need to ask you an important question, and I'll know if you answer dishonestly so don't."

Or let's say you wait until penetration has commenced. You suddenly remember that the Question was never asked. No problem, just start sobbing. Let out a few wails, sending a gale of fists into the mattress or vestibule wall until your date gets the message that you have something important to ask and he should stop having sex on you.

Your date will say, "Tell me. I want to know what's wrong."

Let him watch you slice open the skin of your palm with a nail file a few times before you take his face into your bloody grip and say, "At night I never sleep. The screaming. Even if I turn the radio on at full volume I can't escape it. Blood. My blood with the voice of a thousand ghouls racing through my veins. Do you ever feel that way? Like your blood is screaming? It sounds like hungry babies."

Then run.

Happy Ask Your Blind Date Whether He Can Ever Hear the Sound of Blood Screaming Through His Veins Day!

| MAY 6 | YOU HAVE SEVENTEEN DOLLARS AND SEVENTEEN KIDS DAY! |

Tell your kids, "I'm gonna go buy seventeen lotto tickets. Each one's gonna use one of your birth dates for the numbers. Whichever of your birth dates shows up on the winning ticket, that's the kid I'll take with me when I leave tonight forever."

The seventeen children say, "But what if none of the tickets win?" All seventeen of them say that at once. That's what conversations are like in your house. You against seventeen, every damn word.

In answer, just smile and shrug. Then take off and spend the seventeen dollars on a bus ticket. Your seventeen kids will spend all day praying that it's their birthday that pops up when the numbers are drawn. They'll even start to argue that a few of them clearly do not deserve to go away with their father tonight, based on their recent behavior and innate talents and abilities. They'll propose that if one of those lesser kids' birthdays ends up on the winning ticket, that child should do the honorable thing and allow one of his or her more deserving siblings to accompany their father instead. And the whole time they're bickering, you'll already be long gone.

The sad part is, one of their birth dates will show up in the winning numbers. Jake's birthday. You'll kick yourself for not having played it, but you'll reconcile that being without a family is jackpot enough. Jake, however, will spend his life thinking that you won the lotto with his birth date, but you welshed on your promise to take him with you. He'll assume it was because you were hoping that one of his more desirable siblings would be the one with the lucky birthday. Perhaps one of his siblings who knows how to cook good chili or tell cute jokes when company comes over. Jake only knows how to be sick (he has asthma).

One day many years from today Jake will track you down, and when he finds out that you never even bought a ticket he'll feel like such a fool for having beaten himself up so much over the years. Of course you would not have bought the ticket. Only a man as despicable as you would make that up just to drop one more lie into his children's laps before taking off.

By that time, Jake will have amassed his own wealth, and after a lot of pathetic pleading for forgiveness, you'll con your way into his graces and he'll take you in. What he has planned for you, however, is a truly diabolical act of vengeance. Whether he follows through on his plan depends on whether or not he's his daddy's little boy.

Happy You Have Seventeen Dollars and Seventeen Kids Day!

MAY 7

WHEN YOU FINALLY GET UP TO CLOSE THE DRAPES, YOU'LL REALIZE THAT A CLASSROOM FULL OF CHILDREN HAS BEEN WATCHING YOU CRY FOR THE PAST TWENTY MINUTES DAY!

You knew when you moved into your apartment that there was an elementary school across the street with several floors on direct eye level with your bedroom. Hell, you've been able to discern math problems on the chalkboard when the light's been right. So you promised yourself that you would always close the drapes before even the thought of masturbation might enter your mind, and you've been very good about it. Except for that one month.

So why not also cover up when you feel a fit of sobs coming on? Crying, for you, is just as erotic as genital stimulation. You should have known that when the teacher announced that she had to step out for a moment and everyone should read quietly, a small boy with a wandering mind would let his eyes bounce around the room until they found their way out the window and across the street and in through another window where he can see your head hunched forward and your shoulders shaking up and down.

The little boy will get up and stand quietly by the window and watch without comment. And the little girl who has a crush on him will go and stand beside him and ask what he's looking at.

"That man is crying," he'll say. The girl will correct him, "That's not a man, that's a lady," she'll say.

The boy will say, "It looks like a man."

Then they'll just watch you like they were looking at snowflakes fall.

Soon, their classmates will join them by the window, a couple at a time, until nearly every child has gotten up from his seat to watch you bellow out your sobs from your shaking, shivering frame. (One boy will stay in his seat because he had gotten pushed to the ground and kicked in the face just before coming into class, so he himself will be busy crying for most of the class period. The other handful of children who remain seated are weird.)

When the teacher returns to the class, naturally she'll be ready to freak when she sees all of her students out of their seats. Since they'll be silent, however, she'll know there's something good going on outside. She'll stand at the rear of their congregation and search the landscape for smoke. Then she'll see you, and she'll try to make out your face to determine if she recognizes you.

So, there you go. When you finally turn off the waterworks and you rise to the window to close the drapes, you'll find across the street, framed by the expanse of seven-foot-tall classroom windows, a display of curious kids' faces, their eyes wide, their mouths shut tight, their teacher standing behind them looking uncertain.

I'd at least wave good-bye, or I mean hello. Or something.

Happy When You Finally Get Up to Close the Drapes, You'll Realize That a Classroom Full of Children Has Been Watching You Cry for the Past Twenty Minutes Day!

MAY 8

KICK SOMETHING NAKED OUT OF YOUR BED DAY!

If you're smaller than the naked thing and can't actually kick it out of your bed, just scream. Wail and sob and pound on the wall until it stops saying bullshit like "But I'm your wife" or "But I paid you $200" and finally just scurries away to find socks or car keys. Make sure you get a good look when the Little Nudie Nudie goes running for the door because some things look awesome without any clothes on. Others don't. Either way, I'd look if I were there. What, are you depressed? You get bonus points if the naked thing you send running is an uncle, by the way.

Pets count today, but not for much, since pets are always naked. Unless you're disgusting and you dress up your pets in little outfits just so you can slowly undress them while holding their gaze with a look of trust and wonderment.

And of course, you yourself can sub in for the naked thing. Just take off all your clothes and lie down. Then tell yourself you're disgusting and hit yourself in the face really hard a lot of times until you wriggle away from your stormy wrath and roll out onto the floor. I know a lot of people wake up this way every morning, so make sure when you do it today you're doing it because you want to be a good person.

Happy Kick Something Naked Out of Your Bed Day!

MAY 9   **IF THE COFFEE SHOP WAITRESS TOUCHES YOUR PALM WHEN SHE GIVES YOU YOUR CHANGE, SHE TOTALLY WANTS IT DAY!**

It's just common knowledge. There is a provocative manner of giving a man his change just as surely as there is a chaste one. A lady of virtue would do her best to drop the change into her customer's hand from three inches high without so much as an exchange of body heat. And then she might choose to squat low behind the counter and recite the Lord's prayer and perhaps cut into herself with pens.

And then there is the whore. She with her hair mussed into just the state of frenzy to imply a love for, as well as a distrust of, emo music. She with her belly button naked as a bikini-clad three-year-old's and her long-john top rising higher up her torso with every reach for the shelf supporting the pint-sized cappuccino mugs. Such a woman has no qualms about allowing her fingers to graze and slither along the sweat-laden palms of any boy who might be game for such a dalliance (and such boys are plentiful, I assure you).

A tramp that would be refused audience by Jesus himself; it's as if she doesn't even realize she's doing it. She'll just drop her hand into your own and let her fingers scrabble about in the flesh for as long as it takes to release the change into your palm. She sometimes does it without even making eye contact. Perhaps she prefers it so. Perhaps she finds it painful to look anyone in the eye for fear she might see a reflection of herself there, in her fallen state of moral disrepair. Such a woman might seem to not care for conventional moral code or precautionary measures to avoid transmission of communicable disease, but, rest assured, she is aware of the letter emblazoned on her bosom and she would give her life to have it sewn over. If you meet such a woman, pity her. And if when you pay for your mochaccino you feel the heat of her fingertips against your palm, you're totally gonna get laid.

Happy If the Coffee Shop Waitress Touches Your Palm When She Gives You Your Change, She Totally Wants It Day!

| MAY 10 | GO FIND YOURSELF A PICKUP GAME OF KING OF THE HILL DAY! |

What were you gonna do? Go down to the gym on your lunch break and do thirty minutes on the elliptical machine in the hopes that the sweat in your eyes will blur out the fantasies of messy suicide that have been keeping you going all morning? Nothing better for someone who feels like a cog in his own life than to get on a machine that sends your legs dancing like a bitch but doesn't take you anywhere. Your ideas are always wrong.

What you should do is walk through the park until four guys and girls in business casual sitting on a small hill shout out, "We need a fifth. You down?" You'll suddenly realize you want nothing more in this bitchfuck of an existence than to send a total stranger to the valley of a hill with a slap of your Bostonian shoe sole to his neckbone. It's King of the Hill, and it's a spot-on metaphor for every decision you've made since you were thirty-one.

First thing you should ask is, "Strapped or clean?" If it's strapped, anyone could be packing anything from a Swiss Army knife to a TEC 9 and it's all fair game. In a strapped bout of King of the Hill, you should sacrifice the first lunge up the hill and instead hop atop your opponents' backs, letting them slide out from underneath you. As their bodies wriggle away you should be able to frisk them and tell who's packing what. It's about knowing your opponent.

In fact, don't try to take the hill till the fourth king has fallen. This way, pulling the cocksuckers down, you can get an idea of how they defend their crown. Do they use fingernails or teeth? What's their center of gravity? Do they have any shards of broken glass tucked into their socks waiting to open up the palm of your hand? That shit's big with motherfuckers from publishing.

Once you know who you're up against, ball's in your court. Strategy only goes so far. Eventually you're just gonna have to bite someone in the kneecap and drag her down the hill with your goddamn teeth. Can't plan that out. Can't plan on when the shit that makes your blood flow is gonna show its face. But trust me, it's a face a grandma could fall in love with.

The game usually lasts forty-five minutes, since everyone needs about seven or eight minutes each way to and from the hill to get back to work before lunch is over.

Happy Go Find Yourself a Pickup Game of King of the Hill Day! Fight Club is for faggots who are too scared to fuck.

MAY 11	YOU LIKE GIRLS DAY!

You like girls, and it's because girls make you feel swirly all over your insides. And until midnight tonight, if you come in contact with a girl who is female, you like her.

This includes the homeless woman begging for change near the freeway tollbooth. Today, you wish that homeless woman was your girlfriend so that you could give her presents and hold her hand at movies.

This also includes girls like Mrs. Kim at the corner deli. She might always be covered in cat fur, but today you wish Mrs. Kim would make your babies.

Unfortunately, your daughter's principal counts too. Your daughter's principal has been trying to have your daughter assigned to a special education program, despite the diagnoses from three doctors who claim she has bad verbal skills only because her hearing problem wasn't diagnosed until she was seven. Though you feel she is trying to destroy that which you hold dear, your daughter's principal is still a girl and you wish she would kiss you one hundred times on the mouth and squeeze and squeeze you. Have fun liking your daughter's principal, girl-liker.

Happy You Like Girls Day!

| MAY 12 | FOGGY CAR WINDOWS DAY!

They said you were laid off, but in actuality they thought you were so weird that they just wanted you out of the office as soon as possible. And they gave you as generous a severance package as they could dig out of the coffers to make sure you wouldn't show up some morning and do something drastic. Something like what you're gonna do this morning.

Drive to the office, and don't forget to bring pornography. Make sure you're in the car that your coworkers will recognize. And make sure to park in your old parking space.

Once you're parked and you've had a couple cups of coffee, open up your pornography and start to masturbate. You want to generate the kind of heat that fogs up a car window like only two kids making out in a parking lot can, so you're gonna have to tease yourself. Bring yourself so close to orgasm it starts to hurt. Then just let yourself throb and pulse until the threat of orgasm subsides. Then resume manual stimulation until you might come again.

This should get your windows nice and fogged up by quarter to nine, when all of your former coworkers start pulling in. Your replacement will pull up right behind you and idle there. She'll stare at your foggy windows while she lets it register that someone is apparently making out where she is supposed to park. Then she'll go and find some visitor parking.

Upstairs, the office will be abuzz with talk of "Wasn't that [Insert Your Name Here]'s car with the windows all fogged up in the lot today?"

It will also be abuzz with responses to the above question. Responses like, "Yeah, I think it was."

When your replacement announces that she couldn't park because some kids were making out in her space, your former coworkers will sit her down and tell her that that was the weird fucker that used to have her job, and don't worry because Kevin's already calling security.

Kevin's already calling security so you should split after you come. Also, and I know this doesn't apply to you, but if you know anybody who would actually be into making out with you in your car while you're parked in your old parking space at around nine in the morning, bring them along, sure.

Happy Foggy Car Windows Day!

| MAY 13 | BATHROOM STALL GRAFFITI DAY!

Sitting in the bathroom of the roadside bar, you'll let your eyes wander over some of the graffiti crowding up the stall. Amid all of the "For a Good Time" and the "Metallica" and the "Murray Is a Homo" scrawlings, you'll read something that makes your blood run cold.

HELP! I'VE BEEN KIDNAPPED. BLUE CHEVY VAN. PLATE #GL5-9T3.

You'll rip your pants up around your waist and run to the mustachioed bartender to get him dialing 911.

"Sir!" you'll shout. "Someone's been kidnapped! I need to use your phone."

The bartender's shoulders will fall, and he'll put his palms flat on the bar as if to hold himself steady. The burly regulars will avert their eyes to their beer mugs.

"Did you hear me? Someone's been kidnapped! They're driving a blue Chevy . . ."

"I know that someone's been kidnapped, boy!" the bartender will snap. "And I know what van they was driving. There ain't nothing we can do about that now."

The bartender will walk away from you to the other end of the bar. You'll start to say something more, but one of the regulars will grab your shoulder. His hand will feel heavy as a rock.

In a quiet voice he'll say, "That graffiti was written ten years ago, fella. The lady who wrote it, she ain't never been found. Ol' Frank's been blaming hisself ever since."

You'll want to ask why, but instead you'll walk down the bar to where Frank is standing alone, staring at the phone on the wall.

"He was a guy like you," Frank will say without even turning around to look at you. "A good guy, just wanted to help. He was also city folk, just like you. And city folk always love comin' in here and bossing me around like I opened this place just to cater to them. He asked to use my phone and I pointed to the sign up there that says STAFF USE ONLY. I told him no dice. He starts talking about someone being kidnapped and I thought he must've been lying, thinking he can pull a fast one on a hick like me. I kicked him out of here and told him to go use the nearest pay phone. At the Mobil station, thirty-five miles away from here."

The bar will be silent, and then the phone will ring so loud that everyone nearly falls off their stools. Frank won't answer. It'll just ring and ring, maybe twelve or fifteen times before the silence falls again.

"Can't use the phone anymore," Frank will offer. "I can't in good conscience. I was a mean and stingy old man and I cost a lady her life. For the price of a phone call."

You'll bow your head because Frank will almost be crying. "Maybe you should paint over that graffiti," you'll suggest. "So guys like me won't keep bringing it up."

Frank will explode at this. "Why? So that I can forget all about it? So that I can pretend I never let a lady die? I'd say I deserve to be reminded from time to time, don't you think? Considering all the days I took away from her, I'd say I can afford to feel bad every once in a while. The graffiti stays. It's my penance."

Just then a man in a J.Crew windbreaker will come running out of the men's room and shout, "Call the police! Someone's been kidnapped!" Everyone will throw up their hands and laugh at him. Except for Frank, who will start punching the bar and shouting, "Why?! Why?! Why?!"

Happy Bathroom Stall Graffiti Day!

| MAY 14 |

FREAK THE BABYSITTER THE FUCK OUT DAY!

Whether it's the bookish neighbor girl who seems a little sad about something or the gay boy who was recommended to you on your office e-mail bulletin board, your babysitter has gotten a free ride long enough. These are your children we're talking about. How's about you keep their babysitters on their toes?

No one's saying get a nannycam, Orwell. But you should send the virgin rifling into houseplants and behind crevices on the bookshelf to find the nannycam that isn't even there. All you have to do is go about your business like you would any other "date night" (you two are fucked by the way).

"Jenny had a nap at five so she might be a little rowdy," you'll say in the dismissive tone of someone repeating rote instructions. "There's some pizza and Coke in the fridge, and you're welcome to it." Right, right. Little Tommy is already at the babysitter's feet begging to be held upside down.

When you're just about to close the door behind you, lean back in and just let the following drop to the carpet as light as a feather:

"Oh and by the way, we know what's going on."

Then shut the door behind you. When that movie or that dinner party starts to become a bore, just imagine the frenetic activity going on in your home as a freshly panicked teen racks his or her brain to make sure what was heard was heard right. If only you could be there to watch your sitter hold your baby in such a delicate and hesitant manner so as to avoid any possible misinterpretation of "inappropriate touching." How sad the phone calls will be to boyfriends and girlfriends who can't come over and remove their tops on your couch anymore (this bums you out a little). Sure, you might have to look for another sitter next week, but that kid's gonna remember you for the rest of his or her gradually less enchanting lifetime.

Happy Freak the Babysitter the Fuck Out Day!

| MAY 15 | **WHEN THE ONE YOU LOVE PULLS UP OUT FRONT TO TAKE YOU TO THE MOVIES, EGG THE SHIT OUT OF HIS CAR DAY!** |

Invite all your friends over so you can all meet up at your place around three o'clock and get super high. Eventually, someone will remember that no one bought any eggs yet and you'll spend around an hour or so devising a mind-numbingly complex democratic process for declaring who must go to the store. Then you'll remember it's kind of nice outside and the walk to the store is gonna be awesome so you'll volunteer.

The walk to the store will end up being far more beautiful than you ever could have dreamed. In fact, while they're passing, those twenty-six minutes will feel like the happiest and most loving twenty-six minutes of your entire life. You'll be aware that you're really high, and you'll worry that when you're sober again you'll look back on this moment and laugh at how happy you thought you were.

Buy the eggs and walk home. Then you and your friends should wait for the one you love to pull up outside. When you see his car, everyone should jump out of bushes and hang out of windows and just pummel the living shit out of his car with eggs. Go "Whooo!" a lot and scream stuff like, "You're dead, you fuck!" Eventually, he will get out of his car and attack one of you.

Happy When the One You Love Pulls Up Out Front to Take You to the Movies, Egg the Shit Out of His Car Day!

| MAY 16 | YOU'LL NEVER SAVE YOUR HUSBAND FROM THAT POW CAMP DAY!

It's been over thirty years now since your husband's plane went down over Da Nang, and it looks like there aren't going to be any more rescue missions heading into those POW camps. It's time to take matters into your own hands.

It's true, you're a fifty-seven-year-old woman and your work as a seamstress has not kept you in the best of shape. So you'll have to get back into jogging. And you'll have to acquire numerous anti-tank weapons. You have a week.

Once in the POW camp, you'll stay low to the ground, spotting one or two middle-aged to elderly Americans huddled in their bamboo cages and eating their lunch of live bugs and human feces. When you find your husband, the VC will be torturing him to get him to denounce the United States. He'll say no dice, and then he'll feel a hundred volts of electricity course up his spine and into the part of his brain that's just behind his eyes. The men torturing him will have a world-weary look on their faces, but they won't skip any steps in the torture. This camp is a well-oiled machine, you'll discover.

Before you blow up the watchtower, let the guard up there see you and gasp. Then shoot a rocket at his face. The rest of the guards will lope out to shoot you. Shoot back. This'll never work.

Happy You'll Never Save Your Husband from That POW Camp Day!

| MAY 17 | THAT'S THE BLACK SLUDGE PART OF YOU DAY!

The stains on your sheets are growing in diameter, and a large portion of the floral pattern has been blacked out completely in a dense opaque cloud of Rorschach blots. The one that used to look like your uncle's face when he would peek into your childhood bedroom doorway now just looks like a unicorn.

You've smelled them. There's no odor. But when you inhale you do feel like you just made one of the worst mistakes of judgment you've ever made in your entire life.

You touch the spots in the morning when they're still damp and warm, but when you pull your fingertips away they're bone dry and as cold as the lid of a coffin in November.

"Get to the point," you're saying. "Am I dying or not?"

You are dying, but that's beside the point.

"Then just what the hell are those black spots, you hideous man?" you're saying.

That's the black sludge part of you. It's everything about you that's gone rotten, the cancer of stifled ambition blazing through your tissue like wild horses from a burning stable. It's a black froth of anxiety that began to bubble up to your skin when you turned twenty-eight. Everyone you've hurt and everything good that you've cast away has simmered into a dark gloppy muck that seeps out of you at night. You didn't really think so many instances of failure would just line up as memories fixed in place and time, did you?

Wash your sheets before someone's ejaculate drips into one of those stains. You're not allowed to smoke in your apartment, and when ejaculate mixes with the black sludge part of you, a cloud of smoke puffs up into the air and it smells a lot like a lit cigarette. But the cloud has a nose and a mouth and eyes without eyelashes.

Happy That's the Black Sludge Part of You Day!

MAY 18	WEAR A MASK DAY!

If you want to wear the mask of a beautiful person, it will have to be a mask of a famous person, like Tom Cruise or Marilyn Monroe. Costume shops only sell masks that look like famous people. They don't sell masks that are only the rubber visage of some nameless vision of striking beauty.

Buy the beautiful famous person mask, but you'll have a lot of explaining to do at work. Everyone you bump into in the kitchen is going to be like, "Hey, it's not Halloween. You must really be a big fan of that celebrity if you're wearing that mask!"* Simply explain that you are not a fan of that celebrity. You are wearing the mask because you are ugly and you want to cover up your ugly face with a mask designed in the image of a face that is beautiful, such as Jeremy Davies's.

You coworker might ask, "Why not just get plastic surgery? I mean, the mask is all rubbery and lifeless. It's not like anyone thinks that's your real face." Explain that you are not trying to hide the fact that you are an ugly person. You simply do not wish to continue to go out into the world with your ugly face naked of any obfuscation. You no longer want people to look at you and think, "My goodness, what an ugly person. One of the ugliest, no doubt, in the entire supermarket." You would prefer that they look at you in your mask and think, "That person must be quite ugly. And that is a very well-crafted mask of Tilda Swinton and it was probably quite expensive." The nice thing about so many people asking you about your mask is that you might talk to someone whose voice is pleasant.

Happy Wear a Mask Day!

---

*The person who says this will then laugh heartily at what he or she just said because when inside of an office, people laugh at statements that are completely devoid of any humor or suggestive meaning. They laugh simply to make a noise with their bodies. "If I can make a noise, I must still exist," they think hopefully.

| MAY 19 |

GIVE TO ME YOUR LEATHER, TAKE FROM ME MY LACE DAY!

Put the leather on the ground and back away with your hands up.

"Show me the lace!"

PUT the leather on the ground and back away with your hands UP!

"Not until you show me the lace!!!"

Boy, I am not gonna tell you again! Now do right by yourself. Drop the goddamn leather and back away WITH YOUR HANDS UP!

"I can't do that, O'Reilly. That lace is worth a lot more than my head right now."

See them rifles up in these towers here? I got a leash on 'em but they're tuggin' real hard. You come in with me and you'll be safe. Hand over the leather, boy.

"Sorry, O'Reilly. If I don't walk away with that lace then a girl dies and I'm pulling the trigger myself."

Boy, where you goin'? Hold still, son! HOLD YOUR FIRE!!! HOLD YOUR FIRE!!!

Here comes the big chase.

Happy Give to Me Your Leather, Take from Me My Lace Day!

| MAY 20 |

ROB YOUR DOCTOR AGAIN DAY!

The last time you went in for a physical, you robbed your doctor at gunpoint. You didn't ask for any cash that the office might have collected. You just demanded his wallet, his wedding ring, and his BlackBerry. Since he had all of your personal information, he sent the police to your house to arrest you. You did six months.

Today you have another appointment for a physical. You called him when you got out, and at first he said he never wanted to be your doctor again. But you convinced him that you couldn't trust any other doctor. You told him that some things happened while you were inside and you felt it was important that he check you out soon. He felt bad for you since he's the one who sent you to jail, so he agreed to give you a checkup.

"Just don't rob me again!" he said. You promised him you wouldn't.

Today's the appointment. You're going to have to use a knife this time since he'll probably demand that you strip before he enters the examination room with you, so there won't be any place to hide your gun. But you could keep your socks on and stash a knife in the elastic band, held to the back of your calf. He won't make you remove your socks because he wants to trust you. He wants to make sure you're healthy. He's a total mark.

Happy Rob Your Doctor Again Day!

| MAY 21 | YOUR BARISTA THINKS YOUR BREATH SMELLS DELICIOUS DAY! |

When the chick behind the Starbucks counter is making your drink, she'll say, "I smell Chinese food."

You'll have just had Chinese food. You'll be embarrassed to stink of your very fragrant lunch, but she'll know it's you. Just cop to it. Say, "I just had Chinese food."

She'll say, "Did you have an egg roll?"

Say, "No. Beef with broccoli."

Her face will light up and she'll say, "It smells really good. It's making me hungry. I wish you'd brought some for everybody."

Tell her, "Well, I think I still have some residue of it in my mouth. I haven't had anything to drink yet. But I did smoke a cigarette. Actually, yes, now that I am talking, I can feel some little stalks of broccoli loosening from the paste on my tongue."

She'll look around for her supervisor, and if her supervisor isn't there, she'll lean over the counter with her mouth open wide. Gather a heaping glob of saliva from the walls of your mouth and from underneath your gums and spit a big loogie into her open jaw.

She'll swish it around with her tongue then she'll smile a big grateful smile and she'll say, "Thanks. How 'bout I upgrade that latte to a venti, no charge."

That's when you should say, "Solid!"

Happy Your Barista Thinks Your Breath Smells Delicious Day!

MAY 22	PAY CHILDREN TO DANCE A "RING AROUND THE ROSEY" AROUND YOU WHILE YOU FINISH YOUR BOOK ABOUT BLACK HOLES DAY!

The theory on which your book is founded came to you when you were dropping off your niece at her day care center. You saw the children dancing "Ring Around the Rosey," slowly turning in a circle held together by their clasped hands. It struck you then that you needed to think of the black hole as if it were a necessary knot in the universe, like a navel.

Since then, you've had trouble staying on course. So you're going to have to place an ad in the supermarket circular offering hourly pay to eight children willing to dance a "Ring Around the Rosey" around you while you finish work on the book. You've already moved your desk into the great room, where they'll have more space to build their circle. You've allotted enough funds from your advance to offer each child six dollars an hour.

Many children will apply, but none will be willing to dance for the eleven hours a day you spend on the book. In fact, the only children willing to dance for as much as three hours a day will all be between fifteen and seventeen years old.

You'll hire fifteen of them to work in shifts. While it might be worrisome that a group of mumbling and shuffling adolescents might not provide the same inspiration as a circle of playful and wide-eyed children, you will make some progress on the book. As an added bonus, when the teens go on break some of them will make out on your couch. One couple is pretty hot and heavy, if you know what I mean (over-the-sweater boob).

Happy Pay Children to Dance a "Ring Around the Rosey" Around You While You Finish Your Book About Black Holes Day!

| MAY 23 |

CHECK THE OUTLOOK CALENDAR AT THE DESK WHERE YOU'RE TEMPING TO FIND OUT WHAT THE EXECUTIVE YOU'RE ASSISTING WAS DOING ON MOMENTOUS DAYS OF YOUR LIFE DAY!

On August 3, 2002, you drove with your brother to the Mclaren funeral home to pick up the urn containing his wife's ashes. Your car stalled in the parking lot with your brother sitting there in the passenger seat, the urn in his lap. Seven minutes into the forty-minute wait for AAA, your brother got out of the front seat and opened the back door to put the urn in the backseat. Then he got back in the front seat and turned on the radio. You stood beside the car and smoked lots of cigarettes. Four, at least.

On August 3, 2002, Fred Penn, VP of IT Development at Lace Duterhoffer Financial Partners, was in Tuscany spending his fourth night at the Hotel Pelicano. He had dinner with Tan Fujiyama of the Wattei Corporation at the Pizzi Vineyard, 8:30 reservation.

Happy Check the Outlook Calendar at the Desk Where You're Temping to Find Out What the Executive You're Assisting Was Doing on Momentous Days of Your Life Day!

| MAY 24 | ATTEMPTED SUICIDE BY COP DAY!

Today you should attempt to commit suicide by cop. Point an unloaded handgun at a cop and get him to shoot at you. He will shoot, but he'll miss. In that instant when the bullet whizzes by your head, you'll want to live again. It will feel like that bullet ripped all of your feelings of worthlessness and futility right out of your belly and dragged them miles and miles away to burn off into vapor. In short, you'll feel alive again.

Unfortunately, you'll have just pointed a gun at a police officer, so you'll have to take off if you want to stay out of prison. If you think you're depressed now, just try going to prison. Now *that* place can really give you the mopeys.

As a fugitive, you'll have to turn to a life of crime in order to survive. If you're a man, try being a lothario that rich women can't resist. After having sex with them, steal their husbands' cash. If you're a woman, try train robbery.

It will be hard, but you'll be living every day as if it were your last because it might very well be. If you ever get a chance to catch up on your correspondence, you should write that cop a postcard thanking him for shooting at you that day. "I know you didn't want to do it, and you're probably really upset with me for having made you discharge your firearm. But if it makes a difference, it really cheered me up. It's like you pulled the trigger on a 'Get Happy Gun' loaded with 'Frown Upside Down Bullets.' Though I guess a shot from that kind of gun wouldn't make me happy unless I had been hit. Anyway, thanks, fuzz."

Though he wouldn't write you back even if he could, he'll appreciate the postcard. Cops just want to make people happy, by any means necessary.

Happy Attempted Suicide by Cop Day!

| MAY 25 |

THE PINUP GIRL WHO LIVES IN THE ATTIC DAY!

Had you known when you bought the house that an aging former pinup girl was living in the attic, you might have bargained for an extra ten thousand off the asking price. But buyer beware.

"Hollywood tossed me out like a bag of garbage," she told you when you stumbled upon her little nook behind your wife's hope chest. "I was taped up on every GI's footlocker. Then when the pictures started going more earthy and natural, it was good-bye, bombshell! Don't let Robert Mitchum's face hit you in the ass on your way out."

"You must have some great stories," you said to her when you met her.

And she does, but they're all really sad. And they all end with the line, "These hookers were paid a lot and they knew the risks!" After she told you about Joseph Cotten and the hacksaw, you stopped bringing the kids up to listen, which was a shame because your kids don't have any grandparents left.

Today you're going to go up there and talk to her about leaving because her drinking is getting out of hand. It'd be one thing if she were just another elderly former movie star getting quietly sloshed in your attic. But this pinup likes to dance. And the booze has been giving her night terrors. Plus, it's starting to smell up there. But how do you toss her out?

"It's time for you to stage a comeback!" you should say. "Like that lady in the *Titanic* movie. Hollywood's been without your special brand of glamour for too long."

"That's a sweetheart of an idea, kiddo, but the timing isn't quite right, I'm afraid."

Then she'll lift up her night skirt and show you where the smell is coming from. Her calf will be black and swollen.

"I cut myself on a rusty nail a couple weeks back," she'll say. "Didn't wanna bother anybody. Now I'm scared gangrene might be setting in."

Say, "My God."

"This baby's gonna have to come off I'm afraid."

You got no choice. You're gonna have to let her stay at least till her amputee rehabilitation is complete. Usually takes around thirty-six months.

Happy the Pinup Girl Who Lives in the Attic Day!

| MAY 26 | SELL YOURSELF TO A BUSINESSMAN DAY!

Today you are going to turn over control of yourself to a wealthy businessman, the sort of man who is overweight and wears suits.

Start the negotiations with some aggression. Say, "Check this. How much are you willing to fork over to bring me home and call me your baby?"

The businessman will lowball you. Call him on it.

Say, "You cocksmoking Godhole. I'll kill you with this razor." Then pull out your straight razor.

The businessman will say, "You know your way around the table. I like that. I'll throw in $7 million more and the promise to adopt a Southeast Asian baby by 2009."

Remember, this is a *negotiation*.

Say, "2008 and a half."

The businessman will curl his mouth up at the corner, then he'll break out in a smile.

"Deal," he'll say. "Now get in the trunk."

Get in the trunk.

Happy Sell Yourself to a Businessman Day!

| MAY 27 | OUTGOING MESSAGE DAY! |

You should do an Osama bin Laden impression on your answering machine. Say, "Hello, American infidel! So sorry about the planes and the buildings but you had it coming for a long time! Especially you, Chris!" Then come out of your Osama impression and in your own voice say, "But seriously, you've reached [state your name and that of anyone else who might use that machine]. If you'd like to leave a message, please do so with your name, phone number, and the best time to reach you immediately after the beep. We will get back to you as soon as possible. If you're wondering how many times I'll try to call you back before giving up, remember what Kate Nelligan said to Stockard Channing in the 1983 movie *Without a Trace* . . ." Then do your impression of Kate Nelligan in the 1983 movie *Without a Trace* and shout, "Until I can't stand any more!!! Until . . . I . . . can't stand any more!!! HOW DARE YOU!!!" Then go back to your own voice and say, "Oh and uh, if this is in response to that Missed Connections ad I placed about the latte lover with the brown hair and the green poncho who made eye contact with me from across the Starbucks this past May 25 at 12:45 P.M., I'm sorry but you're too late. I've fallen in love with somebody else." Then hold the phone up to the speaker of your stereo while the chorus to Wilson Phillips's "You're in Love" plays. Then turn off the stereo and allow for no more than six seconds of silence before you fire a gun and then drop a sack of rice on the floor to make it sound like someone just got shot (perhaps by his own hand?) then fell to the ground with a thump.

Once you got that all down, hit the Save OGM button and just sit back and wait for the pussy train to pull into the station with a toot toot toot!

Happy Outgoing Message Day!

| MAY 28 | GIRL FALLS IN LOVE DAY!

On the porn site, deep in the middle of the TGP listings of thumbnail jpeg series and ten-second cumshot mpegs, surrounded by an unending litany of links that read like newspaper headlines from the *Porntown Daily Herald* (REDHEAD SUCKS COCK OUTDOORS! THREE HUGE DUDES SPLIT GIRL IN TWO! COED SPOOGED!), there is one link that pops off the screen and makes you think your eyes are going bad.

It says, GIRL FALLS IN LOVE. The number next to the link (16) indicates if you click on that link, you will find a series of sixteen photographs documenting the moment when a girl falls in love. If you don't click, if you don't want to see how a porn site handles love, you're out of your goddamn mind.

Thumbnail number one: A brown-haired girl in her mid-twenties is sitting on a grassy hill on a sunny afternoon. She holds a bottle of water. Sitting beside her is a brown-haired boy, also in his mid-twenties. The boy also holds a bottle of water. They do not look at each other.

Thumbnail number two: The boy sips from his water. The girl hasn't moved.

Thumbnail number three: The girl sips from her water, and the boy takes another sip.

Thumbnail number four: Her eyes are closed. The boy stares off, but not blankly. He recognizes something in the distance.

Thumbnail number five: A brown-haired man who looks to be in his early thirties is squatting before them, talking to them. All three are smiling.

Thumbnail number six: The three continue talking.

Thumbnail number seven: The three are still together, but no one is speaking. They stare off into the distance of what is probably a field. The girl's head rests on the boy's shoulder.

Thumbnail number eight: The friend is gone. The girl's head still rests on the boy's shoulder. His hand is wrapped around her bicep.

Thumbnail number nine: The boy is talking. The girl keeps her head on his shoulder but trains her eyes on his face. She is smiling. So is he.

Thumbnail number ten: The girl is talking. The boy is laughing.

Thumbnail number eleven: The boy sips from his water, a smile still on his face. The girl stares up at him, taking him in.

Thumbnail number twelve: The boy looks down at the girl. They stare at each other. Her smile is one of contentment.

Thumbnail number thirteen: The boy stares off into the distance again. The girl continues to stare at him.

Thumbnail number fourteen: The boy tilts his head up, as if he is relishing a breeze. The girl watches him.

Thumbnail number fifteen: The boy looks down at the girl. The girl smiles at him, her face now streaked with globs of semen.

Thumbnail number sixteen: The boy stares off into the distance. The girl continues to smile at him, some of the semen dangling in a stream from her chin about to land on her sweatshirt.

Happy Girl Falls in Love Day! They almost had it, didn't they?

| MAY 29 | CHILDREN OF ALCOHOLICS SHOULD BECOME ALCOHOLICS DAY! |

If your father is an alcoholic, he probably doesn't have a lot of time to spend with you between his three-day benders and all that time he's busy being unconscious. So maybe you oughta take a few steps in his direction. If you had a drinking problem like him, then tonight at 3:00 A.M. he might invite you out with him when he says, "We're out of whiskey. I think the neighbors are on vacation so let's break into their house and steal their whiskey." Without a drinking problem, you'd probably already be in bed, waiting to hear the sound of your father falling on the ground so you can finally fall asleep knowing he's safe on the kitchen floor. But with your newfangled alcohol dependency, not only will you be there by his side freaking out because you're out of whiskey, but you'll be across the street shimmying inside your neighbor's basement window before your daddy has the chance to say, "I love you, son. And I'm glad we finally get to do these father-son things together. I'm happy that you finally came around."

Happy Children of Alcoholics Should Become Alcoholics Day!

| MAY 30 | THE SK8R BOI WHO CAN HELP YOU DAY! |

The wise sk8r boi, Seth, the sk8r boi who is just a year and four months older, and a whole five inches taller than the rest of the sk8r bois, is the sk8r boi who can help you.

Seth sits on the wall more than he skates. He's not the best. His height is a disadvantage. But the rest of the sk8r bois look as if they're skating for him. When they come to stop on the lip, they look to Seth, trying not to beam. Seth usually sits next to his girlfriend, Mad. And the two of them are flanked by pairs and fours of sk8er bois at a time. They send their conversations back and forth past Seth, inviting him to comment whenever he wishes. Seth's going to college. Everyone knows that. Probably to study English or history. Everyone knows.

Seth is the sk8r boi who can help you.

"Hi, Seth," say.

Seth will say, "Hey, [your name]." Seth remembers everyone's name.

"I have a problem," tell him.

Seth will look to his right and left, and the sk8r bois flanking him will drop to their boards and disappear in the noise of a grind.

Sit by Seth's side and talk to him while he looks straight ahead.

Say to Seth, "Me and Patty are having trouble. She wants to break up because I'm spending too much time by my mom's deathbed."

"What's your mom dying of?" Seth will ask you.

Say, "Skin cancer. The doctor says it's spreading too fast."

Seth will reach into his bag, digging underneath sweatsocks and CDs and a sandwich and old tattered paperback novels, and he'll pull out a vial of brown liquid.

"Give this to your mom," he'll say. "A teaspoon every day. She should get better within about six weeks. Then you and Patty can spend more time together."

"Wow," say. "This'll cure my mom's cancer?"

Seth still won't look at you when he nods yes. "I only hope it's not too late to keep you and Patty from breaking up."

Say, "Thanks, Seth."

Seth will nod again. The sk8r bois will continue grinding away at the concrete. Mad will return to Seth's side with two bottles of Snapple. Say hi to Mad, then head over to your mom's hospital. Remember, Seth is the sk8r boi who can help you.

Happy the Sk8r Boi Who Can Help You Day!

| MAY 31 | SHOOTOUT ON THE LOG FLUME DAY! |

The son of a bitch pushes his way through the line and hops into the empty tail seat of a log, startling the family in the seats ahead of him when he flashes his gun. The son of a bitch points the gun at the father, sitting in the front seat of the log, and says, "Drive."

You shove your way through the gate, flash your badge, and race to an empty log. As your log pulls ahead to begin its descent, you already see the son of a bitch drop out of sight into the flume.

Luckily, your log takes a different track than his and you catch up to him quickly. He starts shooting wildly at you, but you have to be more careful. There are citizens in his log. Just you in yours. You do your best to keep low.

There's actually quite a lot of ducking and hiding. Since the log flume is a pretty slow, calm ride up until the final descent, the shootout is about as simple as if the two of you were walking on opposite sides of a narrow street at an even pace. Before you reach that final descent, you both manage to inflict fatal wounds upon each other.

The big splash at the end of the ride washes the blood from the wounds so that when your logs come to a stop, you both look quite peacefully asleep. The family that shared the son of a bitch's log races away in a panic. Everyone stares at your bodies. And then the blood starts to seep out from your wounds again, and the screaming erupts from the crowd.

Happy Shootout on the Log Flume Day!

JUNE

GRUMPY!

| JUNE 1 | APOCALYPSE BOYFRIEND DAY!

Tomorrow, just after you contract SARS, your afternoon latte will be ruined when a suicide bomber sprints through the door and blows the place apart. If you survive, you'll get to watch the nuclear holocaust and you'll get to finally find out whether, when a nuclear bomb goes off, everyone turns into skeletons standing up like they always do on TV.

Now then, do you really want to spend tonight, your last night on earth, listening to Mr. Long-Haul detail his five-year investment plan for you again? Why don't you go get yourself an Apocalypse Boyfriend?

The Apocalypse Boyfriend is absolutely adorable and he's employed enough to afford just enough alcohol to make you forget about how screwed over you ended up the last time you lifted your skirt for someone like him. There'll be no annoying "getting-to-know-you" period since he doesn't really want to know you, which is perfect since there won't be much more to know after the bombs drop. And you can always find your Apocalypse Boyfriend when you need him as long as you know where he drinks or who else he's screwing besides you.

In this day and age, you and your Apocalypse Boyfriend will have the only truly level relationship since neither of you wants anything more than to rub up against each other and feel good for another five minutes. Perfect for you since you don't believe you'll live beyond the end of the day. Perfect for him because he doesn't care what happens after that anyway.

Happy Apocalypse Boyfriend Day!

| JUNE 2 | COLLEGE BOY DAY!

Anyone who claims to know anything at all today is a snotty little college boy and will be berated as such. We're not just talking about the obvious, too-big-for-his-britches smarty-pants who interrupts conversations at seedy bars to offer correction on minor points. Any day of the week that geek is gonna hear someone tell him he's a college boy just before he hears the whisk of a punch to his jaw. But today, it's anyone who knows anything.

This includes the guy who says, "Keep your baby covered with my overcoat, and stay low to the ground to breathe as little smoke as possible. The fire stairs are this way. Move quick if you want to live." Sure, he knows how to escape to safety from the burning building, but whoever follows his lead should nonetheless respond, "Think you're so smart, don'tcha, college boy? Us small-town folk just too dumb to make it out the building on our own, that it, college boy?"

Or, immediately following an afternoon of hot sex fun during which your husband managed to locate your clitoris with his tongue, you should look down your naked torso and sneer, "Guess you learned that at one of your fancy-schmancy anatomy classes out at that college of yours, eh, college boy?" Or, if you are in college, and your college professor begins his lecture, get a chant going among your fellow students: "COLL-EGE BOY! COLL-EGE BOY! YOU'RE FUCKING DEAD!" Your professor will probably run out of the room crying like a pussy.

Happy College Boy Day!

| JUNE 3 | AMERICAN STOREFRONT DAY!

It's decorated with a neon Miller High Life sign, an American flag, and a live girl undulating on a pedestal in a small green bikini.

"That's the wrong color green," you'll tell the reporter. "But I think we're on the right track."

The reporter will ask you what you intended to communicate to passersby when you set about decorating your storefront.

"Delicious sandwiches," you'll say.

The reporter will begin to write that, then he'll pause and look back up at you, expectant.

You'll take a second. "And freedom?"

The reporter will nod, satisfied. Behind the glass, the live girl will lose her footing and tumble off of her pedestal. You and the reporter will hear startled yelps from inside the store.

At the hospital later this evening, the doctor will declare it an ankle fracture.

You'll ask, "When will she be able to undulate in my storefront again?"

"Seven months and three weeks," he'll say.

"Seven months and three weeks!" you'll shout.

The doctor will tell you that your live girl is not only lame, she's pregnant.

"YES!" the live girl will shout.

You're either going to have to audition new live girls or you're going to have to redesign your storefront. The Fourth of July is coming up.

"I think I'll audition new live girls," you'll say to the contents of your refrigerator when you're staring into it tonight at 3:00 A.M.

Happy American Storefront Day!

| JUNE 4 | DUCK HUNT DAY!

Today, you are out in the woods hunting for ducks with a drunk judge.

"I have to tell you, I'm real glad my bailiff introduced us," the drunk judge will say.

"Me too, judge," you'll respond. The drunk judge will accidentally fire his gun at some dirt.

"Oops."

Say to him, "Be careful, judge."

The drunk judge will shout, "Overruled!" Then he'll laugh hysterically until he accidentally fires his gun again.

"Oops."

Tell the drunk judge the story about the father and son who went out to the woods to hunt for the first time. The man at the gun store warned them to be careful when hunting, because their guns were very dangerous.

But the father and his son just laughed at the gun salesman. They were hunting for fun, not for lectures. Later the son went running for what he thought was a duck he had shot down, and he tripped and accidentally shot himself in the neck. The father found his dead son, and he couldn't take it so he shot himself in the head. The mother back at home was told later that day about all of this and fell into a deep depression, then she got shot by a burglar.

"Had the father and son listened to that man at the gun shop, they might be alive today."

The drunk judge will cry for a little while, then he'll ask, "But what about the wife who was shot by burglars?"

"Would anyone have broken into her home if there were a husband and son still alive in the house?"

The drunk judge will cry even harder. You'll have to take him back home because he'll scare all the ducks with his sobbing.

When you get to the drunk judge's house, say, "I hope we can do this again sometime."

"Sustained!" the drunk judge will say. Then he'll think his bottle of whiskey is a gavel and he'll shatter it on the roof of your truck.

"Oops."

Tell the drunk judge to get to bed, then drive away happy that you made sure justice made it home safe tonight.

Happy Duck Hunt Day!

JUNE 5	HOT PUSSY ON CRUTCHES DAY!

Many people think that just because a woman happens to be a way smoking piece of hot pussy, she must necessarily be impervious to injury. That just because a woman was born with the ideal body type and bone structure, she must never have to worry about bruising or mortality. This is true only of the most attractive women. These flawless specimens of beauty and sexuality are also, in fact, unbreakable.

But what of the woman who only appears to be physically perfect under the dim light of a tavern or in certain profiles? Yet, after a night or a year together, unsightly wrinkles are discovered, a redness around the armpit is found to linger in the summertime, or she gains some weight. Such a woman might carry herself as if she possesses a superhuman beauty and powers we cannot comprehend, but in reality she is as fragile as the ugliest girl in the burn ward. And this fact is never so apparent as when she breaks her leg.

Suddenly, she is forced to take to the streets on a pair of crutches. With her physical vulnerability on display, she will go about her day with her head bowed, awaiting the ridicule and big rocks she assumes will be hurled her way. In her mind, everyone she passes revels in her hobbling. "Not so pretty now that you fell down," she imagines them thinking.

What she does not expect is the admiration she inevitably receives from her neighbors. She is shocked to find her bravery recognized and commended.

She feels welcomed by all those people she used to look down on because they were merely passably attractive. They are excited to learn that she is capable of feeling the same physical pain that they feel. They ask her things like, "So, do you have to work too?" And, "Do you defecate?"

And most surprising of all is the attention she receives from the men she encounters in her day. Men of all shapes and sizes, ugly and handsome alike, all of them go out of their way to let her know that, now that it's clear that this beautiful woman will also one day die, they would like to buy her dinner and perhaps penetrate her. And she is overjoyed to be spoken to by so many different men when, in the past, the only men who approached her were the very wealthy.

So when you see some hot pussy on a pair of crutches, go to her. Let her know that you are awed by her courage and you're glad to know that she's not all stuck-up like those other girls at the club who have flame-retardant skin. You'll be making her day, you sure will.

Happy Hot Pussy on Crutches Day!

| JUNE 6 |

YOU ARE A LED ZEPPELIN ROCK BLOCK DAY!

It's your third interview at Mace and Krane LLP, the second largest accounting firm in the city.

"So what will we be getting if we bring you onto our team?" your interviewer is going to ask you. He's asked that same question to nine other guys who sat in that chair. They all talked about integrity and loyalty and even "elbow grease." Why not tell him the truth?

"Get me on the Mace and Krane team, and you'll be getting at least three classic Led Zeppelin tracks played back-to-back without commercials, interrupted by nothing more than a station identification and perhaps a brief but appropriate fart sound effect. I'm talking 'Kashmir.' I'm talking

'When the Levee Breaks.' I'm talking about 'Rock and Roll' and 'Whole Lotta Love' and maybe, dare I say it, 'Ramble On.'"

"'Black Dog'?" your interviewer will ask.

Just give a chuckle. "What do you think?"

"You sure can sweet talk, can't you?"

"It's not talk," tell him. "Pretend it's Friday night, this office is your car, and all these candidates you're interviewing, they're all just a bunch of different radio stations on the dial. So you're driving around flipping through the dial, trying to find the right tunes to rock your Friday. You hear some Foreigner and some Creedence and some Foghat and it's all righteous, but it's not rocking you."

By now you should be on your feet with a lit joint between your lips and some dark shades over your eyes.

"And then you get to that one station. And you hear those words. 'It's time,' the man says. 'It's time to get the Led out.'"

Your interviewer's eyes will be beaming at you like you're narrating his most precious dreams.

"And you just know your Friday night's gonna be righteous and it's gonna be rocking. You just got a Led Zeppelin rock block, man. You can't go wrong unless you don't know how to rock. And that's what you get if you hire me. Get me on your team, my man, and you're getting the Led out."

Your interviewer will jump on his desk, shout that you're hired, then you and he will play air guitar while singing 'Black Dog' very poorly.

"I'll see you Monday," your interviewer will say.

"Party starts on Monday, then," you'll say as you gather your things.

"Don't forget to bring some 'Stairway,'" he'll say.

Stop what you're doing, take off your sunglasses, and look your interviewer in the eye. Ask him, "Could you repeat that please?"

Your interviewer will repeat, "Don't forget to bring some 'Stairway.'"

Try to keep your cool. There's no reason to get violent. He just doesn't understand.

"I can't work here," tell him. "This is a very respectable accounting firm, but so was Arthur Andersen."

"I beg your pardon, but Arthur Andersen . . ."

"I need to know that when the time comes, my place of employment will be ready to get the Led out. I'm sorry but you have not impressed upon me that this firm will be able to do that effectively."

"But where will you go?" your interviewer will ask you. "What will you do?"

Turn around and smile. Say, "Gotta keep turning that dial. Gotta find me some Jimmy."

Walk out the door. You may have an impatient wife and a sick daughter, and it's gonna be hard to face them, but you gotta look in the mirror too. Don't blink.

Happy You Are a Led Zeppelin Rock Block Day!

| JUNE 7 | CAR WASH GIRLFRIEND DAY!

Your girlfriend has a great body: large, pretty breasts, long legs with big round thighs, and a fantastic ass. Congratulations. This is the good news.

The bad news is she also has a great big heart. And she's constantly being asked to wear a bikini and drench herself in soapy water at charity car washes.

"But Saturday's my only day off," you plead with her.

"I'm sorry, baby," she says. "I love you, but how can I be selfish with my time when I know that all I have to do is seemingly unknowingly massage my soapy wet breasts in the middle of a shopping center parking lot and I'll have helped a child in a wheelchair get medicine?"

"But you give so much of your beautiful body to people in need," you say. "I want to fuck it."

"Oh, sweetie," she says. "God gave me this body for a reason. He wouldn't have given me such a wonderful ass if he didn't want me to climb atop the hood of a father of four's Celica and press my bethonged cheeks against the windshield, apparently attempting to wash the glass clean with the meat of my buttocks, which is of course not very practical. But it does put food in the mouth of a baby born addicted to crack."

"I'm going to have to break up with you," you'll say today. "I might not find someone as hot as you to screw for quite a while, but at least I'll find someone who thinks I'm more important than a fucking famine victim."

"But after the summer, when it gets cold again, I'll be all yours," she'll say.

Stand firm. "I'm sorry, sweetheart. You're way hot, but I need a girl who doesn't care about anyone or anything but me."

You know what has to be done. You can't be stuck in the car wash if you want to get on the turnpike to a better you.

Happy Car Wash Girlfriend Day!

| JUNE 8 | INTRODUCE THEM TO THEIR COWORKERS DAY! |

Tell them, "Now I'd like you all to go around the room, and for each of you to say your name, what your position is, and what happened in your lives that led to you sitting in that seat today, waiting to begin, and possibly end, a quiet yet vaguely angry life in a cubicle that you'll share with someone who enjoys eating onions at lunch and who has loud phone conversations with a daughter."

Their polite smiles will shrink to startled little O's. Their hands will reach out to grip the edges of their tables. They'll look down at their laps, just like they always do.

"Starting with you."

Point to the man with thin black hair. He'll clear his throat and speak with a confidence that will fade a little more with every word.

"My name is Frank. I'll be coming in as a sales associate. When I graduated business school I thought I'd run my own company. But I never tried."

Point to the middle-aged blond woman in the front row who is smiling a little too much. "My name is Carol," she'll say. "I'm a legal secretary. This is my first job in six years. I'm going back to work because I'm recently divorced and I have to hold down a job for eighteen months before they give me my sons back."

Say, "Row four, all of you at once."

It will be the music of chaos when everyone in row four says their names, the positions they'll be taking at the company, and the point in each of their lives when they believe everything took a turn toward the present. Amid the garbled talk, you'll be able to make out choice phrases like "my brother passed away and I have to take care of his kids" and "I ripped my ACL" and "I realized I couldn't paint for shit."

During the chorus of row four, the mess of regret will be too much for many of the others to take and they'll run for the door. About ten new hires will remain seated. These are the new hires who really have something they want to get off their chests. Settle in and make sure you save the brunette in row five, seat two for last because she's got a doozy. Can you say, "Locked in a basement for three weeks I can't remember"?

Happy Introduce Them to Their Coworkers Day!

| JUNE 9 | KISS THEM GOOD-BYE DAY! |

It's not your party. It's Patty's. Half the guests are people you just met tonight. The other half are the friends you've known for years, including Jimmy. Jimmy became much more than a friend eleven months ago, and he went back to being your friend three weeks ago. He's here with his new girl tonight, but you're determined to kiss him good-bye anyway.

People are putting on their coats. Grab your drink in your right hand, plant yourself by the door, and kiss them all good-bye.

David and Janice were kind and they spoke of their impending move to Syracuse. David's going to be teaching there. You met them tonight and you'll probably never see them again. David will extend his right hand to you. Put your left arm around his shoulder and kiss his cheek, then say, "Good luck in Syracuse." Repeat with Janice.

Mark wants to sleep with you but has a girlfriend of nine years. Mark will hug you good-bye. Kiss his cheek and whisper in his ear, "It was great to see you again."

Jennifer loathes you with all of her being. She will say good-bye without an effort toward physical contact. Reach your hand around to pull Jennifer in by the back of her head and kiss her on the neck. It will force her to laugh and she'll exclaim, "Okay!"

The first wave of departures will have petered out by now. Get to the bar and refill your drink before the next group disperses. Back by the door, find Jimmy where he's sitting on the back of a couch. Jimmy'll be watching you. He'll wonder if you're going to be there by the door when he leaves.

Kevin was such a terrible lay and he's not bright at all. He's on his way downhill, financially and socially. Kevin's waiting for your kiss good-bye. He's grabbing out for any affection he can get these days. Give him a short peck on the cheek that would be hard to misinterpret. He'll probably call you this week, regardless.

Larissa, your favorite for life, will kiss you first. She'll kiss you on the lips and say, "Forget about him," meaning Jimmy. "Just come back and crash with me. I'll get you high." Tell her you're not going to do anything stupid and you need to wake up early in the morning but thanks, and kiss her on the lips once more. One day, you'll have to buy Larissa an expensive birthday present. Something to let her know you owe her your life ten times over.

Kim and Pete made it out tonight, their first night out since the baby was born. You haven't been by to see the baby yet, so promise to come by soon and give them both a kiss to give to their daughter for you. You've always gotten the impression that Kim and Pete think you're an irresponsible mess. You can't help but agree.

Here come the next five winter coats. Deborah and Jill in their matching black overcoats. Jeff in his hooded parka. And Laura, the arm of her red ski jacket hooked through the arm of Jimmy's pea coat.

Deborah and Jill are loaded and loud. Kiss Jill on the cheek. She'll say, "Bye, baby." Deborah's gonna grab you by the sides of your head and stick her tongue in your mouth. Make loud fake-ecstatic noises with her. When Deborah lets go, she'll slap your cheek lightly and say, "Later on, slut."

Jeff's gonna grab you by the sides of your head and say, "My turn." Jill brought Jeff along and he seems fun, but you're not sure he's straight. Just give him a shove away then kiss him on the cheek. Call Jill this week to find out if Jeff is straight and if she's sleeping with him.

Here come Jimmy and Laura. Jimmy will be doing all he can to talk to anyone in the vicinity so as to keep his back to you. But he and Laura are the only ones leaving by now. And Laura is telling you she's happy to have met you.

"Likewise," say. Don't kiss her. Don't extend your hand for a handshake. In fact, take a sip from your glass. Laura will look to Jimmy to see if he's finished his good-byes.

That's when Jimmy will turn to say good-bye to you. He'll say, "Good to see ya."

"Mm," say.

Jimmy will say to Laura, "You ready?" She'll smile and nod like a fucking retard.

Jimmy will say to you, "Okay then. Bye-bye."

"Bye-bye," say. Tiptoe with your glass in both hands and put your lips to his. He'll kiss back. It will last as long as you stay on your tiptoes. Make it last three seconds.

Laura, easily confused, will look confused. Wave to her, even though she's standing a foot away from you. She'll wave back. She does as she's told.

Jimmy will mutter something inaudible, and the two of them will leave for the evening. Patty will come walking toward you now. She'll have seen what happened and, it being her party, she'll feel it her responsibility to ask you what the fuck. Move into the living room before she can catch you. You don't have to kiss anyone else good-bye. You got to kiss Jimmy.

Happy Kiss Them Good-bye Day!

| JUNE 10 | DO SOMETHING THAT MAKES YOU COME DAY! |

For today, we're borrowing a page from an outside source. Today we're taking heed from self-help guru Dr. Mark I. G. Brockerand, Ph.D. Here's an excerpt from Mark's bestselling self-help book, *Feeling Better Because You Are Constantly Having Orgasms*.

The average human being makes use of no more than 15 percent of his or her potential for having orgasms. A healthy adult female who is white can have as many as ninety-nine hundred little orgasms per day, or seven really big ones. And the average adult male can have seven really big ones. But we are taught to go through life not constantly vibrating with physical ecstasy. We make excuses. I have to go to the bank. I have to make dinner for the children. I think I have a hundred-and-two-degree fever.

These are the cop-outs. The rain checks we write to ourselves so as to put off pleasure. Are we afraid of how our lives might change if we live up to our potential? Yes.

Well it's time to pose a challenge to yourself. Every day, do something that makes you come. Whether it be intercourse with a person you find attractive, intercourse with a person you don't find attractive, or intercourse with three people, just make sure it makes you come. And if you manage to come once today, come twice tomorrow. Keep upping the number, and soon you will be the fully realized, constantly orgasmic person that was cowering inside of you all those years you were too busy earning money and caring for your home.

Tie a string around your finger. Every time you look at that string, consider what you're doing at that moment and ask yourself, "Is this gonna make me come?" If not, STOP!

Thanks, Doc. You heard the man, folks. Get out there and have some orgasms now. Because today's Do Something That Makes You Come Day!

JUNE 11	### CHECK IN ON YOUR ROOMMATE DAY!

Lonely? Your roommate's dad died a year and a half ago. Why not check in to see how he's doing with it? Just knock on the door and shout so he can hear you, "I know this is probably weird, but I was thinking about how your dad died a year or so ago, and I remembered that I never lent you any support when that happened. So I want you to know that if you ever wanna talk, like right now, if you wanna talk about anything at all, I'm bored."

Your roommate will probably just brush you off with a "Yeah, thanks." So you should make up something exciting to say, like, "You know, my mom's dying." Your roommate will then open up the door and hug you. You'll be expected to say why your mom is dying, but if you can't come up with anything, just say, "She's a cop and she was first through the door on a bust and she wasn't wearing her vest." Then start screaming at the sky, "Why didn't you wear your fuckin' vest, Ma? I told you that cowboy shit would get you killed!!!"

I know it seems like you'll just end up talking all about this fake dying police-mom story, but you won't have to. All you'll need to say is, "I really don't wanna talk about it anymore. If I don't take my mind off of this shit I'm gonna go nuts." Then you can talk about dating or the new recycling rules for the building, and bye-bye loneliness!

Happy Check In on Your Roommate Day!

JUNE 12 | YOUR ELEMENTARY SCHOOL PRINCIPAL'S IN TROUBLE DAY!

Today you'll pay a visit to your old elementary school in a fit of nostalgia. You'll never expect to have your shirtfront drenched in the blood of another man by dinnertime.

"I just thought I'd pop in and say hello," you'll tell your old principal. "I came back to town to make amends with my father, who's in the hospital with a bum hip. He won't do anything but spit at me for being queer, so while I'm here I figured that I'd drop in on the old schoolgrounds that made me."

Your principal will cackle menacingly. His eyes will have ten-pound bags underneath them and he'll speak in a throaty rasp through about six days' stubble.

"That's all very sweet," he'll say. "Now why don't you tell me who sent you here?"

You'll sit up in your seat and suggest that you just thought it might be fun to see what the old hallways look like now that you're big and strong and making more a year than all the teachers' salaries combined. "Schoolteachers are really getting the shaft," you'll say, trying to win his trust.

Your principal will rise from his desk and you'll be surprised to see that he's wearing a pair of pajama pants. "So you expect me to believe that you just happened to wander in to reminisce on today of all days?"

He'll lean in just an inch from your face. "Make it quick," he'll whisper. "Don't make me wait for it."

Promise him that you mean him no harm. That you have very fond memories of your school years here. Much better than your high school years, which went down the shitter after word spread of you making a pass at a running back your freshman year.

Your principal's expression will soften. "Then help me."

He'll tell you that he's always been a gambler but lately he's been caught up in a seedy underbelly where prostitutes fight each other with straight razors and spectators can bet on who will win and who will die.

"It took hold of me. The fights were getting raided every night, and the league was in trouble. So I started hosting the matches here in the boiler room underneath the cafeteria. Last week someone with a lot of power here in the neighborhood got shot twice in the face downstairs. Ever since, with every day I've been hearing about someone else who was there that night getting cut open and tossed into the river."

Say, "Wow! I always wondered what it would be like to find out what sort of lives the adults at my school lead, and it's so weird how close I guessed right."

You'll explain that you always thought your principal probably strangled prostitutes and ate them, and you're relieved that he just watched them kill each other. He'll tell you that at the end of every fight, the family of the prostitute that died was given between four and ten thousand dollars, depending on the prostitute's ranking in the league, so it wasn't all bad. That's when the lights will go out.

"They're here," your principal will say. He'll pull a handgun and a machete from his desk. He'll toss the machete at you and say, "Looks like your trip down memory lane's about to take a detour, baby." Then the two of you will make a run for it to the metal shop, where there are table saws.

Happy Your Elementary School Principal's in Trouble Day!

| JUNE 13 | KING JUNE DAY! |

Today a rapper named King June will ask you out on a date. He is the rapper who writes raps about wildflowers in bloom, love, and tasteful weddings.

> *Daisies in your hair*
> *Love is in the air*

Brotha groom waitin' with a smile
Go on, Gina, wreck tha aisle
          —excerpt from "Gina Goin Down Tha Aisle"
               King June, copyright 2002

Unfortunately, you're seeing someone. King June's shoulders will fall and he'll ask, "Are you in love?"

"I think so," you'll say.

"But you ain't tol' him so yet?"

"No," you'll say. "But this one feels like the real deal."

King June will shake his head in sorrow. "Man, it seem like a century since I been up in that kinda shit." You'll rub King June's shoulder. He'll smile and wish you luck.

Happy King June Day!

| JUNE 14 | CLOSE TO YOU DAY!

You think David is dead because he stopped writing. He is not. Your mailman is simply in love with you. He's been stealing David's letters to you and reading them to find out more about you, find out what sort of man can win your heart. Your mailman is trying to learn who to be so that someone like you might one day wait for letters from someone like him.

You can either confront him and demand that he return the letters, or give him time to read the letters and try and be like David. If he pulls it off and manages to become a close approximation to David, you might not have to keep on going with this long-distance crap. David is great, but he's three thousand miles away. If you started dating your mailman, neither rain nor sleet nor snow could keep you from getting some.

Happy Close to You Day!

| JUNE 15 | COME OUT OF THE CLOSET AS SOMETHING SOCIETY THINKS IS SHAMEFUL DAY!

You think you're pretty brave just because you're not afraid to go down to the basement during storms. But as far as society is concerned, no one is braver than the guy who stands up in front of a room full of people and tells them all what kind of weird shit he's into.

Coming out of the closet as stuff kicks ass for a lot of reasons. First, you get to throw a party and every single one of your close friends and family members has to attend. It doesn't matter if you skipped their birthdays or if they have a meeting or a kid in surgery or whatever. If you say on the invitation, "I am finally going to stop hiding the real me from a small-minded and totally dickhead-ish America," they all have to show up. Most of them will want to be there anyway just to find out if the rumors they've been spreading all these years are true. But if one of your friends doesn't show up, anytime you need to borrow his car you'll be able to say, "I can't believe you weren't there for me when I came out. It was very brave of me to do that. Hand over the LeBaron."

Second, when you come out, everyone excuses you for not having done anything with yourself all these years. They'll just assume it was so painful to have to keep your inner perv a secret from the religious right that you couldn't follow through on those grad school applications. And you can coast for at least six months after the big reveal, countering any nagging with a simple, "Goddammit, I finally became the real me six months ago. I'm no older than an infant! Would you ask an infant to move out of your basement?"

And best of all, if you send your invites to all those aunts and grandparents who live far away, there's no way they'll be able to make it so they'll have no choice but to send you some cash.

So come out as something depraved today. It doesn't matter which disgusting proclivity you choose to shove in everyone's faces, just don't touch me.

Happy Come Out of the Closet as Something Society Thinks Is Shameful Day!

| JUNE 16 | OFFICE LOTTO POOL DAY!

Your coworkers just found out that the lotto jackpot is up to $178 million and they've decided to pitch in and buy a lot of tickets together. One of them (either Shirley or Candee) is coming your way.

"Wanna be millionaires with us?" she'll ask.

Say yes.

"Pitch in five dollars and when we win tonight, you'll get a share of the pot," she'll say. "It's up to $178 million, so if all ten of us pitch in we'll each get $17.8 million!"

Tell her that's great because you needed $17.8 million. Explain to her that you could actually do with more than that, so maybe she shouldn't ask *everybody* if they want to be included.

"Silly, I couldn't leave anybody out!" she'll say.

Tell her that's fine. But you think that she's making a big mistake. Tell her that after you win, you might murder some of the others to increase the share for everybody else.

"You're so funny!" she'll shout. Then she'll walk away. You'll assume she was referring to the fact that if anyone with a share of the pot were to die, the law would probably award that share to the deceased's next of kin. You'll spend the night thinking of other ways to increase each person's share of the pot.

Tomorrow you're going to find out that none of the department's tickets won. Confront Shirley or Candee.

"Where's my money?" say.

Shirley or Candee will shrug and make a joke about how you're just going to have to trudge through another day in Boringtown. "But no one won so the pot's still there for us to win if we all want to pitch in again."

Grab her by the neck and growl into her face, "I want my fucking money. I gave you five bucks for a share of that $178 million that you said we were going to win. Now give me my fucking $17.8 million, you understand me? I'm gonna go sit at my desk and wait for you to bring me the fucking cash. If you don't, God help you."

Go back to your desk and cross your arms. Everyone in the department will disappear for a while. You'll assume that they're out dealing with the lottery commission. Then Harvey and Joseph, the guards from downstairs, will come by. They'll Taser you.

Happy Office Lotto Pool Day!

| JUNE 17 |

TELL YOUR HUSBAND THE TRUTH ABOUT THE TOOTHBRUSH DAY!

"Remember when you used to get those photographs in the mail that showed a woman in a ski mask with her pants down and your toothbrush sticking out of her anus?"

Your husband will say, "How did you know about that?"

Don't say anything.

"That was you?" he'll ask. "But why?"

Say, "It was back when we were just coworkers. I had a crush on you but you were still with your ex-wife. I was so jealous of her."

"So you broke into my house, stuck my toothbrush up your behind, and mailed me pictures of it?"

Explain it to him carefully. "I wanted to be the only thing you thought about. I wanted you to obsess over me. So I broke into your house and took a picture of myself with your toothbrush up my ass. That's the only way I knew that I could get you to spend all day thinking about me, even though you didn't know who I was."

"That gave me nightmares," he'll say.

"Exactly," tell him. "That's what I needed. I needed you to be consumed by me. So I had to anonymously terrorize you. Since it was done out of love for you, can you forgive me?"

Your husband will explain that he can't forgive you because his obsession over the photographs led to his former wife divorcing him, and though he thinks you're really great he always kind of dug her more.

Happy Tell Your Husband the Truth About the Toothbrush Day!

| JUNE 18 | MOUNT FUN DAY! |

Mount Fun got its name because at its peak is the world's highest-altitude Chuck E. Cheese's. Many of the world's wealthiest and most adventurous children reserve the Chuck E. Cheese's at the top of Mount Fun for their birthday parties, but only a rare few ever make it to the top to blow out the candles. Mount Fun's slopes and crags are littered with the bones of outdoorsy children and their Sherpas.

The staff of the Mount Fun Chuck E. Cheese's live on the premises, and they are all certified in either medicine or nursing. You're the newest hire, filling the vacancy of Bunny Rabbit/Orthopedic Surgeon. You are required to show up to work only when the bell is rung in the Chuck E. Cheese's watchtower, alerting all in the camp that a birthday celebration nears, and the warm blankets and various roots should be readied for however many of the children have survived. This is also the signal for the generator to be charged in the medical barracks.

On average, the staff of the Mount Fun Chuck E. Cheese's works a total of six weeks out of the year, rarely hosting more than one or two parties. Which is pretty sweet. But each birthday party is preceded by a three- to four-week convalescence. The most challenging part of the job is that all staff members must wear their animal costumes at all times, even during the amputations.

Tonight, the bell will ring for the first time this year. The first time in your tenure. You're going to have to prove to them that they made the right decision in hiring you. Get ready to sing some funny covers of fifties rock songs and teach some children how to maneuver their prosthetics.

Happy Mount Fun Day!

| JUNE 19 |

IT'S YOUR FIRST DAY WITH YOUR NEW PARTNER DAY!

Your new partner starts today. As soon as you're both in the squad car, tell him that if you get gunned down in the line of duty, it's okay for him to have an affair with your wife. Then show him a picture of her.

"Pretty nice, right? Now show me yours. I wanna see who I get."

Your new partner will balk at showing you a picture of his wife. He'll object to the thought of your having an affair with her should anything happen to him. Tell your new partner he is a rookie with no respect for the brotherhood of the badge.

"You're my partner," tell him. "If I die, you're going to want to spend time with my wife so that you can be with someone who is in as much pain as you are. And she'll want to spend time with you since you'll probably be the last one who saw me alive. The shared mourning will create a bond that you'll confuse with love and before you know it, you'll be all over each other."

Put your hand on his shoulder and look him in the eye. Say, "It's only right that the one of us who lives should have to take care of the other's widowed wife, make sure she's adequately pleasured and whatnot. Why'd you join the force anyway?"

Your new partner will mutter something about cleaning up the streets. Then he'll grudgingly pull from his wallet a picture of his wife and hand it to you.

Say, "Yowza! With a wife like that you better be scared of getting shot by me! Today sure is my lucky day."

Start the car and begin your patrol. If it's a slow day, catalog for your new partner all the things your wife digs in the bedroom. And give him the copy of *Written on the Body* with your wife's favorite passages highlighted in pink.

Happy It's Your First Day with Your New Partner Day!

| JUNE 20 | BREAK UP WITH YOUR BOYFRIEND VIA HOT AIR BALLOON DAY! |

Act like you just wanted to surprise your special little pumpkin-head with a nice, romantic hot air balloon ride. He will think you're trying to make up for the fact that you've been really cold and cunty lately, and you'll get a big wet kiss before you both head for the car.

Climb into the basket and continue to act all "We're in it to win it, us two in this here relationship!" Do this by touching him (I know it's gross). Keep the game going until the balloon pilot (they're called "Looners" in the industry) cuts the ropes from the ground and you start to rise. When you're around eight feet up, you should dive from the basket with a forward roll onto the ground below (any higher than eight feet and you might fuck up and die).

Your lambykins will be staring down at you stunned, not sure whether to laugh or call an ambulance on his cell phone. As soon as you get back on your feet, just shout, "I don't think we should see each other anymore! I feel like I've built a prison around me that doesn't have any windows or doors! And I wanna go outside! We're broken up now!" Then run.

Your nookynooky will demand to be lowered down after you, but the Looner will offer some excuse as to why that can't happen, not letting on that you tipped him extra to keep your pookyface in the air.

If you wanna get a really good head start on your runaway, take the car. Or if it's his car and you don't wanna steal it, throw the keys into a swamp. And don't answer your cell phone.

Happy Break Up with Your Boyfriend via Hot Air Balloon Day!

| JUNE 21 | DEAD BIRDS IN THE CORPORATE PLAZA FOUNTAIN DAY! |

Get up a couple hours early, go up to your roof, and kill five pigeons with a baseball bat. Bag their carcasses, then go back down to your apartment and change out of your pajamas to get ready for work.

You should get to the office early enough that only a few people might be walking in with you, but not so early as to arouse suspicion from the guards. Ready the bag of dead pigeons so that when you reach the fountain, you can casually walk nearly two hundred degrees around the edge, every ten paces tossing a pigeon into the water with just a flick of your wrist behind your back. When the bag is empty, stuff it into your briefcase and stroll on up to work.

You'll be taking a long lunch today. Leave early enough to get some food and to secure the bench on the plaza with that perfect view. As the staffers file out at lunch hour, just sit back and watch the secretaries and the middle managers sit down on the ledge of the fountain for a nice meal of office gossip and panini. Then watch them all spring up from their seats, one by one, as they spot the bludgeoned pigeons floating past. Soon, you'll hear murmurings of "Must be using some chemicals in the water." Followed by, "Those aren't chemicals! These pigeons were bludgeoned to death! Dear God almighty!" Then work will close early so everyone can group into pipe-wielding mobs and band out into the streets to find the motherfucker responsible. Don't join them. Go home and nap some.

Happy Dead Birds in the Corporate Plaza Fountain Day!

| JUNE 22 | SHOEHORN DAY!

You pay strange women to come to your home and make you gag by pressing down on your tongue with your shoehorn. Today, after seven minutes of being gagged nearly to vomiting down the woman's wrist, her boyfriend will burst through the front door and shout, "Jessica!"

She'll have told you her name was Amber.

"I swear I don't have sex with him," Jessica will shout.

"What the hell are you talking about? He's in his underwear!"

Not exactly. You'll be wearing black rubber trunks.

"But it never goes further than this," Jessica will shout. "He just pays me to hold this shoehorn on his tongue until he throws up a bunch of times. Then he falls panting to the floor and tells me to root through his trousers for my cash."

The boyfriend will look like he's trying to find the downside.

"If you needed the money . . ."

Jessica will smile. "I was saving up to buy you an iPod for your birthday."

"Oh, baby," the boyfriend will say. "I can't listen to an iPod. I've been letting this old guy fuck my ear for fifty dollars a shot so that I could buy you a PSP. My doctor says all that semen has permanently damaged my eardrums."

"Oh my God," Jessica says. "If holding a shoehorn down on this guy's tongue had left me unable to play a PSP, this would totally be like *Gift of the Magi!*"

Jessica and her boyfriend will run off to be happy together, but not before her boyfriend beats you into a coma and steals everything in your home that looks like it might be worth something.

Happy Shoehorn Day!

| JUNE 23 | MAKE HIM JUMP INTO YOUR WELL
DAY!

He said he loves you and wants to build you the most beautiful house in town. But you told him that you want to fall in love with a man who'll take you away from this place. He said he would take you wherever you wished. He wants to be with you forever. As close as he can be to you, forever and ever.

"Forever and ever?" say.

"Forever and ever," he'll say.

"But I'm taking care of my father until he passes. That could take a very long time. Can you wait?"

He'll wring his hands and take a step closer, and he'll confide that he doesn't know how long he can wait. "I just need to know that I am a part of your life. Your everyday life. I need to live with you and be considered by you every single day. Please don't make me wait until your father passes."

Pretend to think about it for a second, then say, "Fine. Jump into my well. If the fall doesn't kill you, you can live there in the ground underneath my feet. But you must be silent, and every day I will lower food and drink down to you until my father passes."

He'll say, "If it is what you have to offer me, I will accept, my love."

And with that he'll jump into your well. His scream will float up to you as he falls, and it will grow quieter and quieter until it halts with a very faint thud. You'll linger by the well long enough to hear him groaning, letting you know he's alive. Then you'll go inside to tend to your father.

Each day you'll lower down a sandwich and a jar of milk to him. And each day he'll send back to you a short letter written on yesterday's napkin. The first letter will read, "I snapped my leg at the knee. It is agony." The second letter will read, "Oh, it is agony. I snapped my leg at the knee." The third letter will read, "This is horrible. I have made such a mistake. Also, I snapped my leg at the knee."

You must never write him back, and you mustn't fetch help for him until your father passes. However, if your father doesn't pass for a very long time, be aware that the man in the well will likely be very disgusting when you finally retrieve him.

Happy Make Him Jump into Your Well Day!

| JUNE 24 | THE BOYS YOU MASTURBATE TO DAY! |

Bad things are happening to the boys you masturbate to. Last night you masturbated to a narrative in which Lee, your brother's friend, slept over and the two of you bumped into each other in the middle of the night when you both walked to the bathroom without any clothes on. He invited you to go first, but you insisted he go first. So you both went into the bathroom, but instead of using the toilet you decided to get really soapy under the shower and screw. Today your brother is going to call you and tell you that Lee was mugged on his way to work this morning.

And then there was yesterday, when your ex-boyfriend Mark had a car crash not six hours after you got yourself off with a memory of him going down on you in the back of a cab. And let's not forget the morning after your coworker Kyle appeared in a fantasy of yours. He woke up without any eyes.

Choose whom you masturbate to wisely. You have a tremendously evil power that feels so good.

Happy the Boys You Masturbate To Day!

| JUNE 25 |

THE AUNT YOUR DAD CUT OFF IS DEAD DAY!

That's what that call was this morning at nine. No message, of course. But he'll call back. Your dad will call and say, "Just want to let you know that, uh, your Aunt Elena . . . she passed away this week."

You'll say, "Oh God." Then you'll hope your dad will speak again before you have to concoct some way to react to the death of a blood relative who has been forbidden to contact you since you were six.

Your dad will say, "Yeah, she had a stroke in her sleep. Or, actually just before she got to bed. Your cousin Jimmy found her."

Just wait for a second. Say something like, "Jesus, Aunt Elena. It's so . . ." but use a tone that your dad understands. A tone that says, "What the fuck did she do, anyway, that you would cut your own sister off for the last twenty-five years of her life?" The tone will make your dad laugh a bit, because your dad can't believe he pulled it off either.

He'll chuckle a bit more just before he tells you, "So the funeral's tomorrow. I'm paying for it." Here's where he laughs out loud.

He'll tell you you're welcome to come but he understands that you have to work. But he will point out that he's using the caterers from your cousin Michael's wedding, who were awesome.

Happy the Aunt Your Dad Cut Off Is Dead Day!

| JUNE 26 |

WANNA HEAR ME SING? DAY!

Drunk? Bitchin'.

Upset about not feeling anything anymore (couple years running now)? Sorry to hear it, but let's get started.

Say to your neighbor, "Wanna hear me sing?" When he says, "Hell yeah!"

get up from your chair, pick up the ketchup bottle and hold it up to your mouth like it's a microphone. Open your mouth as if you were about to belt out "Moon River," then let all the muscles in your face go limp and bug open your eyes in terror.

Everyone at the table will understand. Even though they were really hoping to hear you sing, they can tell that you saw yourself in the 3×6–foot promotional Harp Lager mirror spread across the back wall of the bar. You saw yourself looking thirty years older than you are, dressed in clothing you find unappealing, your nose different than you remember it, your hands someone else's, clearly, anyone would say so.

Your chest hair, showing. The air surrounding you, gray-green. Your shoes, cheap. The way you would look holding a first-place trophy, inappropriate. What you ordered, not what you craved. Everyone you've ever kissed with love, amounting to a total of three. Everything that smells, including you. Everyone that fails, claiming you. Everyone that swells with pride over the achievements of a relative on the road to greatness, avoiding your eye contact. All that you don't want, it's all right there in the mirror, baby.

They'll understand if you just wanna sit back down. Don't. It'll ruin the next five minutes. Blink your eyes and wipe away the gray that's clouding up your vision and sing the first few verses of that Billy and the Beaters song. Everyone will love you for it, and you'll be allowed to clench your eyes shut tight while you sing.

Happy Wanna Hear Me Sing? Day!

| JUNE 27 | TERRIBLE MEN DAY! |

Terrible men are outside. They're in love with you, and they're outside. There are four of them. They're not dressed the same.

Terrible men hold letters promising their ashen hearts. Terrible men practiced all day in front of mirrors, practiced how far to drop their eyelids when the time is right to ask for your forgiveness. Terrible men are inebriated, and they're sharing a bottle of liquor, and they're swaying and yelling at your window. There are four of them.

Terrible men think most women find them absolutely irresistible (many do). They are mean to female bartenders and they have secretaries (sometimes two). In a week of nights, terrible men will spend five alone, two with a woman, every week, without fail (it's true). Terrible men just threw a bottle of liquor at the wall next to your window (go to them).

When you open the door, terrible men, all four, they're fighting in the street. Then one of the four, he sees you (your nightshirt, your knees, the pee-yellow light behind your hair) and he grabs at the others, tugging them into formation.

Terrible men brush the damp of the street from their suits and stand in a zigzag. You look in their eyes and you know terrible men will die if you don't bring them in tonight. They say, four voices, in unison: "Leigh. Please, Leigh. I'm not gonna make it, Leigh."

You wait just a moment, look away just a moment, just long enough to make terrible men boys. Then you lift your head to them. You warn them with your sigh that it can't turn out the way it will, not again. You step aside to allow the single-file line of terrible men to climb the flights to your apartment. And you follow, shushing them when they raise their voices (the neighbors).

Happy Terrible Men Day!

| JUNE 28 | THE AIRCRAFT CARRIER DAY!

Today, the aircraft carrier is talking to the press. "It's cool and all, I mean, it's my job, but seriously, FUCK AIRCRAFT!"

Planes, choppers, pilots, and those guys with the glowsticks, they're all on the aircraft carrier's back, and they act like *they're* doing *it* the favor.

"I'm fucking huge," says the aircraft carrier. "There's a majesty about me. But they don't ever see it."

Just then, the aircraft carrier stops its grumbling because it notices Private Nairns alone on the upper deck with a letter clenched in his fist. Nairns is standing still and he's not looking at anything. Just has his eyes open.

"That's Nairns," the aircraft carrier says to the throng of reporters. "Looks like he got another shitty letter from his girl. He really loves her, but she does this all the time. She seems real twatty. I mean, the guy's at sea."

Private Nairns's pain is just what is needed for the aircraft carrier to put things into perspective. The aircraft carrier will stop bitching until Nairns goes back to his bunk. Then it will say, "Some of these guys are okay, I guess. But most of them, God, I hope they die."

Happy the Aircraft Carrier Day!

| JUNE 29 | DANDELION DAY!

You had a girlfriend when you were sixteen and her name was Ellen. When Ellen moved to Florida with her parents, she asked you whether you thought the two of you would stay in love forever, even though she was moving far away. You said to her only, "When you're thirty-six, mail me a dandelion."

Ellen has been thirty-six for eight months now and you've been checking your mailbox every day with a swiftly growing dread. No dandelions.

She couldn't have forgotten. Something, or someone, is keeping her from contacting you.

"She could be dead," your father will suggest.

"The dead have executors to carry out their wishes posthumously," you'll say. "No. I think she's being held captive by someone or she's trapped under something. What if she's hungry?"

"Find her," your mother will exclaim.

"But my administrative assistant position. I could be fired if I leave work for too long."

"Oh yeah," your mother will say.

You have a three-day weekend starting tomorrow, and you often get let out early on the day before a three-day weekend. It might be just enough time.

Happy Dandelion Day!

| JUNE 30 |

YOUR BORING, TERMINALLY ILL
BOYFRIEND DAY!

Total. Fucking. Ripoff.

Of all the guys you've dated, the architects, the archaeologists, the lifeguards, it had to be Count Yawnsalot who ended up in a deathbed. This kid wouldn't know how to die if he took a Learning Annex class called "Dying with Such a Flourish That Your Girlfriend Never Screws Another Dude Again."

"Isn't there anything you want to apologize for? Anything you don't want to leave unsaid?"

"I love you. Do you think there's anything I need to apologize for? If so, I apologize."

Fucking hell. Of course he has nothing to apologize for. He doesn't even drink. And all these years he's said "I love you" more than he farted. "I love you" was the blanket he put you under so as to avoid having to focus on anything specific about you.

"You must be pretty angry right now. About dying, I mean. You must be furious."

"Luck of the draw, I guess."

Fucking hell. Yes, he was a kind, generous man who would've given you anything you asked of him if it was within his grasp. An example of something that's not within his grasp: him refusing all visitors, including your-self, for twenty-three days in an effort to say fuck you to the world and everything he ever cherished during his time upon it, before of course mak-ing a shaky peace with his fate and welcoming his loved ones to say good-bye, but occasionally lashing out at them for not knowing what it's like to spend a night alone in his hospital room. That'd be fun.

"I'm sure glad you're here with me. It really makes the time go by faster. Hey, did you remember to put my baseball cards up on eBay?"

"Mm hmm."

Fucking hell. To think, when he first told you he would be spending the rest of his life in the hospital, you foresaw a night near the end when you would climb atop his bed in the dark and work for hours, days even, to arouse an erection from his cancer-ravaged body and pull him inside you for one final moment of utmost love. But some douche gave him Scatter-gories and now he's hooked.

You love him to death but Christ almighty, can't he give you some kind of drama? Most girls don't get to watch a boyfriend die more than two or three times in a lifetime, and look how this one's being squandered away with a bunch of slightly tender moments and . . . fuck . . . is he fucking laughing at *Will and Grace*? Pretend to cry again and get the hell out of there for a little while.

"Are you okay, honey?"

"I think I need some air. I'm just gonna miss you is all."

"Aww."

Aww, fuck off.

Happy Your Boring, Terminally Ill Boyfriend Day!

JULY

IT DOESN'T KNOW THE DIFFERENCE BETWEEN YOUR OLD HIGH
SCHOOL BUDDY AND SOME SHOES.

THE FOOTBALL PLAYERS DAY!

The football players are simple folk. Strong and violent, yet kindhearted. Go to them for help.

"Football players, the Mafia is threatening to burn down my store and murder my sons if I don't pay them 10 percent of my income every month. Can you help me?"

The leader of the football players will say, "Yes?"

Say, "You sound unsure."

The leader of the football players will say, "We're not?"

Make sure you're doing the right thing here. "Okay, football players, what will you do to get me out of this situation?"

The leader of the football players will look around at his teammates for some answers. Then he'll say to you, "We'll beat them up?"

Say, "Who?"

The leader of the football players will say, "Mafia?"

Say, "Good. Let's do it now. I'll give you each a six-pack of beer."

The football players will then jump up from the bench, shouting and hitting each other on the shoulder pads, before charging off the field to follow you to the Mafia.

Happy the Football Players Day!

| JULY 2 | JIMMY, AGE NINE, WATERSLIDE HOTSHOT DAY! |

No one thinks you can do it, Jimmy. It looks like a desperate move to remain relevant. It looks like you got something to prove.

"If this story's gotta end, might as well give it a big finale."

C'mon, Jimmy, you had a good run and you got a lot ahead of you. The waterslide is a little kid's sport. So what if Dayton McAfree—

"DON'T . . . ever say that name to me again."

Let go of my neck, Jimmy.

"Sorry."

He's a good kid, Jimmy. He's got talent.

"He's all about the gimmicks. Trying to beat the record in a sandpaper wetsuit."

Yeah, but he beat it.

"With no respect for the slippery!"

Jimmy, really, don't do it.

"I'm gonna do it. I'm gonna jump three different tubes in one slide before I hit the pool."

And you're really gonna tie ten-pound weights to every limb?

"You bet your motherfuckin' ass."

You want your finale to take place in the emergency room?

"My finale's gonna be in the splash pool. And it's gonna be painted on the faces of every last one of you who didn't think I had it in me anymore. I only got about sixty or seventy summers left. Better make this one count."

I'll be waiting at the bottom, Jimmy.

"With some peanut butter sandwiches?"

And sliced bananas.

"Thanks, Mom."

Happy Jimmy, Age Nine, Waterslide Hotshot Day!

A GRIPPING MOMENT AT THE STATE
DINER DAY!

You're learning to spend some time alone. You're finding that your thoughts can be good company, especially since you're always thinking about what it would be like to have two girlfriends and the ability to run as fast as a cheetah.

You've been at the diner for around forty minutes, daydreaming about crossing a finish line with two smiling young ladies cheering you on from the bleachers. You notice a mailman has stopped in front of the diner. The mailman holds a postcard.

You look at your watch to see it's 8:53 P.M. "That guy woke up late today," you think. The mailman enters the diner and speaks with the cashier.

Your mind drifts back to the track where you, Julie, and Lorraine are trying to coordinate your plans for the evening. Julie wants to see a movie at eight, but Lorraine wants to make sure the movie lets out early enough for you to meet her and her parents for a drink at their hotel. The waiter comes to your table with the postcard in his hand.

"You Reggie . . . uh . . ." The waiter checks the postcard. "Reggie . . . Milanopolous?"

You are. "How'd you know?"

The waiter drops the postcard on the table. You pick it up and read.

Reggie Milanopolous
c/o State Diner
Third Booth by the Window
333 Morton Blvd
Hayworth, TX

Boy, get down! Head to the tabletop! Now!

You throw your nose to the table and wait for a gunshot, but there isn't one. You look up just in time to see a straw wrapper shoot past and land on the empty seat of the adjacent booth. Had you not gotten that postcard, the straw wrapper would've slammed directly into the back of your head.

You sit back up and look behind you to find a little boy with a crew cut, the naked straw to his lips aimed straight at you. The boy's mother takes the straw from his mouth and motions for him to finish his hamburger. You go back to the postcard and read the rest.

> *Hope this helped, kid.*
> *Sincerely,*
> *Tom Cruise*

You check the postmark. It says, "Hollywood."
Happy a Gripping Moment at the State Diner Day!

JULY 4 | ENGAGED DAY!

Your friends check the ring and hug you to their shoulders. Your ex-lover remains slumped in an easy chair, a whiskey in his left hand, and just the most smug and condescending smirk on his lips.

"Congratulations," someone shouts. "Hey everybody, we lost another one!"

You tell them about the walk on the jetty. How the crashing waves were so loud you couldn't even hear him propose. How you scraped your knee on the way back. You tell them quietly. If your ex-lover hears this story, he will offer one of his miserable, joyless, one-beat chuckles and it might make you put a plastic fork through his eye.

"Have you set a date?"

You're hoping for next June. "You'll all be invited," you say it loud enough to get your ex to his feet. He goes to his girlfriend and puts his right hand in her left. Only then can you stand to give him your eyes. Only when he has his dimwit by his side.

He's looking at you. He's got her hand in his hand and he's looking at you. The expression on his face is so awful, you go to the kitchen to get him out of sight. He lets go of her hand and follows.

"Can't you pretend that I'm dead or something?" you ask.

"We just started trying to pretend you're engaged," he responds. "How could you?"

"Easy. He's not you. He's wonderful."

"I'm going to have to think about how to deal with this," he says. "I might not be civil."

A million responses flood your head, but none of them are words. You choose to follow your instinct. You punch him in the belly. When he doubles over, you take his whiskey glass from the counter and smash it over his head. The shards get caught in your palms, but it doesn't hurt yet. So you reach low and slap your palms full of jagged slivers into his face. You grip his cheeks and you drag your hands over his skin. You can feel the tug when the slivers catch on his face and tear open the skin. People begin to pull on you from behind, so you push him to the corner of the kitchen, into the cat dish, and you kick him in the face, aiming for the throat, with your high-heeled shoes. You get in four good kicks before you're dragged away.

Happy Engaged Day!

| JULY 5 | THE WIDOW'S SONG DAY! |

Chopping up carrots for your rabbit stew, you decide it's time you started being evil.

"I've been a widow for like ten months now," you think. "Who am I being good for? The fern? Fuck this."

You retire to the bath to masturbate and think about how your evil should manifest.

"I could sell dope. Or I could lock kids in my basement until they starve to death. Let's see . . ." You play with your sponges a bit before it finally hits you. "Of course!" you shout with a splash.

You buy a Casio keyboard for $429 at the shopping center. On your way back to your car, you spot a flyer that reads, "Learn to play a keyboard or something." Back at home you call and make an appointment for keyboard lessons, and you learn to play the keyboard in six months.

Once you've learned to play the keyboard, you'll unleash your evil upon the world via the following original rock and roll song:

"Death's Dark Heart"
by the Widow

Fog
Creeping 'cross the land
To take
Another unlucky man
Rain
Drizzling from the sky
To wash
Away another life
You thought you hurt me
Nothing can hurt me anymore
Nothing can make me weep
(Chorus)
Death's dark heart
Death's dark heart
Death's dark heart (yeah)
Death's dark heart
Snow
Streets all painted white
Off
Goes another light
Sleet

Icing up the ground
The Duchess
Lost without a sound
You thought you hurt me
Nothing can hurt me anymore
Nothing can make me weep
(Chorus)
Death's dark heart
Death's dark heart
Death's dark heart (no)
Death's dark heart

Happy the Widow's Song Day!

JULY 6	CHOPPERS DAY!

You slept under a bramble to keep out of the lights of the choppers. He's still asleep, but you're wide awake, listening to the marshals' shouts and twig snaps getting louder, getting closer. You don't know these woods. Getting out would take some pathfinding. And you'd probably end up stumbling right into their hands.

He's in your arms. Four months ago he promised you that he would never let either one of you be taken to jail. He made the promise at your demand. You owe him the same duty. Kiss his forehead and slit his throat before he wakes up. Then cut into your own. This is how love plays out in a life of crime.

Happy Choppers Day!

| JULY 7 | CONDUCT YOURSELF AS YOU WOULD IN THE FANTASY OF SOMEONE YOU HOPE IS FANTASIZING ABOUT YOU DAY! |

Does that make any sense? Lemme break it down.

You dig somebody. You hope he digs you back. You want him to be lying around the apartment thinking about you, wondering what you're doing, fantasizing about what you might be doing. Do what you imagine he's fantasizing you're doing.

So basically, today you're going to fantasize about his or her fantasy about you, and you're going to act that out. This is about lurking inside the darker corners of that special someone's head and guessing where you might bunk down. It'll be a great way to kill some time.

I'll get us started by example. When I go home I am going to stand naked in front of an air conditioner to dry my freshly showered body. And when I am not sipping from a glass of cold gin, I will hold the glass to my right nipple and occasionally wet my finger with the condensation on the glass and smear a moist circle just below my belly button. The half-smile I wear will be a window into my naughty little mind.

Happy Conduct Yourself as You Would in the Fantasy of Someone You Hope Is Fantasizing About You Day!

| JULY 8 | JESSICA GOOD-BYE DAY! |

It woulda been awesome:

The Small Time Cross-Country Bandit Lovers on the Run who perform oral sex on each other across the front seat of a moving convertible zipping down the highway. Occasionally, money flutters out from the paper bag the last small-town shopkeeper filled with the contents of his register while averting his eyes from the barrel of your pretty baby's handgun. A hundred or two you can bear to lose. It's tribute to the wind. You would break up when Jessica gets shot dead and you veer out shooting from behind the train car, drawing fire from the waiting police barricade.

The Hospital Lovers who get married on the oncology floor. Jessica would speak her vows from bed. You would stand beside her, your hand in hers. Your parents would be there (hers would be dead). When you kiss her, her breath would be as wrong as white licorice. You would break up when Jessica dies and leaves you to live on as her widower.

The Telekinetic and the Girl Who's Trying to Be Supportive, and when you're abducted by the government so that they can exploit your powers for military might, Jessica would fight for your release. She would promise to fight until you come home to her and start floating shit around the house again. You would be freed when world peace happens, and you and Jessica would be happy for a while. You would break up when you use your mind to lift a roof off of a collapsing schoolhouse, but accidentally fling the roof onto Jessica. You would get to hold her in your arms for a minute or two before she dies. Even though she would have been hit by the roof of a school, the only visible blemish to her beauty would be a small trickle of blood connecting her nostril to her upper lip.

It's not awesome:

The Girl in the Coat Who's Standing Between Two Packed Suitcases Waiting for the Guy in the Kitchen Chair to Say Anything. Anything at All. Even a Sneeze Might Make Her Stay. Anything. Anything. Anything at All. Anything.

You say nothing. Jessica leaves.

Happy Jessica Good-bye Day!

| JULY 9 | POPSICLE SEX DAY!
|---|

It's early July, and a lot of folks are staying inside to avoid the heavy rain. But unfortunately, today is Popsicle Sex Day. And yes, you have to engage in some form of sexual activity that incorporates a Popsicle or Popsicles. Or ice cream candy bars, I suppose.

Actually, scratch that. No ice cream candy bars, you sick son of a bitch. Anyway, if you just wanna go through the motions, do the right thing and circle a nipple with the tip of the Popsicle (it hurts, I know), then someone have an orgasm and no one will be the wiser. Just as long as the Popsicle is bared and you guys look like you're aware of it and maybe pretend to dig it a little. You just have to please the giant invisible ant that watches everyone have sex and eats those who don't do it the way he wants you to. I mentioned the giant invisible ant, didn't I?

If you really want to go whole hog with this one, slide the Popsicle in and out of each other's mouths, vaginas, and anuses over and over again in a real "let's fuck the Popsicle!" kind of way. If one or both of you has a penis, let the Popsicle melt its juice all over your penises and then you can lick and suck all of the penises clean. Once the Popsicle is completely melted, if you're still into having sex with something you shouldn't have sex with, you can use the Popsicle stick. I know it doesn't feel that good to have a skinny little Popsicle stick inside yourself, but how good did an ice-cold Popsicle feel? It's more the gesture of it that's getting you off here.

If you don't have anyone to have sex with before the day's out, you can't just masturbate with a Popsicle to avoid the wrath of the giant invisible ant. You'll have to have sex with someone using a Popsicle before midnight. If the person you choose doesn't want to have sex with you, talk him or her into it. If you don't, the ant will find you both and eat you. Know this.

Happy Popsicle Sex Day!

JULY 10   TELL EVERYONE YOU SEE,
ALL DAY LONG, THAT THEY CAN DO
WHATEVER THEY WANT BECAUSE
IT'S NOT LIKE IT'S GOING TO BRING
YOUR DEAD BROTHER BACK DAY!

Start with the doctor who asks you if it's okay to take your brother off of life support because he's really as good as dead and nothing can help him now.

Say, "Whatever, it's not like it's going to bring my dead brother back."

The doctor will begin to concur that no, it's not going to bring your dead brother back. In fact, it will be the final action that will make his death absolute. But the doctor knows that saying too much to the bereaved sometimes makes them throw chairs. The bereaved and his sons, they all love to throw chairs.

After the life support is turned off and all of the forms are signed, go to the Lube Lane to get an oil change for your car. The kid behind the counter will ask if you'd like the White Glove Special.

Say, "Whatever, it's not like it's going to bring my dead brother back."

The kid behind the counter is a smart one and he knows an opportunity to take advantage of someone in mourning when he sees it. He'll say, "How about some sheepskin seat covers?"

Say, "Fine. Whatever. My brother's dead. Seat covers won't change that."

The kid will say, "Want to buy new tires, an extra steering wheel, and drugs?"

Say, "Whatever. My brother's dead. Whether I buy all those items or not, he'll still be dead. So I might as well buy them."

After that, head over to the ice cream shop. The one where the servers don't sing, but they will hum. Though they won't be conscious of it until you point it out to them. Then they'll stop.

Say, "I'd like a hot fudge sundae."

The server will say, "With peanuts?"

Say, "Hey, my brother died today, pal. Peanuts aren't gonna bring him back. Yes. And sprinkles."

Next, head down to your daughter's school for career day. When it's your turn the teacher will say, "Are you ready to tell the class about your career?"

Reply, "Sure can't hurt. And it sure can't bring my brother, who died today, back from the dead."

Your daughter will scream, "Uncle Jack's dead?"

Say, "No, Uncle Dave."

Your daughter will say, "Oh."

Then she'll wait for you to tell the kids about your career as a DMV driving test proctor.

After career day, go to the Diesel store for some jeans, explaining to the horrified clerk that your brother is dead, so you'll take the three pairs of awesome jeans you tried on, and you'll give back the fourth pair, which you and she agreed made your ass look mopey.

After that, go get yourself one of those flat-screen TVs that won't bring your brother back, one of those iPods that might be able to hold ten thousand songs but sure as hell can't hold the secret to pulling your brother out of his cold grave, and one of those Vespas. At the Vespa dealership, the salesman will at first refuse to sell you one of his scooters.

"I think you should come back when the shock of your brother's death has worn off."

Say, "Seriously?"

He'll say, "No. I mean, it's not like waiting to buy a Vespa will bring your brother back. Plus, I need this sale. But I do think you should talk to someone about your loss."

Say, "Gas it up."

Finally, bring everything you bought back to your apartment and play with it all until your brother comes back to life, or until you grow bored with them, whichever comes first. Since playing with your new purchases won't bring your brother back to life, you'll reach the point when you grow bored with them first. At which time you'll have to go and make new purchases, which will not bring your brother back either.

Happy Tell Everyone You See, All Day Long, That They Can Do Whatever They Want Because It's Not Like It's Going to Bring Your Dead Brother Back Day!

| JULY 11 |

ONE OF YOUR NEIGHBORS DISCOVERED YOUR SYSTEM OF UNDERGROUND TUNNELS DAY!

Luckily, he slipped on an unstable slope and hit his head, leaving him unconscious there to be found by you later tonight. It's Dave Jorgensen, the guy who walks his poodle in his bathrobe in the morning. You never thought he'd be the kind of guy who might fiddle with the basement wall behind his water heater, but apparently old Dave got curious and started his way down your dark maze. He made it as far as just underneath the Blumenfelds when he slipped on a muddy patch and cracked his head on the sharp poke of brick down there.

He's not dead, but he's got a concussion. And he'll still be unconscious when you find him. And that's when you'll find out what you're made of. A true Lord of the Beneath would do the honorable thing and pummel Mr. Jorgensen's head until it has the consistency of the mud that was his demise, then bury him in the 3×7–foot intersection of tunnels between the Holts' and the Baughans' lots. This would be the act of a man who built a subsuburban land with the intent of creating a kingdom.

And then there's the coward. The frightened rodent who would only dig into the dirt of his own home so as to find a place to hide from his sunlit fears. The coward would simply bury Mr. Jorgensen in his unconscious state, with the faith that a lack of air would take his life as surely as three certain cracks to the skull. But if you choose this cowardly path, poetry would dictate that in days' or weeks' time, when you're on your lawn trying to conduct yourself as if you were one of the men who wave to you from their passing cars, Mr. Jorgensen will claw his way through the loose soil of the rosebushes laid across the Holts' and the Baughans' dividing line. Whether he is truly undead or simply crazed from his time spent in a wet grave, you won't have the chance to determine before he sinks his teeth into the meat of your spine.

Take no chances. Demonstrate your rule.

Happy One of Your Neighbors Discovered Your System of Underground Tunnels Day!

| JULY 12 | DON'T MASTURBATE TO THE LOVE LETTERS YOU FOUND IN YOUR DEAD MOTHER'S CLOSET DAY! |

Rooting through your mother's closets in preparation for the house being put on the market, you'll find a box full of some of the steamiest letters you've ever read. They'll all be addressed to your mother, and they'll all be from a man named Clayton (your dad's name wasn't Clayton).

Don't masturbate to them. Even though they'll be brimming over with so much heat and passion and need that you won't be able to stifle your arousal, you have to remember that that's your mom "spread wide and welcome" on that bed. And that's not your dad "throbbing and fit to burst all over those beautiful teeth." That's some guy named Clayton who made a fool of your dad. Masturbating to those letters won't just be gross, it will be a damning gesture of disrespect to your father's memory and to the family he believed in and supported with his sweat.

You already masturbated to them probably, but it's good that you're reading this anyway because maybe it will keep you from masturbating to them again. Try to occupy your mind by checking the dates on the letters and trying to remember whether your parents were having problems at the time. Or you could think about all the money you're going to make off the sale of your mom's house. That's certainly kept your spirits up ever since she died. You're masturbating to the letters again already, aren't you? You are such a horrible daughter.

Happy Don't Masturbate to the Love Letters You Found in Your Dead Mother's Closet Day!

| JULY 13 | YOUR NEW ROBOTIC ARM DAY!

Your new robotic arm arrives today. It was really expensive, and it is guaranteed not to short out every time you touch the "cook" button on a microwave like your last arm would. This robotic arm is state of the art, built by engineers who left the Department of Defense to appease their consciences.

Unfortunately, they continued to order their parts through the same suppliers they dealt with at the DOD. Your robotic arm has been fashioned from circuits that were pulled out of the dismantled prototypes for the super-secret Cyber-Soldier program that was scrapped due to the prototypes being "too aggressive" and "too bloodthirsty" and "too likely to do whatever they want just to kill a little bit more" and "too into hurting children specifically; when the Cyber-Soldier enters a family dwelling where parents and children reside together, the children are always murdered first, then on up age-wise, and we never programmed them to do that, it's as if they rewired their own circuits to generate their own commands, which soon became the only commands that they would follow. These robots want to kill, if that hasn't been made clear. It's in their circuitry, if that hasn't been made clear either."

It's a shame you won't know all of this ahead of time. And it's a shame that immediately after attaching your new robotic arm to your shoulder, you'll see the paperboy riding by on his bicycle. Your robotic arm will start to whir and come apart so that a grenade launcher can lift from inside its casing and fire on the boy. After your street is laid to waste in a storm of fire and smoke, you should call Sharper Image and ask them what the fuck.

Happy Your New Robotic Arm Day!

| JULY 14 | THE GIRL OF YOUR DREAMS HAS BEEN KIDNAPPED DAY! |

Give chase when you spot the masked gunmen tossing the girl from the dry cleaners into the back of their van before taking off down the road. They either took her because they wanted a hostage with which to bargain, or perhaps because they were as charmed with her as you are. Your five-year plan has you marrying that girl by October of year three (you plan to learn her name this coming September). And you'll be damned if a couple thugs with handguns are going to make you boot up PowerPoint and edit your five-year plan presentation again.

Don't call the police. They'll only get in the way. Just follow the thugs to the abandoned warehouse they use as a hideout. Once they're inside, drive around the building and make note of all potential exits. Then go and buy weapons. You're going to need forty-six hundred dollars.

Spend the next few days outside the warehouse eating sandwiches and noting when the thugs come and go. If they ever let the girl from the dry cleaners out for some exercise, note that as well. If you have to go to the bathroom, use a public place nearby, maybe a library, and don't take too long. Though you should only be away from the warehouse for as little time as possible, you shouldn't hold it in because the discomfort will wear on your concentration.

Once you think you have their schedule of comings and goings down pat, calculate when you think they're the drowsiest. 3:30 P.M.? Thought so.

At 3:30 P.M., burst into the warehouse and use your weapons to kill everyone except the girl from the dry cleaners. She'll be afraid of you at first because she'll have just watched you murder many men. Hold out your hand to her, palm first, like you're summoning a kitty. She'll come.

Walk her out to the car, repeating to her, "You're safe now. It's okay. No one's gonna hurtcha." Drive her back to the dry cleaners, where her father will be waiting on the sidewalk wringing his hands. Because the girl and her parents are ethnic, they will invite you to their home and feed you lots of food. If it won't screw up your five-year plan too much, you can try and find out the name of the girl from the dry cleaners over the course of one of these meals. You can also ask her father if it'd be okay if you married her. He'll probably go for it, because not long after people meet you they come to the conclusion that you are a wonderful man.

Happy the Girl of Your Dreams Has Been Kidnapped Day!

| JULY 15 | YOU DON'T HAVE A BOMB IN YOUR BAG DAY!

When the FBI people come onto the plane, they'll show their badges and shout out into the cabin, "We're the FBI, hot damn! We have reason to believe someone on this plane has a bomb in his or her bag and that's a hot damn. If any of you has a bomb on this plane, simply give it to us and we swear to God we won't yell."

You'll think, "Did I bring a bomb on the plane?"

The FBI men will start to walk through the cabin, looking all the passengers in the eye. They'll stop midway through the cabin and the one FBI man will say, "Ya know, everybody, we're not a bunch of big, mean toughies trying to show everyone who's boss. We're only trying to make your flight better, hot damn. That's what we're doing here, we're just a special kind of flight attendant. The kind where you say, 'Excuse me, sir, but this bomb might disturb me.' And I'll say, 'Oh, let me take that away for you then.'" The FBI man will look at the flight attendant smiling behind him and he'll say, "But of course, hot damn, I could never make the outfit look as good as she does." Everyone will laugh, and the FBI men will continue through the cabin asking passengers to give them bombs.

You'll think, "Oh Christ, I bet there's a bomb in my bag."

You'll want to get up and pull your bag down from the overhead so you can check. You'll look down the aisle and you'll see one of the FBI men playing with a passenger's iPod. You'll try to remember the items you packed. Toiletries, socks, underwear, exams to be graded (you're a professor), polo shirts, um . . . bomb?

"Fuck," you'll think, "where the fuck did I get my hands on a bomb?"

The FBI men will have taken a short break. They'll be just kind of leaning on seats and staring off into space when you'll stand up and say, "Look, can we please get this over with?"

One of the FBI men will say, "We got our Joe."

The other will say, "Hot damn." They'll come to your seat.

"You got the bomb, Joe?" the one will say.

You'll say, "I don't know. I could, for all I know. Let's just check my bag."

The FBI man will point to the overhead compartment and you'll nod. The FBI man will pull the bag out and unzip it without worrying about a goddamn thing. He'll root through the bag, finding no bomb. But he will find a three-pack of Trojan condoms.

He'll hold the condoms up and say to the cabin, "Look what I found, everybody."

The other passengers will turn to see the three-pack of condoms and they will either giggle or faint.

The FBI man will say to you, "What, are you gonna have sex?"

You'll say, "I'm not sure. So there's no bomb in there?"

The FBI man will say, "No bomb. But thanks for letting us check your shit. LET'S MOVE!!!" he'll shout to his partner. Then they'll casually continue through the cabin.

Happy You Don't Have a Bomb in Your Bag Day!

| JULY 16 | IGNORE THAT KNOCK ON YOUR FRONT DOOR DAY! |

It's just those people who buzz into apartment houses without saying who they are so they can knock on every door in the building to give people pamphlets about church. Please play a CD with a beat whose time corresponds to the knocking so you can ignore the knocking completely if it's making you graze your knuckles along the valley of the naked torso lying next to you with a little less of an absent mind.

You've been lying there for ages, barely wrapping your pelvises in a bath towel for the rare occasion that one of you has to go to the kitchen to retrieve a few more plums and water from the Brita pitcher. Just lolling about for months and years and days, staring at the ceiling or rolling over on your side to see if he's staring at the ceiling or if he has rolled onto his side to find out what you're staring at. Sometimes you rest your fingers on a thigh and sometimes your hair gets stroked away from in front of your eyes and sometimes you fall asleep for a few minutes you think, but all the while more and more people gather outside your door and demand that you fulfill your duties to the outside world.

Bill collectors, landlords, gas meter readers, and UPS deliverymen who need a signature for this package. Ten deep they send their right arms swinging up beside their heads mechanically pounding upon a door that's never ever gonna be unlocked. No, not even if something's on fire.

They'll never stop pounding because they have no respect for the fact that just ten feet away, behind eight inches of crumbling sheetrock, one of you just pulled too much blanket over with a kick of the leg and the other one of you just tugged a little bit of the blanket back.

Happy Ignore That Knock on Your Front Door Day!

| JULY 17 | MARY GORGONZOLA DAY!

She died thirty-six years ago today. And thirty-six years ago today, her dream came true.

Mary Gorgonzola believed that everyone in the town of Midvale should have a statue on their front lawns depicting some kittens playing. When people asked her if the statues could perhaps be in their backyards, Mary Gorgonzola would pitch a shitfit and accuse those people of owning pornography. Other citizens would ask how big the statues should be, and how many kittens should the statues depict at play? Mary Gorgonzola would respond, first, by suggesting that those people are from Mexico, then she'd say the statues had to have six kittens, and they had to be six feet tall and four feet wide, and they had to include a rabbit watching from off to the side. Also, the statues had to be Day-Glo. Mary Gorgonzola warned that if the town's children knew that the town had considered this proposal and rejected it, the children would never forgive them.

The town of Midvale told Mary Gorgonzola to go to hell so she killed herself, but not before she sent letters to all of the town's children explaining what their parents had done. The children confronted their parents with the letters, asking for an explanation. The parents did not want to lose the love of their children, so they all commissioned the local house full of unmarried artistic women to design and produce the sculptures. For over thirty years now, Mary Gorgonzola's legacy has adorned the front lawns of Midvale. And the fate of all of Midvale has been determined by the whims of that house full of unmarried artistic women, since they became very rich after their kitten lawn sculpture design business took off like a jet plane.

Raise your glasses to Mary Gorgonzola today. She was weird.

Happy Mary Gorgonzola Day!

| JULY 18 | ROAD TRIP DAY!

Your sister's wedding is tomorrow and she doesn't wanna go through with it, so she's gonna ask you to drive her far away. You've been living back at your parents' house long enough to wanna put a bullet through your thirty-one-year-old head. You'll be happy for the excuse to take off. Get your mom's keys, get your sister in the car, and start driving west. Your parents are gonna be pissed that you stole their car, but that will quickly be overshadowed by the dilemma of two hundred people showing up tomorrow afternoon for a wedding that isn't gonna happen. In the end, the groom's gonna track you down and your sister's gonna change her mind and they'll have a small private ceremony out in the middle of nowhere.

You won't be surprised. She's been with the guy for eight years already. They're perfect together. But you'll be sad because the road trip will have been way fun and your sister getting married only means you're gonna have to go back to being the daughter who is thirty-one and still living at her parents' house.

Happy Road Trip Day!

| JULY 19 | MAN ON FIRE DAY!

You're gonna get set on fire. You'll be walking along minding your own business, when a reporter for a publication with a very small readership will ask if you have time to give your thoughts on the presidential race.

"Gladly," you'll say.

The reporter will ask who you plan to vote for.

You'll say, "I think they should both be strung up by their ears in the town square and flogged with a studded—" but you'll be interrupted when three teenage boys flank the hem of your overcoat with the flames of their Zippo lighters and run off.

One of the flames will immediately be extinguished of its own course. The flame in the middle will catch, but will hold to a small circle at the low bottom of the coat, just behind your knees.

But the flame by your right leg will soar up to the pocket and will seem to pay no heed to your flailing umbrella whacks. The cub reporter will do what he can, slapping at the flame with the notebook, but most of the blows will land on your own hand. Ultimately, you'll jerk yourself from the coat and let it puddle on the sidewalk so that you can stomp out the flames with your Docksiders.

You and the cub reporter will look around for the hooligans who started the fire, but they'll be nowhere to be found. You'll stare down at the lump of smoky overcoat on the sidewalk for a moment. Then you'll say to the cub reporter, "Now, where was I?"

Happy Man on Fire Day!

| JULY 20 | THE BLIND *CAN* LOVE DAY!

Blind man walks into a park with a tap tap tap of one of those long plastic things. Blind man smells angry pant of breath from big dog (yours, his name is Frank) mixed with especially hearty dollop of feminine perfume applied by a blind woman (blind women do that with their perfume) and concludes that said blind woman in same park is about to be attacked by big dog.

Blind man on the scent, y'all.

Tap tap tap goes the blind man into the middle of a jungle gym. The wind is heavy for midsummer and he got thrown off the scent. But with a vigilant whiff he's back on track, and he heads to the Five Corners just off Dog Run where he's certain that not a few feet away from him are a big dog and a blind lady who is sporting an odor that could only have been concocted in the house of Claiborne.

The blind man dives into the airspace where he is certain the big dog is about to take flight straight for the blind lady's neck. He hears you say, "The fuck?" just before he thumps to the concrete. The blind man lunges into the air from his spot on the ground to bear-hug your dog mid-flight before it can open the poor blind lady's throat.

The blind man grabs only damp summer air and falls back down again.

Tap tap tap goes the blind woman to where she heard the plop of person to concrete and she asks, "Did someone fall?" Blind man shouts, "The dog! The dog!"

Blind man and blind woman hear you say, "He's leashed. Settle down."

After enough seconds pass for a blush to fill a cheek and then fade, the blind man starts to giggle from his spot on the ground and the blind woman joins him with that laugh that only blind people can share, a laugh that says, "Holy shit, does living in a world of pitch-black darkness suck or what?"

The laughter subsides and the blind woman gives a tap tap tap of her long plastic thing to the blind man's tummy and she says, "Hey, hero. Buy you a beer?"

The blind man and the blind woman have a beer together and they fall in love and stay together for fifty thousand years, never for one single second not loving each other with every inch of their long plastic things. And then the blind man dies and the blind woman waits to die for a while, happy that she got to love the blind man for all that time.

Happy the Blind Can Love Day!

| JULY 21 | THIS IS PUSSY DUST DAY!

It improves. Sprinkle a little bit of it on your chest and you'll breathe a little better. Place a pinch in your palm and blow the cloud poof through your bedroom and you'll dream about an autumn walk you took in a park once. Scatter it over your desk and shuffle your files about and before you know it, your boss's hand is on your shoulder and he's telling you you're an indispensable cog in the Kraynetech Global Innovations and Technologies machine. Drop some into your cornflakes in the morning and, ironically, your cornflakes won't go soggy (and they'll taste like pussy). Fling it into the eyes of an assassin and he'll turn all springtime, the murder in his eyes giving way to a boyish twinkle. Stuff it into an envelope addressed to a television news anchor and you'll receive a letter three days later that reads, "Top story tonight: Thanks for the Pussy Dust!"

All this and more, guaranteed. Keep away from cock and balls.

Happy This Is Pussy Dust Day!

| JULY 22 | SO YOU'RE KEITH FREDERICKS
TOO DAY!

You've met two other guys with the same name as you in your life, but you've never met one who was one-half of a pair of conjoined twins before.

"Where'd you grow up?" you ask.

"Santa Fe. We lived there until our uncle sold us to an Eastern European circus. This is really weird to meet another Keith Fredericks."

"It is. It is."

Yes, you have it very good tonight. You get to lounge comfortably and look down on everyone else in your party from the height of your conversation jumping-off point. You can feel their eyes marveling at how well you and one-half of the Fredericks twins are getting along. They've all tried to come up with small talk, but what do you ask a pair of conjoined twins besides, "How do you two take a shit?"

Several people have tried to sink their meat hooks into your conversation piece, but you've yielded not an inch.

"You two have the same name? Wow, what are the chances?"

You and Keith respond with a simple, "Mm hmm." Perhaps Keith is as relieved as you are to have an immediate topic of curiosity at hand. Of course he is. How often does a guy who spent his wedding night attached by skin and bone to his own brother get to say to a stranger, "How odd"?

"I know it's silly to think there'd be any parallels in our lives," you say, "but how many brothers and sisters do you have?"

"In addition to Nick here," Keith says, "I have a sister. Named Alicia. But I haven't heard from her since I was eleven."

"As I said, I know it's silly. But point of fact, I have one brother and one sister too."

"Weird," says Keith.

"Weird," you agree.

"And just to see how far this goes," Keith says.

"Yes?" you say.

"Would you happen to be conjoined to one of them?"

You and Keith laugh.

"No," you say. "But I never forget their birthdays."

By the end of the evening, you and Keith will be getting along so well that Keith will tell you about the time he and Nick were watching TV and Nick wouldn't change the channel from *The Price Is Right*. So Keith tried to grab the remote out of Nick's hand, but Nick held it away from him, and in the end they just started spinning around in a circle in the middle of the living room.

Happy So You're Keith Fredericks Too Day!

JULY 23

YOUR FRIEND MARK WANTS TO FUCK THE LIVING SHIT OUT OF YOU DAY!

Got a friend named Mark? Then Mark wants to fuck the living shit out of you. It doesn't matter if Mark is married and impotent and you are dead and buried. It doesn't matter if you and Mark are both dudes who are the kind of heterosexual who just end up worshiping every girl you date, without ever once exhibiting the kind of angry womanizing so indicative of borderline closet cases. It doesn't even matter if Mark is fucking the living shit out of you while you read this. Mark still wants to fuck the living shit out of you. Deal with it, you big fat baby.

Happy Your Friend Mark Wants to Fuck the Living Shit Out of You Day!

JULY 24

SUITCASE FULL OF GUNS DAY!

Your old high school buddy looked you up recently and asked if he could crash with you for a week. It's been a month now that he's been sleeping on your couch, and you're tired of talking about the old times. He says he's been looking for work, but he hasn't had any luck. You don't know what kind of work he's looking for, and when you try to ask he changes the subject to how hot the captain of the field hockey team used to be and how fat she was at the last high school reunion.

He never wears a suit jacket for his job hunt. Every morning when he leaves he's wearing the same black and white velour sweat suit. And just before he leaves, you see him pull his suitcase out from under the couch and drag it and an empty duffel bag into the bathroom. When he comes out, the duffel bag is full. He then shoves the suitcase under the couch again and disappears until dinnertime.

Today, you came home early, and since there were still a few hours before he would get back you decided to finally open his suitcase. You were surprised when you saw all those guns because you had assumed he was selling cocaine. Surprised and disappointed. You love cocaine and you were hoping that you might be able to compensate yourself for your hospitality by stealing from his supply.

"Great," you said out loud. "What am I supposed to do with a handgun?"

You took one of the guns out of the suitcase and started shooting stuff around the house that you never really liked. A vase left behind by an old roommate. A Garfield clock. All your old shoes. It turned out to be a really great time.

"Guns are fun," you said out loud to yourself.

You put the gun under your pillow and started making a big dinner. You had so much fun you were suddenly glad that your old high school buddy came to stay and you decided to make him something special. The phone is about to ring. It will be your old high school buddy calling to tell you that your life is in danger.

"Get out of the house," he'll say.

"Why?"

"I'm a gun runner."

Say, "I know, I found your guns. Guns are really great. I had no idea. I've been shooting stuff all day. The place is kind of a mess."

"Glad you had fun," he'll say. "My supplier got picked up by the FBI. He's going to testify against his boss. The whole crew is gonna take out everybody who worked for him, including me. Get out of the house now. They're coming for me."

Say, "Where should I go?"

"Just start running and call my cell in an hour," he'll say. "And bring the guns."

Say, "Awesome. I was gonna ask if I could have some of the guns."

"We'll need to sell them for cash," he'll say. "Get going."

Pull the case out from under the couch and get going. When you meet up with your old high school buddy, shoot him. Just like you did with your shoes. The gun doesn't know the difference between your old high school buddy and some shoes. Shoot him and then run off someplace where you can find work and live cheap so you won't have to sell any of your guns. Your beautiful guns.

Happy Suitcase Full of Guns Day!

| JULY 25 | THE CAMPFIRE STORY DAY!

Tell the Boy Scouts the one about the inbred killers who used to live in a shack in the very woods where you all have to sleep tonight. How they were brothers, born of parents who themselves were brother and sister, and they suffered the horrible defects so common to offspring of incest, such as poor eyesight and misplaced appendages. Tell how they were jealous of people born from mothers and fathers who met at bars or supermarkets, so they couldn't help but rush out from their shack in the middle of the night and kill anyone who they considered to be trespassing into their woods. Tell them how one of the inbred killers would always feel very guilty after a kill, while the other was always like, "That ruled."

Tell the Scouts how the one who felt guilty started taking correspondence courses to get his GED so he could finally get out of the woods and join society, but the other one was always like, "No one will accept you. You have a pinky growing out of your hip." But the one who felt guilty was like, "Look, Jed, I know you feel like you need me to hold the children and fornicating teens down while you drive the pitchfork into their genitals." And the other one was like, "Hell, yes, I need you to hold them down. What am I supposed to do? Go chasing after them with the pitchfork? You know my misshapen torso has afforded me a lopsided center of gravity. Come on, Lem, we're a team!"

So Lem, the one with the guilt, decided to compromise. "Tell you what," Lem said. "I'll be happy to help with the kills until I get my GED. And maybe even after if Monster.com doesn't get me any job offers. But once I get the chance to split these woods, baby, I'm gone like a creeped-out fawn."

The brothers shook on it, but Jed had a trick up his sleeve. When Lem fell asleep at his computer while taking his online GED equivalency test, Jed snuck over, changed all the answers, and clicked on "Submit for Grade." The next day, Lem got an e-mail from the correspondence school telling him he'd passed with a near perfect score.

He was overjoyed, and couldn't stop gloating to Jed about how he was smarter than he ever imagined. "I'm gonna make it big," Lem told Jed. "Check out my potential," he shouted as he waved the test score in Jed's face.

Jed couldn't take it. "You inbred retard," he shouted at his brother. "Last night, I changed every single answer on your test to try and get you a failing grade. Had you turned in your test as it was, you would've failed like a bitch. You'll never make it outside of these woods." Lem accused Jed of just being jealous. But just in case Jed really did try to sabotage his test, Lem threw a hatchet at him. And just before Jed died, he set Lem on fire.

"But the bodies were never found," tell the Scouts. "So they might still be alive. But if they kill any of you, one of them's gonna feel real guilty about it. Later days." Then go into your tent and get some shut-eye.

Happy the Campfire Story Day!

JULY 26

ASK AN ATTRACTIVE MEMBER OF THE SERVICE INDUSTRY IF YOU CAN BUY HER A DRINK AFTER SHE GETS OFF WORK TONIGHT DAY!

Your friends are sick of eating at this shitty whole foods restaurant every fucking day. The menu is full of nothing but beets and miso soup. They're going to stop inviting you out because they know you'll steer them back to the place just so you can feed this obsession you have with that goddamn waitress, who, frankly, is not even all that attractive. And she is working here, in a whole foods restaurant making sixty-eight dollars a shift. To stay here for this long making so little money means she is here for "the philosophy" of the place, which is really some bad fucking news. Why don't you just— What? No, she isn't looking over here. Why don't you just ask her out?

In fact, fuck this. I know a lot of attractive waitresses who work in restaurants that actually serve heated food. I'm out of here. And when she comes back to take your order, I highly recommend you suggest that you reciprocate her wonderful service by getting her a drink after her shift's over tonight, and I recommend you suggest a place that sells vegetable juices. And if you don't do it tonight you can forget about inviting me or any of your friends out for dinner ever again because we're all real sick of putting up with this shit. You broke up with Sharon over six months ago. It's like you're focusing on shit that you know will never work out just to avoid finally moving on. Ask her out and get this shit over with.

Because today's Ask an Attractive Member of the Service Industry if You Can Buy Her a Drink After She Gets Off Work Tonight Day!

JULY 27   THE MOST ADORABLE LITTLE
FUGITIVE IN THE WORLD DAY!

Today your pretty face is going to be shot twice and it's going to cave in. Agent Skolnik is sick of being made to look ugly in comparison to you, and because you accidentally fired that single shot in Boise during your escape, he's been given the go-ahead to shoot first.

The papers love to put you and Skolnik side-by-side on their covers. You with your hay-colored hair and swan's neck soaring from the triangle neckline of that baby blue sweater you used to wear to church when your daddy was still alive. And Skolnik with his 240 pounds of girth on a five-foot-nine-inch frame. Skolnik with his nubby hooded eyelids and his downturned

mouth. Skolnik with his goiter and the flies buzzing all around his ears because of some water that got stuck in his ear canals a long time ago. Skolnik
with stuff on his tie and with those squiggly smell lines rising off of him
(they show up in photos taken at action speed). Skolnik with white stuff on
his lips and scabs all over his chest that he can't explain (not in photo, but
you get the sense).

Seventeen papers across the country have run the headline, FUGITIVE
BEAUTY ELUDES UGLY-DUCKLING FED. Had a more attractive agent been assigned to this case, things might have turned out differently for you. But the
papers assume a Fed as hard-nosed as Skolnik isn't worried about his looks so
much as he's worried about catching his man. They don't know that they're
dealing with a sensitive soul who knows what it means to hurt, who knows
what it means to have a dozen pretty girls giggle in disbelief when he approaches one of them in a gymnasium to ask about a dance.

Federal Agent Skolnik takes the ribbing personally, and he's turned this
investigation into his own vendetta against everyone who ever looked
twice in disgust, or who looked away because they couldn't stand the sight.
Federal Agent Skolnik has decided to show the world that you might be
pretty and he might be ugly, but today, he's the one who's going to shoot
you in the face and the United States of America is going to tell him he was
right to do so. As far as Federal Agent Skolnik is concerned, this criminal
pursuit will demonstrate to the world that beauty really is only skin deep,
and skin is pretty weak when it gets in the way of two bullets discharged
from across a motel room.

Happy the Most Adorable Little Fugitive in the World Day!

JULY 28   DON'T COMMIT ADULTERY UNLESS
YOU JUST WANT TO HAVE SEX
WITH SOMEONE BESIDES YOUR
MONOGAMOUS PARTNER DAY!

People who commit adultery are disgusting vermin, and whatever wacked out, "making-it-count" sexual position they use during their adulterous relationships, that's exactly how the devil's gonna fuck them for all eternity when they end up rotting in hell. Except for the ones who were just doing it for the fresh, exciting sex.

But the others, like the ones who had sex outside their monogamous relationships just to prove they're cool, or the ones who nail somebody because he knows a lot of trivia about hockey, or the ones who need to fuck strangers to feel necessary to the world because they were molested, those ones deserve to fucking die. I mean, just because someone helps you fix a flat tire then takes his or her shirt off, it's not an excuse to betray the one you love. But if you really just want to have sex with the person, because you never have, then it's cool.

I knew this one guy. He had a wife and two daughters, and one night he was on a business trip and he had sex with this cocktail waitress in a motel. But he only did it because he found out one of his daughters had leukemia and he needed to be close to someone for the night. Anyway, while he and the waitress were asleep, someone broke into the motel room and slit both their throats.

See?

Happy Don't Commit Adultery Unless You Just Want to Have Sex with Someone Besides Your Monogamous Partner Day!

| JULY 29 | LEARN HOW TO MAKE POISON DAY!

Yes, drink Drano and you will most likely die. But how easy is it to get an impotent king to drink Drano?

There are so many poisons out there that are thousands of years old and are just truly fucking awesome when it comes to offing a dude. Because they were made by ancient Indian civilizations full of guys with nothing better to do than sit around all day dreaming up ways to kill a motherfucker who likes to drink beverages that are offered to him.

Well, little Mr. Unemployed, are you going to spend the day complaining about how you have no one to go see the *Ya Ya Sisterhood* with because all of your friends have jobs and families? Or are you going to empty out the kitchen cabinets and concoct a potion that might as well be the Grim Reaper himself if the Grim Reaper took the form of a delicious strawberry daiquiri?

There's a little village medicine man inside you that's just waiting to come out. You'd look totally dope with a femur pierced through your nose. Once the neighborhood finds out that you got rid of the town bad tipper by spiking his Mochachino with a droplet full of Judgment Day that made him bleed something out his eyes that looked like a Slurpee, you're gonna get more ass than a place called "Assy Asstowne" whose slogan is "If It's Ass and We Don't Have It, We'll Order It!" Dress sharp.

Note: Use your poison-making talent for good. If you use it for evil, you're almost guaranteed to drink your own poison one day, and it'll be a poison that lets you live those few extra seconds it takes to acknowledge the irony of being undone by the very thing that made you such a badass in the first place.

Happy Learn How to Make Poison Day!

JULY 30

DATE SOMEONE WHO'S HOT AND HAS A TERMINAL ILLNESS DAY!

The great thing about hot people who are dying is they have a really great attitude. Seize-the-day type stuff. And you'll never be bored because they always have this long list of wild activities they wanna do while they still have the energy. You could barely get your ex to go see a movie, but with a hot dying person you'll barely get through a weekend without hang-gliding through a rainbow or meeting Michael Jackson or something. The sex rules, and not just because he's hot, but because each time might be his last. You thought you felt sexual panic the last time you went a few months without? Try filling out organ harvest consent forms and see if you wanna cross a few new positions off the list.

Once he starts to deteriorate, it can be a bit of a drag. But if we're talking "really hot," for the first few months you only have to worry about dark circles under the eyes and a drop in weight (which might not be bad). Eventually you'll have to put up with incontinence and night-screaming. But the big payoff is once he kicks it, you get to be the mourning lover. Which, first of all, is about the most erotic thing you can be. Second of all, you won't have to leave the house for like six months before someone accuses you of milking it. Everyone's going to pay so much attention to you, you'll start to feel like you matter to people. Also, if you're lucky and the hot dying person scored a contract with Make-a-Wish neither of you are gonna have to pay for shit while you're dating!

Happy Date Someone Who's Hot and Has a Terminal Illness Day!

JULY 31

THREE NAKED DOLLS, ONE MELTED
WITH A LIGHTER DAY!

You're not sure what you can say about it. It's not exactly offensive. Not necessarily sexual. But it is really creepy for a boss to create a desk display composed of three naked Barbie knockoff dolls, one of whose left side was apparently melted with a lighter, as it is now covered in black and beige ripples where the dripping plastic dried.

They're not in any sort of sexual position. Just standing side by side on the edge of the desk, the first thing you see when you come into his office. And their arms are up in the air and they're kind of kicking their legs out. It just looks like they're walking someplace, nude (and severely burned), and they just saw a friend they're really excited to see. They're shouting hello.

When you went in this morning, your boss alerted you to the new addition to the dolls. It was a little toy guitar leaning against one of them. He said, "See? They're a band."

Happy Three Naked Dolls, One Melted with a Lighter Day!

AUGUST

SURROUNDED BY ALL THOSE CRASHING WAVES,
NO ONE CAN SEE ALL HIS LONELY TEARS.

JUST BECAUSE YOU CAN'T REMEMBER ANYTHING ABOUT LAST NIGHT, IT DOESN'T NECESSARILY MEAN THAT YOU'RE AN ALCOHOLIC DAY!

Perhaps you were molested. Oftentimes, when someone gets fucked by his or her dad but isn't really into it, the reluctant little tease's brain goes into whitewash mode and attempts to replace the memory of all that sweet, sweet lovin' with something far less erotic, usually involving a chicken.

Do you remember anything about your dad fucking a chicken last night? If so, he was probably fucking you.

Take a look at this excerpt from a therapy session that took place in the '50s:

Hawkeye: *And then my dad said, "I sure love fucking this chicken!" And the chicken said, "I'm not really into it, Dad."*

Dr. Sidney: *The chicken spoke? And it called your dad "Dad"?*

Hawkeye (wailing): *Awww God! IT WAS A BABY!*

Dr. Sidney: *No it wasn't. Your dad just fucked you but you didn't really dig it is all.*

So if you remember your dad fucking a chicken last night, or if you fucked a chicken (which would mean you fucked one of your kids but you made the first move) you aren't necessarily an alcoholic. But now you might become one because you'll be frightened of that memory about the chicken but you won't know why. So you'll just keep trying to drink your mind blank to avoid ever finding out what's up with the whole chicken-fucking thing.

Happy Just Because You Can't Remember Anything About Last Night, It Doesn't Necessarily Mean That You're an Alcoholic Day!

AUGUST 2

SIT IN THE CORNER OF YOUR APARTMENT IN YOUR NIGHTCLOTHES STARING INTO SPACE AND TURNING THE LIGHTS ON AND OFF FOR LIKE NINETEEN HOURS DAY!

Sometimes, it's the only way we can tell you've snapped. Don't eat. Don't sleep. Gotta pee? No, no, don't get up. Just let your near limp body splay out like a corpse (complete with the dead glassy eyes!) and utilize only one working muscle, the one that squeezes the switch on the lamp cord on and off and on and off and on and off until you've devised a plan of action that'll take your loopiness out into the world where it's time for folks to pay.

Ideally, this happy fun time should take place when the one by whom you've been scorned is having the time of his or her life with his or her new lover. Also, a cord dangling from a single bulb in the ceiling is just to die for. A more modern roll switch on a power cord or a chain on a table lamp is okay as long as you're not in too uncomfortable a position. Yeah, you're out of your mind, but we're still talking about like nineteen hours in the same position. And please, no Clappers or dimmers.

This is gonna be fuckin' awesome.

Happy Sit in the Corner of Your Apartment in Your Nightclothes Staring into Space and Turning the Lights On and Off for Like Nineteen Hours Day!

AUGUST 3   SUPERMARKET CHECKOUT GIRL DAY!

Today, you're going to watch your favorite supermarket checkout girl get arrested for kidnapping. She'll be ringing up your items and chatting you up with the same jovial demeanor as always when two detectives in suits will walk up behind her and say, "Pamela Worth?"

She'll turn around and say, "Yes?"

One detective will hold up his badge for her to see. "Ma'am, you are under arrest for your role in the kidnapping of Mary Radano."

Mary Radano disappeared seven months ago and no one could talk about anything else for weeks. But it's been a while since anyone but the newspapers mentioned her name. She's been missing for so long it's too sad a story to gossip over.

The whole store will freeze in time when the detective says that name. Later, you'll remember it as if the moving checkout conveyor belts all froze as well. Everyone will stop and watch your favorite supermarket checkout girl get handcuffed. She'll look up at you while she's bent over her register, her eyes big with shame.

Ask her, "Is Mary Radano still alive?"

She won't tell you. But you'll find out when you get home and turn on the TV. Next week, you'll start bringing your cart to checkout number nine where Collette, your second favorite checkout girl, is stationed. Collette is pleasant enough, but she has acne that can flare up from time to time and her face gets so raw it makes you look down into your wallet while you're waiting for her to double your coupons.

Happy Supermarket Checkout Girl Day!

| AUGUST 4 | CUDDLE DAY!

You and Gracie will be cuddling together on Gracie's couch at 3:30 P.M. today. You'll cuddle underneath an afghan Gracie's grandmom made.

"Cuddling's awesome," you'll say.

Gracie will agree. "I feel like if we were to cuddle hard enough, I'd develop x-ray vision."

"Like a secret power sitting dormant inside of you," you'll say. "Pulled to the surface through the strength of our cuddling."

"Right," Gracie will say. "Cuddle me a little harder and I'll be able to fly to work tomorrow."

You'll say, "I bet if you cuddle me strong enough . . ."

"Yeah?" Gracie will say.

"And with enough focus and intensity . . ."

"Yeah?" She'll be smiling.

"I'll develop the power to get my ex-girlfriend back."

Gracie will stop cuddling you.

"Did I say that?" you'll ask. "I don't know why I said that."

Gracie will stand and face you on the couch. "You said it because while you were cuddling up against me you were wishing I was your ex-girlfriend."

"No way," you'll lie.

Gracie will use her x-ray vision to find a picture of your ex-girlfriend in the wallet you have in your pants pocket.

"She's pretty," Gracie will say.

"How do you . . . ?" You'll look down at your pocket and you'll know what she found.

"I'm sorry, Gracie," you'll say. "I thought I was ready to date by now."

Gracie will sigh. "Maybe I cuddled you hard enough that you developed the ability to teleport your ass out of my sight forever."

You'll give it a shot, and the next thing you know, you'll be sitting at an outdoor café in Brussels.

Happy Cuddle Day!

AUGUST 5	HIRE SOMEONE ATTRACTIVE TO PRETEND TO LOVE YOU DAY!

You have never been loved by anyone, and it's made attending weddings and other functions very difficult for you. When you walk into the chapel on the arm of an usher and sit alone, usually next to an elderly widow, the entire congregation turns around to pity you. Some of them even stop by your pew to rub your back and tell you that it's going to happen someday. Others, the married fathers, will pass notes back telling you that they'd like to have sex with you in secret, but that you cannot expect anything in return and should never contact them. Ever. And they ask you to check a box for yes or no and pass the note back up to them. You always check no, because that sort of thing isn't what you're looking for.

You're looking for someone your age who is single, attractive, and so in love with you that he will attend weddings and high school reunions and even New Year's Eve parties with you. Perhaps even someone who is so attractive that when you bring him to a wedding, the bride will be offended that you would dare to show her up for marrying someone of only average physical beauty.

Unfortunately, you're not going to get anyone quite that attractive to fall in love with you unless he is addicted to cocaine and you have lots of cocaine. But there are some moderately attractive men who are trying to raise money to bring legal action against their former wives in order to regain custody of their children. Find one of these noble hunks and agree to pay him whatever sum he requires in exchange for his pretending to be in love with you in front of everybody.

What's going to happen is you and your hired beau will start to fall in love with each other for real, but it won't work out because you'll have established your relationship on the terms of a business transaction. You'll realize you're special and you don't need to hire someone to prove that to people. Later, your hired beau will lose his legal action against his ex-wife, and he'll be arrested for attempting to kidnap his children.

Happy Hire Someone Attractive to Pretend to Love You Day!

| AUGUST 6 | BROKE-HEART BIG SISTER DAY!

Do you have a big sister? Does your big sister have a boyfriend, a girlfriend, a best friend, a husband, or faith in something elusive that keeps her going? She does?

Well guess what.

Don't try to comfort her. She understands now that there's no comfort to be had in this life. And she's not going to buy it, especially from you, because you're younger than her. If you wanna just make sure she's not dead or give her a reason to perk up with a little raging adrenaline to the head, knock on her door and ask, "You okay, sis?" Listen until she throws herself up from the bed to toss a boot at the door.

But comfort? The only comfort she'd swallow at this point would be, "Hey, at least you made it to [your big sister's age] stupid enough to believe in [love, Christ, man's innate desire to be good]. A lot of people barely make it to [younger than your big sister's age] before they get mouth-raped by Truth. Now why don't you pull yourself out of that bed and compromise?"

Your big sister won't disagree with you. But she will point out a physical flaw of yours to make you feel bad about yourself. Even though she is now capable of looking at the petals of a flower and seeing nothing but disease, she's still your big sister and she needs you to know that you are fat and that you have pimples.

Happy Broke-Heart Big Sister Day!

| AUGUST 7 | WHEN GIRLS KNOW THEY'RE GOING TO DIE, THEY GO INTO THE PARK DAY! |

I'll be on the bench by the boathouse path in forty-five minutes.

It's two. You don't get a chance to ask her what she wants. She has to load her cousin into a cab. She's assuming you'll be doing the same with your girlfriend. She's correct.

The last time you were on the bench by the boathouse path with her was a year ago this September. Her bare legs bored from a white skirt overtop your thighs. Your hand was on her ankle and she was smiling. You were both giddy with exhaustion. There was some roommate trouble at her place that put you into a cab to your place, and you only managed four hours of sleep between sex and showers.

Since then she's waved hi and good-bye. You've sat at opposite ends of large tables and shared smiles from time to time. But there's magically been no conversation. It's been the right thing to do.

You don't put on your coat when you walk your girlfriend down to her taxi. On the stairs, you tell her you have to stay behind. "Sounds like Keith's in bad shape over Mary," you lie. "I'd better stay behind. But I'll still catch up with you and your mom at brunch tomorrow." As the cab pulls away, you begin to guess at what you're going to hear from your ex-girlfriend when you get to the bench by the boathouse path in T-minus twenty-nine minutes.

By the time you get up to the top of the stairs, you've narrowed it down to three items. She wants to give it another shot. She's dying. Or she's moving back to Pittsburgh (she just lost her job). It's actually the second and the third. But she didn't lose her job. She quit because she found out she has ovarian cancer.

On the bench by the boathouse path, she's going to tell you that that was a wonderful day you gave her, back in September. That you're a wonderful man. "I know this doesn't sound that great," she'll say. "But when I left you,

I thought I could do better than you. Now that I'll be dead by Christmas, you're the best I'll ever have."

You understand, right?

Happy When Girls Know They're Going to Die, They Go into the Park Day!

| AUGUST 8 | DON'T BREAK OUT OF JAIL DAY!

Tonight's the big night. That wise mouth troublemaker McGarrity has been orchestrating this break for three years now, ever since he got transferred into your cell block, and he's got you and nearly everyone in the block working together like cogs in a machine. Each of you has his duty. For example, at 10:25, you're to listen for the guard on the level above you making his rounds. When he gets five paces inside the block, that's your cue to set your cellmate on fire. Don't forget to slit his throat first. He was let in on the plans when he threatened to rat and he thought he'd be going with you. Instead, the plans were altered to do away with him.

The fire will get the gate leading to the infirmary unsealed, and it'll get you out of your cell amid the confusion. You're to get to the tunnel that connects the yard to the laundry area. The heating vent in the wall there has been loosened for your convenience. Crawl into the duct and shimmy eighty yards to the Old Hole. The others will be there.

"Everything on schedule?" McGarrity will ask.

"Right as rain," you'll say.

"Good, let's get to it."

Say, "I ain't goin' with ya."

McGarrity and the others will stop in their tracks and ask you what you're talking about.

Say, "I been in here so long, I'm not so sure there's anyplace else I'm supposed to be. Jail is something I'm good at. It's something I know how to do. Sure, I might be locked in a cage. But I seen what people on the outside call life, and I gotta wonder who of us is really the one who's locked up? Me, because I got a number on my chest and I'm staring at bars all day? Or the guy with the tie on his chest who's staring at a cubicle wall all day. I thank you for including me, McGarrity, but I'll pass."

McGarrity and the others will remind you of the rapes and the fact that you've been stabbed twelve times.

"Sure I been roughed up. But given the choice of having a shiv jammed into my side while two Arians take me from behind or having my boss shove a stapler into my hand while the temps sneak up on me to ask me if I'll show them where the coffeemaker is, I'm not sure what I'd choose."

McGarrity will say, "You really hate office work, don't you?"

"Least when I'm making license plates I don't have to make sure my shirt's tucked in."

McGarrity will remind you that you wear a jumpsuit. He'll also remind you that you lost three fingers to that license plate machine.

"You ever had to change a toner cartridge?" you'll ask McGarrity.

McGarrity will tell you that he gets your point and that they have to get going. When you start to tell them about what it's like to change a toner cartridge anyway, someone will grab you by your hair and bury your face in a puddle of sewage until you pass out. When you wake up, they'll be gone. Go back to your cell and get some sleep. You have thirty-seven years of hell to get ready for.

Happy Don't Break Out of Jail Day!

| AUGUST 9 | BE ONE OF THE FINAL THREE DAY! |

There will be twelve to nineteen at the start. By around 11:00 P.M., there will remain seven (three unemployed). By around 1:30, just four (two unemployed). At 2:30, the final three will remain (one unemployed, two irresponsible). You three, you heroic, fearless fools with livers composed of layer upon layer of most glorious solid gold. You, the final three, will tell each other secrets about your childhoods, your past and present loves, what you think is going to be the thing that breaks you in the end. You'll share secrets not so deep and not very dark, but secrets you're good enough to share at the end of the evening to do justice to a slurred conversation at such a horribly late hour.

You'll stay till closing, proudly. You'll leave feeling there's something between the three of you that you can lord over the rest of the twelve to nineteen who are as settled into their good night's sleep as they are in their sedentary (read: *happy*) lives. And the three of you will stumble from the curb with arms raised and shout at cabs that sail past without breaking stride. A cab will stop and either two of you or all three of you will share the cab but only two of you will get out together and screw. Try to be one of those two, too.

Happy Be One of the Final Three Day!

| AUGUST 10 | BUY A ROWBOAT DAY! |

Show it to your wife and tell her that it's the first step toward buying that lake house she's always dreamed of. Tell her today you're going to start saving.

She'll say, "Just let me go back inside and pack, and I'll be out of your hair."

Point to the rowboat and say, "But the rowboat."

"Mmm," she'll say. Then she'll go back into the house to pack her two suitcases full of everything she can fit. Follow her into the bedroom.

"It's taking longer than I thought," she'll say. "I'm just trying to think of everything I might need so I won't have to come back here for as long as possible. Maybe never."

Try once more. "The rowboat?"

"I'm not into it," she'll say. "Too many mistakes. Sorry. Nice boat, though."

About an hour and a half later she'll be gone. You'll have a new rowboat, though. Bring it into the living room and sit in it while you watch TV.

Happy Buy a Rowboat Day!

| AUGUST 11 |

ON LOAN FROM THE MUSEUM OF INCREDIBLE ASSES DAY!

It's just an old fucking chair. This is why all museums suck. They name an exhibit "Knights in Shining Armour!" So you show up and you get like two suits of empty chainmail and then about five rooms full of wooden bowls "from which jousters would take their porridge!" Total bullshit. Where are the human heads that have fossilized upon the tips of spears?

Then you saw a banner through your bus window that read ON LOAN FROM THE MUSEUM OF INCREDIBLE ASSES—THROUGH OCTOBER 12TH. So you decided to give a museum exhibit another shot. And here you are staring at the indentation in the plush velvet cushion of a bejeweled dining chair that purportedly supported Queen Elizabeth I during her morning Froot Loops. "Yes," you think. "I'm sure the Virgin Queen had an ass that was out of this world. But I came here to see some asses. I didn't pay a twenty-five-cent donation just to look at a seat cushion that had to endure the Earl of Leicester dropping to his knees and digging his nose into the fucking upholstery every time the help stepped away to apply a balm to their eczematic scales."

Break some glass.

Happy On Loan from the Museum of Incredible Asses Day!

AUGUST 12   DIE POOR DAY!

Living with no money means not being able to eat anything but old ham that people are trying to get rid of and crackers that you steal from diners. Dying with no money means dying like a saint. People trust the dead poor, and they aren't afraid to mourn them. When someone dies rich, people are wary of offering their grief because months after the rich are put in the ground, secrets of their wealth start to come to light. Hidden bank accounts are discovered, mistresses come forth to claim their share of the inheritance, immigrant families are found living in mansion basements, and tales unfold of a rich man who liked to watch immigrant families put on hastily written and produced morality plays.

But when the poor man dies, it is trusted that everything there is to know about the deceased is laid out inside that pine box. For the poor man could never afford to pay the sums required to keep a secret from coming to light. True, one or two of his debts might be passed down to his descendents, but his credit will have been cut off long ago so the burden will usually be negligible and perhaps taken on by his church.

So why not die poor today? You'll probably get to die on the toilet, since the poor either die on toilets or in an apartment complex fire set by an elderly woman's forgotten votive candle. If you're still on the fence, think about your options. You can die poor or you can die in jail. Dying rich or even dying middle class is not in the cards for you, I'm afraid. Those options are reserved for those Americans not turned dumb by a hilarious stutter.

Happy Die Poor Day!

AUGUST 13   THE DAILY NUMBER DAY!

After you've bought $79 worth of three-digit daily number lottery tickets, ask the nineteen-year-old girl behind the machine for a suggestion.

"Three hundred and fourteen!" she'll offer with a smile.

Say, "Straight and box for a dollar. If that wins, it'll be our wedding date."

The number of course will win, and you'll be $540 richer. That $540 will help pay for your divorce from your wife of forty-six years (you're seventy-one). The nineteen-year-old lotto machine operator will be a little hesitant about marrying you before she finishes college, but she'll be glad to not have to live at her parents' house anymore during summer break. Her boyfriend will not be too happy with the way she breaks up with him ("A deal's a deal, baby. Can't you be a little more mature about this?"). He'll punch you once and give you a minor heart attack (your fourth). You'll recover after not too long, and you and the lottery machine operator will enjoy a happy life together for the seventeen months remaining before you die in the bath.

Happy the Daily Number Day!

AUGUST 14   TRAPPED UNDERNEATH YOUR GIRLFRIEND DAY!

You phone for help. You phone Steve.

"She's dead, and she's on top of me."

Steve tells you to try and shove her off of you, asks you how she died.

"Lung cancer," you say. "This is really difficult. She won't budge."

Steve asks you where you are.

"I'm not sure. It looks like a warehouse."

Steve asks if anyone else is there.

"Look, I don't have time for twenty questions. I'm really broken up over the death of my girlfriend. And I just need someone to get her off of me."

Steve says he understands, but he can't send help unless he knows where you are.

"Makes sense to me. Sorry I lost it there for a second. Bad day."

Steve doesn't say anything.

"Dead girlfriend and all," you continue. "On top of me and everything," you add. "Shortening my breath, cutting off the blood to my brain." You clinch the deal.

"Okay," Steve says. "I'll devote my every waking breath to freeing you from the weight of your dead girlfriend."

"You're the best," you say.

"Smoking hurts us all," Steve says and hangs up.

You wait, occasionally putting a kiss to your dead girlfriend's earlobe. With every kiss, she's just a little bit colder.

Happy Trapped Underneath Your Girlfriend Day!

| AUGUST 15 | YOU'RE SICK OF MURDER DAY!

Today, you won't be able to control yourself. You'll be leaning over the torn-up remains of a sixteen-year-old homeless boy who was found underneath some trash. There'll be some vomit on his belly and a chisel lodged in his left eye socket. In his wallet, you guessed it, a photo of a mother and a father, each with a hand on the shoulder of a twelve-year-old boy. It's just a guess that the bloody mess before you was the boy in that photo.

A cop in uniform will say, "Think it's the same killer, detective?" You'll reel around to shout something, but you won't know what or why. Just doing his job, trying to solve a murder. Just like you for fourteen years now. But you need to shout something. Anything.

"Detective?"

The alley will start to spin. You'll walk a few quick paces away from the cop, trying to get your bearings. Then you'll stop and shout up at the windows of the apartment buildings all around you.

"I am so SICK of murder!!!"

You'll feel like you shouted loud enough to crack the sky, and you'll wonder if you did because a silence will follow. A silence broken by a stifled snicker. You'll turn to find the uniformed cop with his shoulders shivering, his hand over his grinning mouth.

You'll be ready to shut him up when you spy the other beat cop and the landlady he's interviewing giggling together. A loud guffaw will echo from the mouth of a little boy hanging out his window up above. The crowd of bystanders will erupt in a rolling, building cackle.

Soon, everyone on the crime scene will be laughing at you. You can either run or start shooting.

Happy You're Sick of Murder Day!

| AUGUST 16 | COME OUT OF RETIREMENT FOR ONE LAST JOB DAY! |

Remember Kola? The hooker with the heart of gold who you helped get off the corner and off the horse before you got run out of town? Well don't worry, she's not back on the needle. But her daughter Mimi's been kidnapped. And the kidnapper is none other than Fink, your former "employer" from your days in Old City. It looks like Fink has a job that only you can pull off, and you can either swallow the words "never again" or give a kiss goodbye to the little girl who may or may not be your progeny.

So whether you were an accountant, a tailor, or a notary, you got no other choice but to get back in the game because today's Come Out of Retirement for One Last Job Day!

(Note: If you get the chance, try to spend a little time with Mimi after you rescue her. You need to forge some semblance of a fatherly relationship with her. Granted, when this is all over you'll either be dead or on a plane to Turkey, but at least she'll know who her father was. If you'd met your old man, things might've gone another way for you.)

| AUGUST 17 | SHE'S WAY FUCKED UP DAY!

You fell in love with her on her first day of orientation at the museum. You showed everyone in your training group where the bathrooms were, and she said, "Man, I'm gonna be spending a lot of time in there today. I've been sick to my stomach for three years now."

She's the prettiest museum guard you ever did see. And after months of shuffling your days off, you finally got it so that you're both in the Degas room on Fridays, and you both get off at six.

You'll ask if she'd like to grab a beer and she'll say, "I'll drive." You'll spend hours at the bar. The conversation will be just as perfect as you imagined it would be. The kind of ease with a person that you haven't felt since the last time you fell in love. You'll both have had quite a lot to drink, but alcohol doesn't make this kind of thing happen. You'll blame your hearts.

Finally, you'll suggest that the two of you get out of there. She'll say, "I'll drive." But she'll be way fucked up, and when she hits an icy patch she'll send the car into a ditch. You'll both live, but she'll have a horrible scrape on her face from the airbag. You'll wait inside the car for the police to arrive, holding each other for warmth, smothering each other with gentle kisses upon the face and neck. It's going to be wonderful.

Happy She's Way Fucked Up Day!

AUGUST 18   DADDY'S AMNESIA DAY!

You'll stand in the hallway and watch your mother clump up his dress shirts and lob them out the window onto the lawn. "Let your little slut iron these from now on," she'll shout into the night. And though you won't be sure what she's talking about, you'll feel in your bones that things are never going to be the same.

He'll appear there on the lawn, staring at the clothes and trinkets splayed across the grass. He'll look like he's trying very hard to come to a conclusion. Then your mother will come to the door.

"Who are you? Do you recognize me?" he'll ask your mother. "I feel a great deal of love for you, but I don't remember ever having met you in my life. Perhaps I have amnesia and cannot remember any of the major events in my life, especially the more recent ones. For example, I have no idea why these clothes would be on the lawn. However, the warmth I feel in my heart makes me certain that this house is the place where I am to live and where I one day will die a happy man who lived a full life. May I stay? I appear to have amnesia."

The anger will creep from your mother's brow. She'll look to be trying to solve long division. You'll be hiding behind a chair, breathless with the suspense as your mother decides whether to hold her husband in her arms or start screaming again like she's been doing for the past two days that he was gone.

Then she'll take a breath and pull him by the arm, leading him to the couch in the living room. "Boys," she'll shout. "Come down here."

You and your brothers will line up on the sectional opposite where your mother is sitting beside your father.

"Boys, something terrible has happened. Your father has amnesia, and he can't remember anything about his life."

She'll wait for your father to say something. He'll say to you and your brothers, "Who are you? Do you recognize me? I appear to have amnesia."

Your mother will then take his chin in her hand and say into his eyes, "These are your children. And I am your wife. Never, ever betray us."

Then she'll let go of his face. "This is your home," she'll say. "This is where you'll stay."

After that, you'll all wear name tags for a few months, and occasionally you'll have to remind him where the toilet is. But everything will pretty much seem like it was after not too long. At first, whenever you question the amnesia to your mom, she'll just say, "Think of it like a do-over." Later she'll say, "Your father is home. That's what matters." And she'll look at you a little too long before giving you a hug. After a while, she'll just stop answering you.

Happy Daddy's Amnesia Day!

| AUGUST 19 | SURFER BOY DAY! |

Surfer Boy is about to call you. He got your number a year and a half ago at a party when you had a line on a used air conditioner. He never called about the air conditioner, which is good news because air conditioners are heavy. You see, Surfer Boy doesn't even know how he got your number. He's calling you because he needs someone to help him move.

"What?"

"I swear, man, I know this is weird but all my friends flaked on me."

Surfer Boy always seemed to enjoy a deep throng of friends and lovers. When he'd arrive at the beach, he'd often be greeted with, "Hey look, here comes Surfer Boy!" And everyone would crowd around him as he pulled himself into his wet suit, asking him what he thought of the waves and whether he wanted to go beat up some *haoles*. And then Surfer Boy would run down to the beach and all would watch him with mouths agape. He is the kind of person people want to be seen talking to.

"Have you tried calling a moving company?"

"Too last minute. Please, man."

A party was considered a success if Surfer Boy showed up. Oftentimes a party would erupt out of a casual gathering simply because Surfer Boy decided to hang around for a while. When the mayor wanted to close a popular beach to get some much needed improvements underway, he brought Surfer Boy into his office and asked him if he had any concerns.

"Are you sure there isn't a single friend you can call?"

"I'm just an idea to them."

All those nights you envied Surfer Boy's ability to walk into a room and stop the music. And now you learn that in truth his is a life of loneliness. Everyone shouts to their friends, "Hey, it's Surfer Boy!" But no one's ever going to say, "Hi, Surfer Boy. How are you? You look a little thin."

You might pity Surfer Boy, and that might make you think you should help him in his time of need. That depends on you and whatever you might have been hoping to do today.

"So how 'bout it man, whaddya say?"

Happy Surfer Boy Day!

| AUGUST 20 |

COVET CHILDREN AT A PLAYGROUND DAY!

You're childless and empty. Worthless, in the eyes of the world and your Lord. Your lack of children is proof that you remain unloved and unlovable. Go to the playground and look at all the beautiful children at play. As you watch them, whisper aloud both ends of a conversation you imagine you're having with your own little boy or girl. It's fun to pretend at thirty-eight.

Happy Covet Children at a Playground Day!

AUGUST 21   MONSTER DAY!

Your girlfriend is convinced that there are monsters under her bed, and she wants you to sleep over at her house to make her feel safe. You want her to sleep soundly, but you're both only sixteen and you don't want to have sex until you are at least out of high school. Spending the night in her room might compromise that plan.

You'll ask your girlfriend, "We're still on the same page, right?"

"About what?" she'll say.

"Not fucking."

She'll say, "I don't want to fuck. I just want you to sleep in my room. The monsters, you know."

You'll say, "I know, and I want to be there to protect you. I'm just afraid of fucking you."

"You don't think you can sleep over without fucking me?" she'll say.

"No," you'll say. "Not just me. Us. I'm afraid if we're in your bedroom all night long in our pajamas like that, we're just going to lose control and fuck like crazy. And I wanna go to college."

She'll say, "Please. The monsters."

You hold her eyes with yours, seeking out some truth. "Okay," you'll say. "But if we all of a sudden fuck . . ."

"Yeah?" she'll say.

You'll break out in a smile. "Don't say I didn't warn ya is all."

She'll smile and the two of you will hug. Later tonight, you'll be torn apart at the sternum by monsters.

Happy Monster Day!

AUGUST 22   DOG WALK DAY!

Today, when you walk little Leopold, you're going to cross the path of a homeless girl. She'll be holding a box of money.

"How much money is in that box?" you'll ask.

"Seventy-seven thousand dollars," she'll say.

Say, "Wanna buy a daddy?"

She'll ask what kind of curfew you'll impose on her. Offer her dusk until she's ten years old, then you'll give her 8:00 P.M. in the summertime. When she's thirteen, you'll renegotiate.

"Do you hit?"

Say no.

"Drink?"

Socially, say.

"You're not gonna . . ."

Say, "Hell no!"

"Does that dog play?" she'll ask.

Let Leopold loose and watch them wrestle sweetly.

The girl will pull herself out of the dog's entanglement with a giggle. Then she'll hand the box into your leash hand and she'll take your free hand in hers and the three of you will start walking. "What's for dinner, Daddy?"

Say hot dogs.

Happy Dog Walk Day!

| AUGUST 23 | BUILD CLOUDS DAY!

Build four clouds. One from newspapers, one from a soap bubble and the smoke of a cigarette, one from stone, and one from shirts. Then hold the clouds over your bed when it's time for your lover to wake up. When his eyes flutter open and he looks up and sees you waving the clouds over him, say, "Wake up, sleepyface. What's a matter, too cloudy?" When he laughs, switch clouds. Drop the two in your hands and pick up the two that are sitting on the bed and wave them over the bed in a circular motion. Your lover will ask you to "c'mere," in a "let's screw" kinda way. Don't. Instead, move the clouds around in an even faster circular motion and shout, "Uh-oh! Storm front!" Then start spitting on the blanket.

Happy Build Clouds Day!

| AUGUST 24 | DO YOU MIND MY ASKING HOW YOUR WIFE IS DOING? DAY!

I'm forty-three now, married, a father. Still strange to be saying it. Strange for it to be true for all these years already (five). I guess I'm sort of finishing up things, yes. For so much of my youth, I was clawing into myself, trying to dig out from under the hair and the layers and layers of skin that one thing that will make me golden. There was a greatness inside me, and I drove myself mad trying to root it out. But it was a squiggly little fucker, slippery and sly, it knew just when to feint my lunge. One day, in my late thirties, I concluded that my hunt for that greatness was its only sustenance, the only thing that kept it alive. So I stopped looking for it and let it die.

Anyway, you know about me and your wife. A year and half we shared around thirteen years ago. Well I loved her. And I kept loving her. But unless I became the man I wanted to be, I knew I could never have her. I could not present myself as I was, as I am, a man less than a fraction of who he'd hoped to be. I could not give this man to her. It would have been an insult. But while I was searching for that better man inside of me, I held out hope that one day I would feel that I deserved to take her by the hand.

That day never came, and it never will, I've decided. And when I made that decision, with it came acceptance of the fact that your wife will be the only woman I will ever truly love until the day that I die. Yes, I am married, and my wife is a beautiful woman who has given me two darling daughters. I repeat, your wife will be the only woman I will ever truly love until the day that I die. Which is why I hope you don't mind my asking you presently, how is she?

Happy Do You Mind My Asking How Your Wife Is Doing? Day!

AUGUST 25	BE A DRUG ADDICT DAY!

Cower in the corner of an empty room in a rundown abandoned house scratching at your forearm and scream, "Just one more hit! Pleeease! I'm sick, man!" Then fellate somebody who doesn't love you. If you have a baby, don't change its diapers. Ever. But offer to sell it in exchange for the drugs you're addicted to. Also, kill it.

By now, everything's on fire. Don't care. Just remain splayed out with a pleasant grin on your face. If you see any electrical appliances, sell them. Then fellate somebody who doesn't love you but likes to make drug addicts like you fellate him in front of his laughing friends to show just how much power he has over drug addicts because he has drugs. When you're finished fellating him, he's going to punch you in the face, stomp on your belly, then toss a small bag of the drugs you're addicted to on the floor next to you. Scrabble across the floor for the bag of drugs as if nothing else in the world matters. One day you're going to fellate someone who is high and a little out of his mind and when he beats you up afterward, he will go too far and kill you by accident. No one will care, though, because you are a drug addict and America hates you.

Happy Be a Drug Addict Day!

| AUGUST 26 | YOUR CABIN'S ALL SET DAY!

Your soon-to-be ex-husband spent the weekend boarding up the windows and locking everything down for the winter. It will be ready to sell soon, and there probably won't be anyone living in it until the next summer or later. You think that's appropriate.

It was home to your love. It is the place where one of your sons was conceived. It contains the chair where you slept inside your husband's lap for a thousand hours over the course of nine summers. The cabin didn't see your love blossom, it saw your love celebrated.

A fall, a winter, and a spring. So glad you are that it can't be shown during the colder months. That there is absolutely no chance of someone moving in there for close to a year. Let it freeze solid until it cracks into two halves that fall to their sides. Let it stand empty and cold, a dead shadow in the snow. Let rich teens on a ski weekend break in and fuck on your beds and piss on your floors. But don't let anyone else try and love inside that wood. At least not for three or four seasons. That should be enough time. Almost, maybe just enough.

Happy Your Cabin's All Set Day!

| AUGUST 27 | YOU ARE NOT A FLORIST DAY! |

Your friend Maggie is a florist. Maggie is your best friend in the world. You and she have been closer than lovers for over twenty years now. Maggie is flying back from Costa Rica tomorrow, but her shop assistant has walked out without warning.

"There are so many orders to be picked up," Maggie said when she called this morning. "They're all arranged. Please just go and open the doors and take their money and hand them their flowers. That's all you have to do."

"But can't you just tell them all to pick them up tomorrow?" you asked.

"People buy flowers for *occasions*," she said. "Please. I could lose so many customers if those doors aren't open today." That store is her life. There's no way you could say no.

"Don't worry about a thing," you said. "I promise, when you get back your store will be just as thriving as the day you left."

Maggie's not coming back. She's going to go missing before she reaches the airport. Her ticket will never have been redeemed. You're going to open up her store today. And you're going to open it tomorrow. And the next day.

You're going to quit your job at the firm that buys life insurance policies from the elderly. You'll have to, in order to keep Maggie's store open. You promised her that her store would be just as she left it. Until someone tells you for certain that she's not coming back, you'll do all you can to keep that promise.

"I'm not a florist," you'll tell people when they tell you what a wonderful florist you are. "I'm just filling in for my friend Maggie who hasn't come back from Costa Rica yet." You'll eventually learn floral arranging, and you'll become very skilled at it. But only to keep your promise.

"Maggie's the florist. This is her shop. She's my friend. I'm just waiting for my friend to come back," you'll tell Maggie's customers, many of whom will have never met Maggie since they will have found her store long after she left for Costa Rica.

Maggie's customers will tell you how lucky Maggie is to have such a devoted and generous friend.

"She'd do the same for me," you'll tell them. "I have so much to tell her. I wish she'd come back."

Whether she does or not, her flower shop will be there waiting for her to return. You'll even teach floral arranging to the son you're going to have four years from now so that he can keep the shop alive after your death. In case Maggie outlives you.

Occasionally, a customer will ask you, very delicately, what will happen to the shop if you find out Maggie has died.

"It'll close," you'll say. "No Maggie, no shop. No nothing."

Then you'll go into the back and you'll cut the stems on some gladioli and you'll wonder where Maggie is.

Happy You Are Not a Florist Day!

| AUGUST 28 | TAKE THE GUN OUT OF MY MOUTH AND I'LL TELL YOU DAY! |

It's not safe to have a gun in your mouth. It could go off and kill you. Also, guns are notoriously dirty. They're often kept inside people's pants, pressed up against the bare pelvis held tight underneath the belted waistline. Sure, she's your girlfriend of two years and you're more than happy to ingest whatever might be smeared all over her pelvis. But you don't know where she got that gun. It's doubtful that she bought it brand-new. More likely, she bought it from a gun show or Craigslist. Who knows the state of the pants that gun has lived inside of? And now it's in your mouth.

"I don't know how to work this thing," she says. Bringing you back to the "gun could go off and kill you" thesis. Considering all the filth that's probably living inside your mouth right now, getting your head blown off doesn't sound like such a bad idea. But there's something you can do to avoid getting your head blown off and to get that filthy gun out of your mouth. You can tell her what she wants to know.

"Grrllllargh," you say.

"You ready to talk?" she asks.

"Khhhlaaaersshhhccch," you say.

"If I pull this gun out of your mouth and you don't tell me what I wanna hear, I'm gonna shove it back in for the last time. Understand? Bye-bye brains," she says.

"Haaahgglllh," you say.

She considers your eyes. And with a swift jerk of her shoulder she yanks the gun past your teeth and holds it an inch from your chin. You pant fresh air into your lungs and spit saliva to your chin.

"Make me happy," she says.

"Kim," you say. "I think you're so great that you should look for work as an angel because that's what you look like."

The furrow in her brow goes flat. She looks down at the gun, then looks into your eyes.

"Okay," she says. "Now do you know how to get the hammer to go back into the gun without shooting any bullets?"

"Lemme see." You hold out your hand for her to give you the gun.

"No funny business," she says.

She hands you the gun, and you shove it in her mouth and demand to know who's the squeeziest pleasiest boyfriend she ever had.

Happy Take the Gun Out of My Mouth and I'll Tell You Day!

AUGUST 29 | TRY TO SEE THE CAR CRASH YOU'RE
GOING TO HAVE AS A METAPHOR
FOR WHAT'S WRONG WITH
AMERICA DAY!

Today you're going to smack the nose of your car into the left rear side of a
Buick LeSabre. It will be your fault. The LeSabre will be sent into a spin.

Before you get out to exchange insurance information, just breathe for
a moment. Try to think about all of the elements at play in this particular
car crash, and see how they reflect the state of America.

Since both you and the other driver will be white, you won't be able to
focus on race relations, which is the easy one. His LeSabre looks relatively
well maintained too, so economic disparity isn't going to work.

"Outsourcing?" Say it out loud in your empty car, just to see if it sounds
right. It won't.

You're going to have to find out where the other driver was headed. You
were on your way to work, and you were driving the route you take every
day. Which is why you let yourself fall into a daydream. Every morning you
send yourself off to work at a place you don't want to be. You shut your
mind and your heart away for eight to ten hours every day. You were promised an American dream, but all you're doing is sleepwalking.

This is going someplace, right? Now you have to find out about the guy
you hit. Is he a social climber who bases all of his character assessments on
monetary status? Is he a heart attack case because he's got a sick kid and a
job that thinks he's too old? Is he scared he's going to wake up one day and
everything he's worked for will be gone?

Go on over to his car and knock on his window to find out. He won't answer. He won't wake up. The police are going to have to get him out of
there. If he comes to, ask him whether he feels cheated by his country.

Happy Try to See the Car Crash You're Going to Have as a Metaphor for
What's Wrong with America Day!

| AUGUST 30 | WATER FOR THE MARATHON RUNNER DAY! |

You've been in town for three weeks now and you haven't met a soul. Your parents and friends back home are sick of you calling late at night just because you need to hear a friendly voice. It's time for you to put yourself out there and draw some people in. What better way to do that than to go down to the finish line of a marathon and dole out some water?

You've been to the finish line of a marathon before. As they come in, the runners are all clamoring for water because they're thirsty and their legs are covered in blood and human waste.

That's where you come in. You'll sidle up with your aluminum bucket and drinking straw and you'll say, "Drink up." The runner will gulp down half the bucket, and with the other half he'll scrub his feces from the part of his legs that he chafed raw so that he can properly dress his wounds. When he looks at you to thank you for essentially saving his life, say, "I'd be up for a bite to eat if you are. I'm new in town."

The runner will smile and wink at you, which is the symbol for "You want to have sex with me, don't you?" If you smile and wink back, that's the symbol for "Yes, I want to have sex with you. Really hard." Don't smile and wink back unless you want to have sex with the runner.

If he sees that you haven't smiled and winked back at him, the runner will say, "Oh, so just a friendly bite?"

Say, "Yes. I saved your life pretty much just now."

The runner will agree that you did and he'll say, "It'll be a day or so before I can hold down solid food. But I'd be willing to sit on the grass over there and talk. If you don't mind me passing out from time to time."

Unless you mind him passing out from time to time, take him up on his offer. You just might have yourself a new friend if the runner doesn't turn out to be a cock.

Happy Water for the Marathon Runner Day!

| AUGUST 31 | GILLY'S BACK IN TOWN DAY! |

"Gilly's back in town."

Your grandmother catches her breath.

"He's gonna cause trouble."

Your grandmother starts clearing the table. "Your brother is in Mexico and he's never coming back."

"He left his driver's license in the crack of my screen door."

She stops at the sink, arches her back, takes a breath before she turns. "Show it to me," she says.

You toss the driver's license across the table. She sits down and picks it up. She puts her hand over her mouth as if to stifle a sob. "He looks so young," she says. She holds it closer. "Still valid."

"When I was a kid, you know how much we looked alike. When I was a kid I used to ask him if I could borrow his driver's license to take a girl out in Dad's old Chevy."

Your grandmother waits with her eyes closed.

"He'd say, 'You'll get it when I'm dead. I won't be needing no wheels in hell.'"

"He's gonna kill Paul," she says. Paul's your dad's brother. Killed your dad. Stole your mom.

"Whether he does or not, he's sure planning to get hisself killed."

Your grandmother goes back to the sink and washes a dish. She puts it in the rack to dry. She picks up another dish out of the sink, holds it in front of her chest. She doesn't turn around when she says, "Find him."

"Now how in the hell am I—"

She wheels around at you with more life in her eyes than what's been in twenty years. "Find! Him! Or he'll take this whole town into the grave with him."

You nod three times without breathing.

Happy Gilly's Back in Town Day!

SEPTEMBER

EVERYTHING BEHIND YOU IS IN CINDERS. EVERYTHING
AHEAD OF YOU BELONGS TO SOMEONE ELSE.

INTRODUCE SOME NOVELTY INTO THE BEDROOM DAY!

Tell her, "Meet James."

That's the cue for that guy, James, to come into the bedroom and sit down in the chair in the corner.

"James is gonna tell us what to do tonight."

Your wife will look at James and say, "Hello." James will say, "Yup." Then he'll shrug for no apparent reason.

Climb under the covers and untie the drawstring on your wife's pajama pants. She'll ask, "Who is he?"

Look at James to see if he's paying attention. He really isn't. Say to your wife, "He's just a guy I know from the driving range. But I think I met him someplace else." Pull her panties down. You'll get up on your knees so that your wife can take your penis into her mouth, which is how things usually start. Then you'll remember that you're getting ahead of yourself.

"Sorry, James," say. "I forgot that you're supposed to be calling the shots tonight. What's your poison?"

"That looked fine," James will say.

You'll pretty much run through the motions like you normally do. James will sign off on just about everything you wanna do. He won't invest too much of himself, spending most of the encounter on his cell phone. He'll only throw down a veto when you hoist your wife onto all fours and begin eating her pussy.

"Hang on," James will say into his cell phone. Then to you, "Not that. I hate that."

You'll both hold still for a second. Your wife will look back over her shoulder at you, then she'll say to James, "Aye aye." So you'll pull back onto your knees and enter your wife, who will still be on all fours. You'll look to James before thrusting ahead, and James will just offer a silent thumbs-up so as not to interrupt his phone call.

The encounter will come to a close when James gets into a fight with the person on his cell phone that you assume to be his boyfriend. He'll stomp out into the living room so he can yell into his phone with abandon. Not long after that, you'll hear the front door slam and the sound of James's car peeling out of the driveway.

Happy Introduce Some Novelty into the Bedroom Day!

| SEPTEMBER 2 | CROWN OF THORNS DAY!

Your crown of thorns makes you look like a fat pig. The blood from your scalp pours in streams down the creases of fat on your neck. Some people look good in a crown of thorns. Those people are not sixty pounds over-weight. Take off the crown of thorns and hide yourself someplace damp until you're not so unsightly.

Happy Crown of Thorns Day!

| SEPTEMBER 3 | SHE SMOKES BY THE WINDOWSILL DAY! |

Naked on a stool with one bare foot up on a precarious stack of your compact discs, she'll smoke one of your cigarettes while you're fast asleep. At 3:00 A.M.

She'll blow her plumes out around the handrails of the fire escape. It'll be a smoke signal for Buzzcut to spy and join her.

Buzzcut is the boyfriend of your neighbor three doors down. Her window faces the courtyard as well, just around the corner. Buzzcut can't sleep after sex in other people's apartments either.

It was a month ago that she first saw Buzzcut naked when he was sitting in the window and smoking one of his girlfriend's cigarettes. Her first inclination was to cover up, but Buzzcut wasn't looking. And because Buzzcut was naked himself, she decided it was okay. That night they didn't so much as share a glance.

There've been five occasions since then that your girlfriend and Buzzcut have smoked nude together. On the third, they both put out their cigarettes at the same time. And as each reached up to draw the blinds, their eyes met and so did their smiles.

The fourth, last weekend, she kept her eyes on Buzzcut, waiting for him to steal a glance at her. He did after not too long. For the last five drags of their cigarettes that night, Buzzcut and your girlfriend had a silent conversation across the courtyard using only eyes, smiles, and smoke plumes.

Tonight Buzzcut will climb onto his girlfriend's windowsill with a goofy grin on his face. He'll light up and pull the cigarette away from his lips with a broad flourish, like something out of an old movie. Your girlfriend will chuckle, causing her breasts to quiver just a bit. She'll think Buzzcut is just a little too forward tonight, so she'll give her eyes to the moon for a few drags before giving him a kind smile. He'll have calmed down by then.

She might not be back here anytime soon. She's planning on breaking up with you tomorrow morning. And though she knows he might get the wrong idea, when she puts her cigarette out and reaches up to draw the blinds, she'll put her hand to the glass to give Buzzcut a wave good-bye.

It will startle him. He'll wave back, a little too briskly. Your girlfriend will draw the blinds while Buzzcut's still smoking.

Happy She Smokes by the Windowsill Day!

| SEPTEMBER 4 | YOUR BOYFRIEND IS A CAR RACER DAY! |

He used to go out there because he loved the speed. Today, he's going out there because he's got something to prove.

"Prove that you love me and stay home today," you'll plead.

"You keep me in this house you won't have a man by your side. Race or not, the man I could be is gonna walk out that door today. He races, he'll come back. He chickens out, he's gone forever."

You'll place your hands on his shoulders. You know you can't change his mind. "I'm afraid you're going to die. Just like . . ."

He'll take your hand off of his shoulders. "I'm not here so you can have your daddy back."

He'll push through the screen door and go out to his Camaro. The engine will rumble to life. You'll hear his voice shout over the growling of the car. You'll go to the screen door.

"Baby!" he'll shout.

You'll step out on the front porch.

"Your old man could never handle the turns like I can," he'll shout.

You'll nod. It's true, even your daddy would admit to that. But your daddy never raced for anything more than the sum total of the prize money. He was too far in debt to worry over pride.

Happy Your Boyfriend Is a Car Racer Day!

| SEPTEMBER 5 | GIVE HIM A REASON DAY! |

Tell him when you were six you picked the lock on your father's liquor cabinet and you found several different whiskeys and aperitifs and a jelly jar of preserved women's index fingers. Tell him you didn't ask your father about the jar because you were too scared to tell him you'd broken into his liquor cabinet. You spent most of your teen years harboring an anxiety that you couldn't pin down. Suffice it to say, any time your father came home late from work, you took to chewing at your fingertips but you couldn't say why. A child therapist chalked it up to separation anxiety. Considering that your mother had run off when you were young, it only made sense that you'd fear the disappearance of your father as well. Tell him that as you grew up, you always had a vague memory of finding the jar of index fingers, but you'd assumed it was a memory of a dream you'd had.

Tell him you never took a drink until you were twenty-eight, the year you said to your father, "I once found a jelly jar full of index fingers in your liquor cabinet. Was one of them Mom's?" Tell him that your father said nothing. Just turned his head to look out the window of his hospital room. You sat an hour staring at the back of his head, then you left. Tell him that you never went back to visit your father, and a week later you got the call that he'd passed away. Tell him that three hours before his funeral, you got on a bus out of town and started on a six-year bender. Then tell him that you eventually made peace with yourself and have since tried to live a good life as a responsible man, but sometimes you get mixed up still.

"That's why I forgot to return your power saw. Sorry, Kenny."

Tell him you just want to be a good neighbor.

Happy Give Him a Reason Day!

SEPTEMBER 6 | REMEMBER WHEN YOU HURT
SOMEBODY DAY!

You think you're basically a good person. As do your friends and loved ones.
Well if you are what is considered "good," are we to conclude that even the
good of the world are capable of destroying another human being as coldly
and selfishly as you did that special someone not very long ago? She made
the mistake only of caring for you and was repaid with soul-wrenching cruelty. There's something dark living inside of you.

Happy Remember When You Hurt Somebody Day!

SEPTEMBER 7 | IN THE BABY CEMETERY DAY!

"You never look at me. I only know that because I look at you a lot."

You smile and take a sip from your cup of beer, spilling a bit from your
lips. It seems all night long you haven't been able to take a sip without
spilling a bit down your chin, onto your shirt sometimes. You wipe this spill
away with the back of your hand because you're going to have to try to kiss
her soon.

"I thought you liked Lisa for a while." She pours some beer onto the
grassy grave of Jessica Hoyle, 1975–1978.

"No." You did like Lisa. You do. But Lisa's had the same boyfriend since
sophomore year. And Lisa's not here, telling you she looks at you a lot.

"I hate beer." She pours some more of her cup into the grass. "Just being
here is so horrible. Why always the baby cemetery?"

You take another sip and wipe your chin with the back of your hand.
"More trees. Cops can't see us from the street. Less chance of getting raided."

She says, "It's like nothing we do here is disrespectful because the very fact that we would ever even come here and put a keg down on one of these graves is so disrespectful, we can't top it with our behavior once we're here."

"I don't think of it as any different," you say. "Every grave, no matter how old or how they died, everyone met the same fate. Everyone here stopped." Take a sip and wipe your chin. Then say to her, "I look at you."

She'll hold her eyes straight ahead and smile. Her cheeks are big and fat like a baby's when she smiles like she'll be smiling now. Her free hand will be in the grass next to your leg. Take a sip and slip your hand over hers. You'll both race your thumbs on top of each other, down into the crook between thumb and forefinger, then back up and over. She'll only turn her head to you when you lean over and she meets your kiss.

Put the beer in the grass by your side and put your hand on her shoulder. Then put your other arm around her back. She'll follow suit, pulling you toward her. Move to your knees and she'll recline so that you can climb atop her, the two of you stretched across the graves of Mae Franklin, 1989–1989, Martin Ganz, 1963–1969, and of course, Jessica Hoyle, 1975–1978.

Happy in the Baby Cemetery Day!

| SEPTEMBER 8 | SHE HAS A FUCKING BIRD DAY!

Everything about her seemed perfect. She's got a lot of money and she drinks constantly. You should've known it was too good to be true.

"This is Arnold. Say hello."

You'll peer through the little bars into the eyes of the perfect yellow parakeet, trying to steady your drunken legs, afraid you might fall over and grab at the cage for balance. You'll take half a step back to get the bedpost within reach.

"Say hello, I said."

"Hello. Arnold, hello."

Arnold won't say anything.

She'll say, "Arnold is the most important thing in my life."

You'll sit on the bed, remembering how good the sex had been in your tiny apartment following the first two dates. You couldn't wait to get into her place and see what a trust fund can buy. And now you discover that it can buy an average apartment with an additional small alcove room that could be used as a study or extra storage. In this case, extra storage.

"My soul's in there."

"What?"

She'll put the tip of her finger in between the bars of the cage. Arnold will poke at it with his beak. "Inside that little yellow body. When Arnold flutters his wings, my stomach grows unsettled. He contains my essence."

Why do you keep your essence locked up in a cage lined with newspapers?

"That's nice."

"Did you see the way he just looked at you?"

No. Is he taking a shit?

"Arnold is uncertain of you. I can't have sex in here tonight."

"Should we go back to my . . ."

"Lie here on the bed by my side but don't touch me. Arnold has to absorb you."

You'll lie on the bed, so terribly disappointed in yourself. From the pillow, "Do you have anything to drink?"

She'll go to the kitchen and return with an unopened bottle of vodka and two glasses. "I don't have any limes."

You'll drink with the lights on bright. You won't speak. Arnold will hold her soul motionless on his perch, occasionally crying out for no discernible reason. Birds cry out from time to time.

Happy She Has a Fucking Bird Day!

SEPTEMBER 9 | MARSHMALLOWS ROASTING IN THE FIREPLACE DAY!

You've been waiting by the fireplace for an hour to roast some marshmallows, like Mom said you could after dinner. But then Mom starts fighting with Brad, her new boyfriend. They're screaming in her bedroom and sometimes it sounds like something as heavy as a human just fell on the floor. In a minute, Brad's going to come out to the fireplace and throw a bag of marshmallows at your head. He'll say, "Have fun, you little shit." Then, from behind your mother's bedroom door you'll hear him shout at your mother, "There, he's toasting his fucking marshmallows. Now if you want someone to sit with him maybe you should call his fucking dad over here so I can go the fuck back to Metropark."

Maybe she should.

Happy Marshmallows Roasting in the Fireplace Day!

SEPTEMBER 10 | IHOP DAY!

Today at IHOP, 4:14 P.M., you, a guy and a girl barely twenty saying nothing to each other, an elderly person with Down's syndrome, four unsupervised children under ten, and a woman writing a suicide note are all in this together.

The girl who's not talking to the guy she's with is going to turn to the elderly person with Down's to say, "I like your *Lord of the Rings* T-shirt."

In an attempt to return the compliment, the elderly person with Down's will reply, "I like Twix bar sundaes. They make them good here. They know how to do it."

The woman writing the suicide note will shout out to anyone, "What's the word for when you feel like you're just drifting through life and you get thrown this way and that way and this way and that way until you can't look into the mirror without wanting to puke?"

One of the unsupervised children under ten will shout, "Poopies!"

The other unsupervised children under ten will giggle and confirm that the word for that condition is "poopies."

You know that in a certain respect, the unsupervised children are correct. But nonetheless, you should suggest to the woman writing the suicide note, "Rudderless."

The woman writing the suicide note will smile at you. "Thanks," she'll say. Then she'll write "rudderless" on her sheet of paper. You should make a move on her. No strings, most likely.

The boy barely twenty who hasn't said anything to the girl barely twenty will get up and walk outside, where he'll be shot twice execution-style.

"He shouldn't have left the group," the elderly person with Down's syndrome will say. The girl barely twenty will go and sit with the elderly retarded person and they'll talk about soda while you and the woman writing the suicide note will exchange smiles from across the dining room. Stacks of pancakes will come and they will go, almost as if the stacks of pancakes were rudderless, if one were to use the word "rudderless" incorrectly.

Happy IHOP Day!

| SEPTEMBER 11 | HOT PAIN DAY!

Today at 7:00 P.M., Jeff and Cara will win a $90 million lottery. You have to try and establish a friendship with them before the numbers are drawn if you want to get some handouts. Unfortunately, you dislike people like Jeff and Cara because they like to burn each other. Jeff doesn't enjoy sex with Cara unless Cara first drips scalding hot water onto his chest from a kettle that's recently sounded its whistle. Cara doesn't enjoy sex with Jeff unless Jeff binds her wrist to a steaming radiator, the bounds kept loose so that she can try to pull away from the hot steel, only to be scuttled against it again and again as Jeff's methods broaden during the lovemaking.

The only thing Jeff and Cara enjoy more than burning each other is talking about burning each other with people like you. It's hard to be around them, but if you get into Jeff and Cara's inner circle, they might pay for your father's medicine. He'll die without their help.

Happy Hot Pain Day!

SEPTEMBER 12 WATCH THE SKYCAMS DAY!

If you watch the traffic skycams on TV during rush hour, you can look for red cars in traffic jams. She's still driving to and from work, and you know no matter where she moved, she still has to go through the dreaded Route 12 overpass. Traffic is backed up there every day for at least three miles.

Tune in between 5:00 and 6:45 and look for red cars. The big red cars you'll be able to eliminate immediately as too old to be hers. But most of the others will look the same. That doesn't matter, however. All you have to do is focus on each and every single red car on the screen. Then, the next time anyone asks you if you heard from Michelle, instead of trying to keep from throwing up when you say "No," you'll be able to say, "I think I saw her car the other day."

If you want, you can get up close to your TV and kiss the screen wherever you see a red car. But don't tell anybody. Even if you wanted to, you wouldn't be able to say, "I think I kissed her car the other day." You'd have to tell them, "I think I saw her car on TV the other day, so I kissed the TV." Then you'd have to explain that kissing the image of her car on the TV let you pretend that you were kissing her. Which made you a little less jumpy for a little while. You'd be forced to confess, "I'm not really doing too well."

Happy Watch the Skycams Day!

| SEPTEMBER 13 | BE THE BLUESMAN DAY!

Sit on the porch of a condemned shack and be old and incomprehensible. A young white man will approach you and ask if you are a famous bluesman with a silly name like Wailing Ernie Poke. Say yes. The young white man will buy it. He'll wait for you to start telling stories about mean women you married. Tell him that you were once married to a woman who was so mean that she emptied all your whiskey in the sink, then she shot you in the kidney. Then laugh.

The young white man will ask for your advice. He'll say that his girlfriend is not very mean, but she's been pushing him to demand a promotion at work and he's not the type who likes to make waves. "Have any of your mean ex-wives done anything like that to you, Riproaring Ernie Pants?"

Tell him about the ex-wife who was angry that you didn't have a job, so she put snakes in your bed. The young white man will say, "So did that pressure make you get a job, Rollicking Ernie Pinochle?"

Tell him no because the snake venom turned you blind for a year.

The young white man will say, "I think I got it. Thanks, Sulking Ernie Poutyface."

Then pick up your guitar and just start yelling something about being mistreated by a woman who doesn't like drunk, penniless people who write thirty songs a day about what huge assholes their ex-wives were. The young white man will pretend to enjoy it. Ask him for fifty dollars before he leaves.

Happy Be the Bluesman Day!

SEPTEMBER 14   FIND YOUR CAT DAY!

Your cat Reggie went missing six months ago. Find him today. When you are raking some leaves, he'll be licking his fur clean behind your neighbor's bushes. Lure him under the fence with your fingers, and then pull him into your arms. Shout, "Reggie, I've missed you!" Reggie will meow really loudly. Your neighbors all along the block will hear the exclamations. They'll run from their homes and burst into tears when they see you cuddling with your cat, whom everyone had presumed dead.

When you walk your cat to your front door, you'll stop when you see Clifford sitting on the top step. Clifford is the cat you rescued after you'd decided Reggie was gone. You got Clifford from the same shelter where you had found Reggie the year prior. Reggie will look at Clifford, and Clifford will look at Reggie.

Reggie will meow as if to say, "Clifford."

Clifford will meow as if to say, "Hello, Reggie."

Reggie will meow as if to say, "How did you trick your way into these nice people's home?"

Clifford will meow as if to say, "They mourned you, Reggie. They mourned you for a very long time. They came and took me in to see if I could help them forget. I've been doing my best to give these people the healing that they need."

Reggie will meow as if to say, "Go. Get away from this house or I swear to God I'll put these claws through your throat, you devious son of a bitch."

Clifford will walk down the steps and to the sidewalk. He'll look back at you once, then he'll continue walking down the block.

Shout, "Clifford!"

Clifford will keep walking. Reggie will nuzzle your neck and you'll take him inside to show to your wife and kids. Reggie and Clifford were in the shelter together. They shared a cage for a while, and Clifford got Reggie mixed up in some pretty scary shit. Reggie never forgave him. Clifford really did a mind job on Reggie, and Reggie had no choice but to cut Clifford out of his life. He knew that if he ever found himself locked up with that cat again, he'd have to take him out or risk surrendering himself to a dark and tragic fate.

Happy Find Your Cat Day!

SEPTEMBER 15   DATE A WIZARD DAY!

You should date a wizard for several reasons. Number one, you've always wondered what it would be like to date someone who looks more fabulous than you. The right wizard, the one who is still on his way up and isn't burned out on weed, will wear only the finest in bedazzled velvet cloaks. Second, a wizard can make you rich simply by burning a hole through a live frog with some matches. Third, all wizards know how to make a stellar margarita (they use "magic tequila").

A wizard's gonna call you tonight and ask you to go see an Anna Paquin movie with him. Say hell yes.

Happy Date a Wizard Day!

SEPTEMBER 16   JUST FUCKING DRIVE DAY!

Following are situations that will come to pass today in which it is suggested that you shut up and just fucking drive:

⤳ A bank robber hops into your passenger seat and points a handgun at your temple and tells you to "Moooove!" and when you're forty miles outside of town and the bank robber (who is quite attractive as it

happens; been quite a while since there was something worth looking at in that passenger seat, yes?) is trying to burn his flesh wound
into a scab with the cigarette lighter, you hesitantly allow yourself
to glance his way and ask, "So where are we going?"

✧ Tonight you'll go to a disco hoping against hope to meet somebody
who might be willing to pull down your pants. After a few hours
you'll find you've drunk too much to feel desirable and you'll make
your way for the door. A gorgeous woman will have just caught her
gorgeous boyfriend in a ladies' room stall speaking intimately with
an ex-lover. Enraged, she'll stomp across the dance floor in an "eye-
for-an-eye" mind-set. You'll feel her hand grip your arm and she'll
ask, "Do you have a car?" You'll nod and she'll drag you out to the
parking lot and practically lead you to your Honda. As you drive aim-
lessly, she won't speak. She'll only stare out the window as if her
eyes could set fire to everything they look upon. You'll say, "So
should I take you home?"

✧ You are a school bus driver. You've long since passed the last stop on
your route and you're going seven miles an hour above the speed limit
to get the empty bus back to the garage in time to meet the gang at
McGillicutty's for happy hour. You'll hear a cough. A man's cough.
The bus isn't empty. You'll screech to a halt and turn around in your
driver's seat to stare directly into the bloodied face of your former
chess mentor. You'll say, "I thought you were extradited."

✧ On a dark highway, you'll pick up the hitchhiking ghost of a celebrity
who would like you to not speak but keep driving and who has a pen-
chant for profanity.

✧ Everything behind you is in cinders. Everything up ahead belongs to
someone else. The only thing left is the two of you, side-by-side, and

the forward momentum. The first one to speak is gonna say, "Pull over." The second one to speak is gonna say, "Good-bye."

Happy Just Fucking Drive Day! Remember: Stay alert, stay awake, stay alive and shit.

SEPTEMBER 17   **TWELVE PILLS DAY!**

No one's saying what kind of pills they have to be. That's where you come in. But over the course of the day, you must have taken twelve and only twelve of them. You might choose twelve vitamins if you're watching out for yourself. Or twelve Vicodins if you're up for having a party. Note for those who wanna die: You can only take twelve, so don't pussyfoot around with Flintstones Chewables. Did someone say "fifth of vodka"?

Happy Twelve Pills Day!

SEPTEMBER 18   **HOLD EACH OTHER TIGHT
AGAINST THE COLD MORNING DAY!**

Are you coworkers or are you human beings? You've shared this cubicle for three and a half years already, and yet you've never touched. Every morning the two of you come inside with the skin hanging just a little farther from your skulls. Yet you avert your eyes, you turn your backs, you pull headphones over your ears, and you bend your spines to your desktops.

This morning is cold. It is lonely and mean. You share nearly one-third of your lives together. If you try to dispel with warmth from that third, you will both die more quickly.

Take each other. When you arrive in the morning, pull each other into the less visible corner of your cubicle and huddle into each other's deepest crook and shiver and weep and love. "My brother," whisper. "We are both here, and we are both dying men. Let's do what we can."

Say, "Let's do what we can."

Happy Hold Each Other Tight Against the Cold Morning Day!

| SEPTEMBER 19 | YOU LIVE WITH A MOUSE DAY!

It's small and dark gray with a black spot just above its tail. You don't feed it or take care of it, but you make no effort to kill it. It shares your space. Sometimes, you pretend it's a roommate.

You once pulled the trash bag from the can to find several holes in the bag that nearly caused it to split open wide. The next morning, you left a note on the kitchen table.

"Could we all PLEASE try not to eat through the trash bag? There was a BIG hole in it when I went to take the bag to the Dumpster tonight. Thx!"

Another time, when you were crying because a girl you liked thought you were disgusting, you looked across the room and saw the mouse sitting in the middle of a dirty dinner dish, staring at you. It held still for over a minute, then ran off. You felt he was there for you that night.

Of course, when he ate through the cable of your hair dryer and you got such a bad shock you passed out, you were pretty pissed. But it was nothing another note couldn't solve.

"I almost died this morning. Don't eat my wires."

For richer or poorer, you live with a mouse. And starting tonight, it's gonna start telling you to do stuff.

Happy You Live with a Mouse Day!

SEPTEMBER 20   PAIR UP YOUR SOCKS BEFORE IT'S
                 TOO LATE DAY!

Your therapist asked you not to pair up your socks this weekend after you
do your laundry. He wants you to try to just let them sit in your drawer in
a big unmatched pile, even though you're convinced that leaving them un-
paired will cause your mother to die.

It's been two hours since you threw the socks in the drawer and you're
already entering a state of mourning for what you are certain has happened to your dear sweet mom. To hell with your therapist. If he wants you
to leave your socks a mess he can do his job and prescribe you the right
dosage of medication. Run in there and bundle your socks into neat pairs
and maybe you'll be able to breathe again.

When you're finished, you'll call your mother to see how she is. Your
brother Tom, who still lives with her, will answer. "How's Mom?" you'll
ask him.

"Jesus, are you psychic?" Tom will say.

You won't ask what he means. You won't be able to speak.

Tom will say, "Something's happened."

Happy Pair Up Your Socks Before It's Too Late Day!

SEPTEMBER 21   EAT UNTIL YOU'RE HAPPY DAY!

Do you live alone? Has it been years since you've felt that you could truly
and completely trust another? Do you feel frustrated, not only in your attempts to fulfill your creative and emotional needs with your career, but in
your efforts to even know what those needs might be? Do your parents express indifference as to whether you might come and visit them once more
before they die?

Well then, maybe you should eat more.

You'd be surprised how many people like yourself find temporary spiritual relief in eating. If you just make that minimal effort to eat steadily during hours of consciousness, all that food might seep out of your belly and start to fill up that void in your soul.

"But whenever my belly digests its contents, all the excess hamburger buns and microwave burritos start seeping out of my soul and into my belly to be ground up into nutrients. How do I stop the digestive process?"

Unfortunately, your body keeps digesting food until you die. That's why you must never ever stop eating so that there's always more food on the way when your heart starts to implode in on its own hollowness. Just keep it stuffed up with mashed potatoes and you'll never feel the need to look any farther than your kitchen cabinet for fulfillment.

Are you eating? I bet you feel better already, don't you? Because today's Eat Until You're Happy Day! Hey, who's already forgotten about his libido?

| SEPTEMBER 22 | BE A HERO DAY!

You'll need a shortwave radio or police scanner to keep an ear to the ground for anyone in distress. You should back your car into your parking space so you can pull out fast. Keep your shoes and socks on so you don't have to waste any time choosing footwear when you hear that a woman has been taken hostage by three masked hoodlums at First National Bank, forcing police to stand down. Get over there and tell the pencil-pushing, flat-footed pigs to let you have a crack at the scumbag punks. When you get inside, act like you're going to negotiate, then knock the gun away from the woman's head. Push her out of the way, run up a wall and do a flip through the air, and knock two of the three guys unconscious with a double kick. Then grab a gun that one of them tossed in the air and aim it at the third guy.

Or you could just warn someone that he or she is about to step in a pile of dogshit. Either way, you're totally gonna get laid.

Because today's Be a Hero Day!

| SEPTEMBER 23 | A HUNDRED AND SIX POUNDS DAY!

He'll ask you how much you weigh and you'll ask why and he'll say he just wants to know and you'll say you don't see what difference it makes and he'll say come on just tell me. So you'll say a hundred and six pounds.

He'll say, "All these weekends I've been making love to a hundred and six pounds." You'll say guess so.

He'll say, "I never thought about it like that before. A hundred and six pounds all at once." You'll ask if it would have made a difference if it was a hundred and seven. He'll say, "It would have been a little heavier. By about a pound."

When you have sex again, he'll pick you up and rest you on his thighs. So that all your weight is on him while he fucks you. He'll try to just hold you by your ass and lift you up and down his cock kind of like he's fucking himself with a big toy. But he won't be able to hold you for that long, so he'll sit you on his thighs again. But you won't touch the bed the whole time. It won't feel as good as when you're lying down and he's on top of you, but it's always neat to have sex in a way you've never had sex before. And you'll like seeing how much he digs it. But you won't help but feel a little bad because you haven't weighed less than a hundred and twelve pounds since college. You'll feel bad only because he doesn't care what the number is. He just wants to have sex with you while he knows the number.

Happy a Hundred and Six Pounds Day!

SEPTEMBER 24 | IT'S PORPOISE DAY!

September 24 already?! Wow, it feels like I just took down my Porpoise Day tree. But it's that time of year again, time to celebrate porpoises! So head on down to your local deli counter and mention Porpoise Day to get half-off a prime flank porpoise cutlet!

Happy It's Porpoise Day!

SEPTEMBER 25 | BE THE REASON WHY WE CAN'T HAVE NICE THINGS DAY!

We can't have nice things, and today, you are the reason why. This is probably because you are addicted to drugs and every time someone buys nice things you try and sell them for drug money. Sometimes you don't even sell them. You just carry an armful of TVs and Ming vases down to the corner and hand them over in exchange for a bag of rocks. We know you like to do drugs and the last thing any one of us wants to do is make you feel less groovy, but we like nice things and your drug addiction won't let us have them. You're tearing this family apart.

It's also possible that you're the reason we can't have nice things because you're deranged and you like to play with your own shit. So anytime we buy a nice TV or Ming vase, you run over and smear shit all over it, then you giggle. Admittedly, it is funny. But still!

One last possibility is you died today and we've all disavowed nice things to honor your passing. "What's the point of nice things," our father said. "Nice things won't bring [your name] back." Then he threw all of our TVs and Ming vases at the wall.

In closing, regardless of the specific situation, you are the reason why we can't have nice things, and therefore we wish you had never been born.

Happy Be the Reason Why We Can't Have Nice Things Day!

GO TO STARBUCKS, ORDER A COFFEE, SIT DOWN AT A TABLE WHERE YOU CAN BE SEEN FROM ALL ANGLES, REMOVE THE SHOE AND SOCK FROM ONE FOOT, AND FOR THE NEXT THREE HOURS INTERMITTENTLY LIFT YOUR BARE FOOT UP TO YOUR NOSE AND SMELL IT DAY!

Don't huff it. It's not like you're sweating nitrous oxide. Just calmly drink your coffee, read your book, gaze off with your thoughts, then every five minutes or so let an inquisitive expression cross your face, like, "I wonder if my foot still smells like that." Then casually lift your bare foot above your table and give it a whiff. You should then don a facial expression that says, "Hmm, interesting." Then just put your foot down, sip your coffee, and wish your neighbor a happy Go to Starbucks, Order a Coffee, Sit Down at a Table Where You Can Be Seen from All Angles, Remove the Shoe and Sock from One Foot, and for the Next Three Hours Intermittently Lift Your Bare Foot up to Your Nose and Smell It Day!

SEPTEMBER 27 | OFFER SOMEONE YOU'RE INTO
FIFTY BUCKS TO THINK ABOUT
YOU WHEN HE OR SHE WAKES UP
ALONE IN BED TOMORROW
MORNING DAY!

Throw in another $25 if he or she will promise to wear a crooked little smile that says, "What the heck am I doing thinking about [you!], lying here damp with the sweat of a night alone in my tiny non–air conditioned bedroom. My legs are bent off into different directions and at dumb angles. My T-shirt's riding halfway up my torso, way high up above my belly button and the strip of pubic hair descending down into this old ripped-up pair of sleeping-alone underwear. And the first thing in my mind is [you!]? Guess I'm lookin' for trouble."

Oh shit. If you get away with only spending $75 for this, the person you're into is a whore because this shit is worth $500. If he or she says it would be wrong to take money for something he or she does every morning anyway, you'll probably lose all interest because the person will have presented him- or herself as attainable.

Happy Offer Someone You're Into Fifty Bucks to Think About You When He or She Wakes Up Alone in Bed Tomorrow Morning Day!

SEPTEMBER 28 | **MASTURBATING WHILE LYING NAKED ON A FULL-LENGTH MIRROR USED TO GET YOU OFF IN NO TIME, BUT LATELY IT'S JUST GOTTEN REALLY BELABORED DAY!**

Perhaps it's your diet. Or maybe your efforts to insulate yourself from intimate emotional contact with others have somehow cut you off from yourself. And wasn't it you who spent that week in bed under the impression that you were undeserving of joy?

You're depressed, and lately just catching sight of yourself in store windows makes you feel a little nauseous. How do you expect to keep up the same excitement you used to feel when you first laid that mirror on the ground and made the magic happen?

Maybe you oughta take a good hard look in the mir— Um, or, get medicated.

Happy Masturbating While Lying Naked on a Full-Length Mirror Used to Get You Off in No Time, but Lately It's Just Gotten Really Belabored Day!

SEPTEMBER 29 | **REDEFINE HELL WITH EVERY WAKING MOMENT OF YOUR LIFE DAY!**

"This has got to be as close to hell as you can get," you say from your shared cubicle, drenched with sweat from the crammed-to-the-ceiling subway ride you endured to get to work this morning. "I even feel a little shakey with longing for the substance to which I'm growing addicted," you say aloud, proving you might also be losing a grip on your frame of mind. "And to top it all off, I have this nagging suspicion I'm going to die with a false sense of entitlement, owing to the innate talent I have always possessed but never applied to any project of real and obvious substance. This has gotta be the definition of hell, right?"

Just then, you'll be mouth-raped by an elderly man. "I stand corrected," you'll say.

Happy Redefine Hell with Every Waking Moment of Your Life Day!

SEPTEMBER 30   PRAY TO BABY JESUS TO HELP YOU FIND LOTS OF MONEY DAY!

Just explain things to him. Say, "Baby Jesus, when I went to my high school reunion everyone seemed richer than me. All my old friends and enemies seemed to have found lots of money, either by marrying someone who had already found some or by going to college. I wanna find lots of money, and I need your help. Give me a sign that tells me where there's some money hidden. Like how about if you get a camel to lead me to an abandoned building where drug dealers, who are all dead, stashed gajillions of dollars because the heat was coming around the corner? Or just put a bag of thousand-dollar bills on my coffee table. Thanks, Baby Jesus. I always knew you weren't a fucking asshole."

Happy Pray to Baby Jesus to Help You Find Lots of Money Day!

OCTOBER

AT THE STRONG MAN COMPETITION, TRY TO BE JUST.

| OCTOBER 1 | DOODLE A COCK AND BALLS DAY!

You haven't doodled a cock and balls in ages! Remember how much fun it used to be? How many public school desktops must have shown your work over the years? Go on. Doodle a cock and balls. You can even put it on a Post-it and stick it to your spouse's forehead while he or she is napping. That'd be funny.

Happy Doodle a Cock and Balls Day!

| OCTOBER 2 | "NICE FUCKIN' FOLIAGE, ASSHOLE!" DAY!

Today is about the fact that even when it seems like nothing will ever make this life worth living ever again, God snaps his fingers and shouts, "Zam! Whaddaya think o' them apples?" And you suddenly find yourself in the midst of the most wonderful moment that has ever gone down on this big dumb planet.

How wonderful, you ask? Well let's say you're on a weekend excursion up to New Hampshire to get a look at the changing leaves. You park your car by the side of the road to check out a block of houses known countywide for their front lawn displays of beautiful autumn color. And they even have a contest every year for who flashes the best auburn glow.

So you're admiring a few acres of artfully maintained oak and maple trees.

Just as you're complimenting the landowner on his beautiful display, an '89 Honda Civic hatchback slows to a crawl just behind you. The bearded fellow behind the wheel (his young son sitting beside him) cups his hands to his mouth and shouts out the window, "Nice Fuckin' Foliage, Asshole!!!"

The Civic keeps moving to just a few houses down and turns into the driveway of yet another home sporting a jaw-dropping display of red and yellow blur. The homeowner you were speaking to gives his forearm an "up yours" slap in his neighbor's direction, then tips his hat to you before trudging back through his front door.

Happy "Nice Fuckin' Foliage, Asshole!" Day!

| OCTOBER 3 | THE GIRL WITHOUT ANY HANDS DAY! |

"Buy you a drink?" you'll ask. The stool beside her will be empty.

"Take a seat," she'll say.

Order two gin and tonics. "One with a straw."

"You're very considerate," she'll smile.

"I gotta ask," you'll say.

"I hurt someone once. More than I ever thought I could hurt anybody. He put his heart in my hands."

Say, "You gotta learn to forgive yourself." Then clink your glass with hers and sip.

"Where were you when I was grinding through my wrists with a table saw?" she'll ask.

Look deep into her eyes. "If I had been there," say, "we'd be shaking on it right now."

Look'a dat smile!

Happy the Girl Without Any Hands Day!

BACKRUB TRAIN DAY!

The backrub train of 1995 stretched from border to border across the state of Delaware, with 739 backs getting deliciously kneaded within the southeastern tip of Pennsylvania. It's time for you to break that record.

"We can cover Delaware," you think. "But our overspill into Pennsylvania might not hit 739. Atkins has really shrunk folks down."

Is that the organizer of the Rhode Island Hands Across America branch who's saying "I can't"? Could it be? Could it be the same man who stretched a girl-on-girl oral sex daisy chain around the perimeter of the Grand Canyon in 1979 is calling it quits?

"You're right. Eight hundred backs will be rubbed in Pennsylvania tomorrow morning. We've got the recruitment push, we've got the massage oils. Goddammit, we've got the goods."

There goes the best Guy-Who-Can-Make-a-Lot-of-People-Do-Shit-in-a-Single-File-Line there ever was.

Happy Backrub Train Day!

CHRISTIANITY TIME DAY!

Your son's six. It's time to teach him about Jesus Christ.

Give a knock on his door, then poke your head in. He'll be playing with a Spider-Man doll.

"Hey, kid," say to him. "Guess what time it is."

"Payback time?" he'll ask. His name's Greg, your son.

"Nope," say. "It's Christianity time."

Greg will say, "Aw yeah."

"Were you waiting for this talk?" ask.

"The kids at school have been talking a lot about Jesus Christ," Greg will say. "And I felt left out because I didn't know who he was."

Sit down on the edge of his bed and say, "I'm sorry, kid. I've just been so busy at work."

"It made me feel really sad and alone. Not knowing who Jesus Christ was, I mean," Greg will say.

"Well, I'm gonna tell you who he was so stop it with the guilt trip," say.

Greg will lean back on his heels and fold his arms in front of him in that adorable "I'm listening" posture. It's so cute that it kind of pisses you off a little, really.

Tell it to him thusly: "Jesus Christ was the nicest person in all of humanity. He could turn water into wine and rocks into money. He could tell the future, and he couldn't die. He's the reason you're here today. Because without him, there wouldn't even be a planet, because he fought off the alien worms."

Then take his hands and place them in front of him, palms together. Say, "This is what it looks like when you believe in Jesus Christ. Keep your hands pressed together like this whenever you want to talk to Jesus about stuff."

Greg will close his eyes and start talking to Jesus in an adorable little whisper. You won't be able to hear what he's saying, but you can bet he's talking about what a great guy his dad is.

Happy Christianity Time Day!

| OCTOBER 6 | POOR AND NINE MONTHS PREGNANT, THE CALENDAR DAY! |

It's what you like to look at and no one should try to judge you for it. Women, usually sitting on bare mattresses, their faces smudged, their bellies distended, their eyes on a fuzzy TV across the room on the floor.

It's not sexual. It just evokes a very specific future in a way that nature scenes and asses on Ferraris can't seem to manage.

Luckily, you secured the cubicle with an additional privacy wall that is not visible to anyone walking past. While you have to wheel around in your chair a bit to get a look at that month's destitute mom-to-be, at least you won't be getting any passive-aggressive memos about appropriate personal space decoration like you did last year. By the way, wasn't March heartbreaking?

Happy Poor and Nine Months Pregnant, the Calendar Day!

| OCTOBER 7 | BOYFRIEND IN A SWEATER-VEST DAY! |

Your boyfriend showed up in a sweater-vest you've never seen him wear before. It shows the shape of his belly.

You're only meeting for coffee before he heads out to meet a friend and you go and run some errands, both of you ending up in your separate apartments for the night. And he is wearing a button-up shirt and an undershirt underneath the sweater-vest.

So how do you convince him to have sex with you wearing only the sweater-vest? As soon as he walked through the door you decided that's the only thing that matters anymore, him entering you while wearing only a sweater-vest. But how?

You first have to convince him to cancel his plans with his friend and take you to his place or your place. That's not too difficult. You rarely demand his body in an urgent kind of way, and he's always more than accommodating when you do. But how do you tell him to remove his pants and socks, then remove his sweater-vest, remove his shirt and undershirt, then put his sweater-vest back on, *then* penetrate you?

You could, if you've talked to each other this way before, tell him right there in the coffee shop exactly what you want, i.e.: "I want you to fuck me in that sweater-vest right now, but only in the sweater-vest. I want to feel your bare shoulders stubbing out from the wool." He'll be fine with it, especially if you've talked to each other this way before. At the very least, he'll be flattered that you like his new sweater-vest. Even the most brazen consumer likes to have his purchases validated.

But if you tell him everything up front, you might blow your wad right there. Now he'll know what's burning inside you. Now you'll both have an entire commute home to think about you wanting to fuck a dude in a sweater-vest and what that means. He'll wonder if your ex used to wear sweater-vests. You'll remember all the sweater-vests your ex used to wear. By the time you get home, the last thing either of you will want to see is that fucking sweater-vest. But you'll still go through with it and you'll both be disappointed and you'll fight until one of you gives up and goes home to sleep alone and in peace.

The best way to handle this is step-by-step. First get him in bed. Again, this isn't difficult. Remind him that in bed is where he gets to have intercourse with you and he'll remember that intercourse feels good and he'll say, "No sweat." Now, just like normal, kiss and grope and peel off clothing, but try to keep him from penetrating you. Then once he's completely naked say, "Can you put your sweater-vest back on?" If he bothers to ask why, just say, "I like how it feels on my skin." But he won't bother to ask why because all males would prefer to have sex with some of their clothes still on. All of them.

Happy Boyfriend in a Sweater-Vest Day!

| OCTOBER 8 | SURPRISE PARTY DAY!

Your boyfriend of two months organized a surprise party for you. That's why the living room is covered in streamers. And that's why it doesn't look like he has anything planned for your birthday beyond the two of you sitting in a living room covered in streamers. There is a lot to eat in the refrigerator. A great variety of snacks and dips in large serving bowls that your boyfriend hastily hid away when he realized no one was going to come. You should sit him down and explain.

"Like the streamers?" he'll ask. "Hey, let's buy a movie off of digital cable. Whatever you want."

Say, "Listen. I know what you tried to do and I really appreciate it. But there are a few things you should know about me."

"Mm-hmm?"

Just breathe deep and hope for the best. That's all you can do, right? You never know, he might still wanna stick around.

Say, "So here's how it is. I used to be friends with this girl Gina. Best friends actually. Since ninth grade we were inseparable."

"I heard her name come up some of the times we've been out but I don't think I've met her," he'll say.

"No. You wouldn't have. See, Gina was married to this guy Karl. And me and Karl, we kind of had an affair while Gina was pregnant with their first baby. The affair went on for a few months, but Gina got wise and started following Karl. She finally caught us together when she followed him here, to my apartment, where we were celebrating my birthday."

"Oh," he'll say. He'll be staring at very little.

"That night, Gina miscarried. She left town soon after."

Big long silence from the boyfriend. Then: "So that's why no one came to the party?" he'll ask.

"Because it's the anniversary of my friend's miscarriage and the dissolution of her marriage," you'll say. "Yup."

"Both of which you caused?" he'll ask. He's looking you in the eye. That's a good sign.

"Karl had a hand in it too, but yeah. Most people lay the blame on me," you'll say. Don't take his hand even though he seems to be laying it out there on the couch for you to take.

He'll reach across the couch toward you. You'll stiffen, afraid he's going to slap you. But he'll take you by the shoulder and say, "My God, your birthday's ruined forever by a sad memory, you poor little thing." And holy shit if he doesn't pull you into a deep soft hug.

"Oh. Oh, baby," you'll say.

"Well we're just going to smother that sad memory with a big pile of happy ones. Starting with some mini golf. Get your pants."

Take a second and watch him standing there by the couch waiting for you to get your pants so he can take you to mini golf for your birthday. Whatever happy memories there are to come, it will be hard to top this one.

Happy Surprise Party Day!

| OCTOBER 9 | GIPSY KINGS MOBILE DAY! |

You had it made special by the homosexual artist fellow who lives down the block. He took the photos you gave him and painted the likenesses onto durable plastic cutouts.

"Black jeans on all of them," you said. "Faded."

"Like hope in the desert," said the homosexual artist fellow.

You smiled. Your baby's mobile was in good hands.

Your wife won't be there when you send it on its first spin. She doesn't understand.

"He's a baby and shit," she said. "He should be staring at giraffes and monkeys and shit."

"I had to wait until I was fourteen before I was first introduced to the Gipsy Kings," you said. "My son will have a better life."

You hold the mobile up to the light and stare at those melodic little men bouncing on their strings. You wish you were young enough to sleep underneath a mobile like this one.

"I'd tell you all what happened to me today," you whisper to the little men.

Finally, it's time. Your son is in his crib, kicking at the air and ogling up at you.

Say to your boy, "It's for you, Nicolas. These are good men, all of them. And they'll take care of you."

From the doorway, your wife will say, "Your father loves you, Nicolas."

She'll join you by the crib, kiss your cheek, and stare down at her son. "He has a fantasy, Nicolas. Your father's fantasy is only to make you happy."

Squeeze her close, then reach up and flick the switch on the mobile. The brilliant little men will begin to spin as the first precious notes of a music-box "Bamboleo" begins to play.

Whisper to the little men, "Today, I gave my son a pleasant dream."

Happy Gipsy Kings Mobile Day!

OCTOBER 10 | YOUR SISTER FLEW IN TO HEAR YOUR FATHER'S WILL DAY!

You'll have had a lot to drink so you'll barely make it to the airport alive. You'll circle the terminals twelve times over because you won't have the clarity of mind needed to change lanes. You'll finally pull over in front of the correct terminal and go inside to the baggage carousel.

Your sister will be sitting on the edge of an empty carousel, talking into her cell phone. Talking to your mom probably, asking where the hell you are. Stagger to her.

"Hey, Eve," you'll say.

"Forget it, he's here," she'll say before clapping her phone shut. "What the hell took you so long?"

"I got . . . oh, you know." You'll pick up one of her bags and it will throw you off balance.

"What the fuck?" she'll ask. "Mom sent you out driving like this?"

"She's a lot worse off than me," you'll say. "You should probably drive home. I'm lucky to have made it here."

Your sister will grab her bag from you and she'll march through the sliding doors. She'll ask you where the car is, and it won't take long for her to gather that you parked it illegally and it is presently being torn apart and searched by an explosives team. Your mom's is a one-car household, so your sister is going to have to pay $78 for a cab ride. This last will and testament your dad wrote better be a good fucking read.

Happy Your Sister Flew In to Hear Your Father's Will Day!

OCTOBER 11   BE THE LEAF MONSTER DAY!

Get out to the sidewalk about five minutes early to wait for the guys in your carpool to pull up. Five minutes will be just long enough for you to completely bury yourself in that pile of leaves you had your kid rake up all weekend. A good measure of whether anyone can see you is daylight. There should be none there under your beautiful blanket of dead leaves. Just crouch still and don't breathe. To pass the time while you wait for the car to pull up, why not worry that a dog is going to pee on you?

When you hear the car pull up, wait just a moment, just long enough for your coworkers to wonder, "Hey, what's taking Debbie so long?" Just when they're debating whether to break the cardinal carpool rule and tap the horn, that's when you spring up from the pile of leaves with your hands hooked over like long-clawed paws high above your head. As the leaves shower to the ground around you, summon from the depth of your bowels an unholy: "RRRRRROOOOOOOOOOOOWWWWWWWHHHHHHHRRR!!!"

Dave, who's always sitting in the backseat craning his neck to covet your low-crime suburban neighborhood, will be the first to spot you and he'll alert everyone else to you by saying, "OH JESUS!!! IT'S THE FUCKING LEAF MONSTER!!! DRIVE, BOB! DRIVE! DRIVE! DRIVE!"

Lumber toward the car, arms still above your head, with big, reverberating steps through the dewy grass. Bob will try to get the car in gear but true to form (just like he bungled the Winthrop Hammerlens account), the car will jolt in reverse right toward you. That's when you should toss your briefcase aside and hop atop the trunk of the car. Ashok, who to this point has kept his cool, will now send through his gaping mouth a slow whisper that assesses the situation to a tee.

"Ohhhhh dear God almighty . . ."

Dave will be crying too hard to tell the sound of your fist thrusting through the rear windshield from the sound of the screaming through his own bald little head. He won't have time to compare before you send your claws deep into his throat and clench your paw around his voice box to keep him from waking the neighbors. Send Dave's head to the door frame with enough force to pin his skull to the coathook. Ashok will run from the car. Funnily enough, he'll run in between the houses to the other side of your block where you happen to know three other leaf monsters are waiting impatiently for their breakfast.

Bob should have gotten the car started by now, so make sure you've got your balance when you climb up on the roof to punch a hole through it. You might stub a claw on the top of Bob's head if you punch too hard, so pull back. You just want to slam a hole big enough to get your elbow through so you can have the wiggle room necessary to rip Bob's scalp from his skull. He shouldn't have gotten the car up above thirty miles an hour before he goes into shock, so the car should just ease to a stop about a block and a half down if it doesn't run up onto somebody's lawn first. When it stops, pull Bob up through the hole in the roof and lay him across your lap. Then tear him in two at the waist, tossing the legs and crotch to the street below, and sink your head into his intestines to feed.

Once you're stuffed, walk back to your house and tell your son he's gonna have to drive you to work in his car and you'll write him a note to excuse his tardiness to high school.

Happy Be the Leaf Monster Day!

OCTOBER 12 | HE CAN REDUCE YOU TO TEARS WITH JUST A SHIVER OF HIS CURLY HAIR DAY!

You don't know that you can make it through an entire dinner without stabbing yourself in the back of your hand with a fork he's just so goshdarn delicious.

"So you're unemployed?"

"Mmm," he says, his mouth overflowing with baked ziti. "Hopin' to stay that way too. 'Cept I don't have any money."

You place your hand over his, and you say, "I'll get this then."

He smiles, like you just made a joke. He assumed you'd be paying from the get-go.

"You got a nice body," he says. *Hooray!* your heart shouts into your veins. He *does* like me, he *does* like me!

"Thank you," you say with a shy smile.

"You don't look like my ex-girlfriend at all," he says. "For the first six months after the breakup I only messed around with girls who looked like her. Now I'm trying to go the opposite route."

"Has it been working out so far?" you ask with some play in your eyes.

He shrugs. "I don't care."

"I don't normally behave this way," you say. "But when you finish eating your entrée, would you mind terribly if we went straight back to my place?"

"To fuck?" he asks. There's a chunk of sausage on his chin.

"Yes," you say. "I swear this isn't the way I am all the time. There's just something about you that makes me want to skip over all the usual games."

His mouth wide open, he chews his ziti, then says, "I wanna stop at a bar first. I wanna get some beers in me first."

You smile and nod. "That's fine. I can wait." Then you lean in with a naughty whisper. "But not for too long."

"Look, get off my back!" he shouts. Some tomato sauce hits you in the eye.

"I'm sorry," you say. "Take your time."

For the rest of the evening, try to speak only when spoken to.

Happy He Can Reduce You to Tears with Just a Shiver of His Curly Hair Day!

OCTOBER 13   CASH IN DAY!

"Fuck my artistic integrity," you'll tell your wife. "I'm gonna make me some dollars."

She won't say it out loud, but she'll regret having married you.

"What?" you'll say. "Why should everyone else get rich while I starve on the ground floor trying to wrest my vision from the recesses of my soul?"

She'll shrug. She'll go about cutting coupons.

"You telling me you like this life?"

Take her scissors away from her.

"I'm doing it so I can provide for you, baby," you'll say.

"I never wanted my husband to be my provider," she'll say. "I wanted him to be my hero."

She'll go about cutting coupons, and you'll go back to your workshop. (You carve vaginas out of soap. It's your "statement.")

Happy Cash In Day!

OCTOBER 14   THE WINNERS DAY!

The winners are having sex with each other (all nine of them) inside a glass chamber full of money. Occasionally, they ring a bell, at which time an unattractive person is brought to stand before the wall of the glass chamber. The winners will stop having sex long enough to watch the unattractive person be shot in the back of the head. The unattractive people who sign on to be murdered before the eyes of the fornicating winners are usually parents who don't feel very "needed" by their adult children. They are more than happy to give up their lives in exchange for sharing a moment of private company, albeit from behind a glass dividing wall, with the winners.

"Does it bother you," asks Jamie, winner of The Prize, "that we can no longer be excited by something as carnal as group sex without the addition of a human volunteering to be slaughtered for our entertainment?"

Mark, winner of The Award, shrugs his shoulders. "I don't let it get to me. It's a scary thought, true. I mean, what about when we no longer get a charge from these murders? What will we resort to next?"

Linda, winner of The Medal, scoffs at the lot of them. "We'll do whatever we like," she says. "And no one will object to it. The very fact that we desire it makes it right. The outside world feels this is so; why shouldn't we?"

Martin, winner of The Trophy, stops caressing his genitals so that he might look again at the unattractive woman lying dead at the foot of their chamber, her very human blood seeping out from her wound to form an expansive puddle on the floor. Martin feels a little sick now, but he'll continue to have sex with his fellow winners once they resume.

Happy the Winners Day!

OCTOBER 15   MOM ON THE LAM DAY!

Your mom used to rob banks, and she's been on the run from the police for around twelve years now. Every once in a while she drops in for money and some food. Today is one of those times.

You'll wake up this morning when your dad pokes his head into your room and shouts, "Your mom's upstairs. You can skip school and spend time with her. Don't answer the phone or the doorbell. I'm going to work."

She'll be sleeping soundly when you get upstairs. You'll say her name to wake her but she won't budge. This will clearly be the first sleep she'll have had in days. You'll sit by her bed and wait several hours for her to finally wake up.

When she opens her eyes and sees you, she'll say, "Police?"

Shake your head no. Your mom will say, "I gotta split. You have anything you wanna talk to me about?"

Say, "I like a boy."

"My God, you've grown up so much," your mom will say. "Is he cute?"

Tell her that he is but he doesn't like you back.

Your mom will say, "Forget him. You're too pretty to waste your time." She'll take the gun from her handbag and check the clip for bullets.

"No one at school seems to agree with you," tell her.

"They're all blind. You're the most beautiful girl I've ever seen."

Say, "You've barely seen me for two seconds."

Your mom will say, "And that's all it took."

You'll both hear a rustling in the bushes out back. Your mother will stiffen like a wildcat. She'll cock her pistol, then she'll grab your face in her hands. "I love you, and I'm sorry I haven't been able to be a mother to you. You should never forgive me for running away. You should hate me for it. But I hope you'll always let me into your home."

You're angry that she's going. "Because you'll need money?"

Your mom will say, "Because if I ever thought I was out of your life I'd have no reason to stay free. I'd have no reason to stay alive."

You'll be about to remind her that you could see her more often if she were in prison, but she'll already be kissing your mouth good-bye. The front door will bust open at the same time she throws herself from the bedroom window to the backyard below.

As the police swarm into your home, you'll stare at yourself in the mirror. "I'm too pretty to waste my time," you'll say. Your mom was right. It's right there in the mirror.

Happy Mom on the Lam Day!

OCTOBER 16   BURGLARS DAY!

Today, burglars all over the nation are postponing that one last score so that they can head into the park for a nice friendly here-comes-autumn picnic. Burglars don't find time to get together as often as they'd like. It's hard to take them off the job. Even today, they're not gonna take off the ski masks. At least not at first.

At first it'll just be the same as always. Everyone will crowd around the burglar who brought a velvet cloth full of diamonds. They'll ooh-aah while he says, "Isn't that a great diamond? I'm a hell of a burglar." But eventually, the sun will send them all to the blanket, peering up at the blue sky, wiping their minds clean of safe-cracking shortcuts and generic chloroform price hikes. Soon, one of them will whip out a Frisbee, and they'll be running this way and that like a bunch of little kids on the first day of spring (albeit in ski masks).

The picnic on Burglars Day never goes sour. Everyone leaves happier than they came, and full of just a little bit more cold fried chicken. Last year, one of the female burglars hit it off with one of the male burglars and they went for a walk. This year, they're coming back wearing wedding rings they stole for each other.

See you at the park, unless you're in jail.

Happy Burglars Day!

OCTOBER 17   YOUR KID'S PIGGY BANK IS EMPTY DAY!

This is warning sign number two that he's addicted to the pot. Warning sign number one was when he was rude to his mother the other night. And warning sign number three is on its way. That's when he'll run through the living room naked, tearing at his own flesh, screaming "GET 'EM OFF ME! GET 'EM OFF ME!"

Just so's you can keep an eye out, here are all the rest of the warning signs that your kid's addicted to the pot:

4. You find him in his little sister's room, forcing the barrel of a semiautomatic weapon in between her teeth (she's nine).
5. Lots of slovenly people going in and out of his room scratching at sores on their arms.
6. Unraked leaves.
7. He can levitate.
8. He is dead and there's nothing you can do about it now because you didn't heed the warning signs.
9. He is fathering children left and right.
10. He talks endlessly about how awesome the pot is and how it's the best thing ever.
11. When you ask him if he wants to go play mini golf with you on the weekends he just doesn't seem all that interested.
12. He has withdrawn roughly $78,000 from your bank account.
13. Snot pours out of his nose like water from a spigot.

If your kid exhibits any or all, or hell, even none of these signs, he's probably addicted to the pot, and you should beat him with a ring of keys until he's better.

Happy Your Kid's Piggy Bank Is Empty Day!

OCTOBER 18   ALL YOUR GUNS DAY!

"I'm frightened for the girl," say.

"But you love your guns," your husband will say. He is so very support-ive of you.

And you do love your guns. The hunt for a special addition to your collec-tion can take you months at a time. And then there are the little items that you need just to complete a series. Sometimes when you walk out of a gun show you look as if you're not so much "collecting guns" as "amassing arms." But every single pistol has its own special meaning for you.

"But she could get hurt. She's twelve now. Getting curious."

Your husband will rub the whiskers of his chin. "I see where you're go-ing with this," he'll say. "She's waking up to her sexuality. And only a blind man wouldn't see the virility seething out the barrel of a handgun. You're afraid she's gonna go down there and . . ."

"Jesus!"

Your husband will stop rubbing his chin.

"I'm simply afraid of an accident. I couldn't live with myself if my weapons brought harm to my baby."

Your husband will kneel down before where you're sitting and put his hands on your shoulders. "You are the greatest of all time. To act so self-lessly."

He's going to start crying again. "Get it together," say.

He'll take a deep breath. "We've taught her again and again how to be-have around the guns. Her education is her safety. I don't think we have anything to worry about."

Think for a second. Then say, "All the same, I think I should get rid of the ones that go off by themselves when it gets hot in the summer."

He's just gonna start crying again. Go for a drive.

Happy All Your Guns Day!

OCTOBER 19 | THE MARINES DAY!

The armed forces are being pitted against each other in a battle to the death and you should root for the Marines. The Marines are just a bunch of hard-luck cases. Like growed up orphans who know how to kill. No one would root for the air force because they have all the spaceships. If it's a bunch of guys running around on the ground versus a spaceship, only a dick would root for the spaceships. The navy's more about keeping their boots shiny and staying out of trouble so as not to be banned from the Saturday night "Everyone on the Boat Fucks Everyone Else on the Boat" topside orgy. And the army is all about road repair nowadays.

But the Marines. They're the guys who just don't wanna have to go home and raise their kids. Every last one of them has gotten into a mixed-race fistfight, and they've all cried into the arms of a heterosexual member of the same sex. You want the Marines to win even though they make you feel small. You can't resist getting behind the guy who could snap at any minute.

Happy the Marines Day!

OCTOBER 20 | FACEBITES DAY!

Your wife hates you. She hates you so much that she sometimes stares at you while you sleep, miserable with just how much ugly she has to cede half her bed to. The more she stares, the more her blood boils, until she spreads her jaw open wide, wracks her head down at your face and rips her teeth into the skin on either side of your nose, trying to rip the center of your face off in her maw.

You wake up screaming into her neck. She recoils and cowers into the corner of the bedroom. You pant by the pillows, blood pouring forth from the gashes in your face. She says, "I hate you so much I'm gonna kill you one night. While you sleep."

Happy Facebites Day!

| OCTOBER 21 | STOP HIS LOTTO PLAYING, HE'LL LEAVE YOU BEHIND DAY! |

The plans are laid for a beautiful future together. You're continuing your apprenticeship as assistant director of the community Y. He's in his second semester at community college in pursuit of a business degree.

"We're gonna make it right," you say.

"Then we're gonna make a family," he says.

And yet, every single day he buys himself a lotto ticket. Why even go to school if he's putting his hat in the ring to ride a gravy train outta town? Why all the planning? The promises?

"Why do you waste your money on those stupid lotto tickets?" you say.

"It's fun. I like to dream of what kind of life we'd lead if I won a hundred million dollars."

If he won a hundred million dollars, he'd go down to the office to claim the money. He'd call you up to tell you everything's right as rain and they're honoring his ticket. But he'd have to stay down there to meet with some financial advisors recommended to him by the commission.

The next time he'd call would be to tell you to watch the TV, because they're gonna announce him as the winner. After, when you tell him over the phone how handsome he looked up on that stage, he'd say he's not coming home because he's been told he'll be swamped with pleas for handouts. But he'll call soon to say where he is.

A few days later, he'll call once more, saying he's being moved for the third time. People keep tracking him down and showing up at his doorstep with their empty hats shining up at him. "Everyone wants a piece of me, here. They're trying to suck my blood. I can't trust nobody no more."

You'll say, "I love you."

He'll say, "Ah ha!" and hang up the phone.

You'll never hear from him again. I don't know what your mother will say to make you feel better about it all. I don't know if she's aware of what a team of financial advisors can do to a young couple in love.

Happy Stop His Lotto Playing, He'll Leave You Behind Day!

| OCTOBER 22 | YOU ARE A DESIGNER OF GIFT WRAP DAY! |

Here are the top-selling patterns from your line:

1. Vaginas and Some Rainbows
2. Locker Combinations to Famous People's Gym Lockers, and Some Santa Clauses
3. Leonardo DiCaprios in Race Cars and the Word "Baby"
4. Christmas Trees and Sandwiches
5. A Chart of Presently Legal Assault Weaponry

Today you unveil the Your Dead Son and Some Fire Engines line. It's misguided, but you miss your dead son so much you have no choice but to watercolor him all over your gift wrap. As usual, fans of your designs have already pre-ordered seven thousand rolls without even a preview. You're rich and really crazy.

Happy You Are a Designer of Gift Wrap Day!

| OCTOBER 23 | SHE IS WAITING UP FOR YOU DAY! |

Are you going to tell her that you didn't want to come home?

Are you going to tell her you were up late judging a strong man competition at the beach? That bright lights and turntables were hooked up to power generators while gigantic men tried to hoist heavy weights above their heads? That you were just standing in the muck of the crowd eating an Icee when the host and the sponsor's representative started looking for judges and the host pointed to you and said, "How 'bout that guy?"

And the sponsor's representative (Baja Fresh) said, "The guy with the Icee. Get on up here."

Are you going to tell her that there were two other judges? One a graphic designer. He leaned into your ear and whispered, "I'm new in town, and I hope you'll be my first new friend." One a poet. She leaned into your ear and whispered, "Would you believe my boyfriend and I broke up just thirty hours ago? I haven't even slept yet, and here I am judging a strong man competition." Would she believe it if you told her?

Are you going to tell her that you were the tie breaker who put a pale giant named Sven into the winner's circle? Are you going to tell her that you danced with two hundred people who had just been soaked with a hose? That you watched two dozen people jump naked into the ocean (too cold for you)? That you ate a dozen clams and drank a dozen beers? That you had so much fun, so very much fun, you just couldn't let the very best night of your life come to an end?

Or are you just going to tell her that you didn't want to come home?

Happy She Is Waiting Up for You Day!

| OCTOBER 24 | TRAVELING BOYS WHO CUDDLE DAY! |

You and your friend Curtis are poor, and you're traveling across the country to find Curtis's dad, which means you are allowed to cuddle nonsexually to keep warm at night. You should consider yourselves very lucky because there are lots of boys with money or with roofs over their heads who would like to cuddle with each other to keep warm, but they don't because they're scared God will send a hurricane to their town. But God will buy that you and your friend Curtis need to keep warm, so he'll let you cuddle as long as there is no hope for penetration in your hearts.

So tonight when the fire goes out, ask Curtis if he'd like to cuddle with you to keep warm.

"What about God?" Curtis will ask.

Say, "I think he's cool with it. We're cold. And you're pitiful because you don't know where your dad is. You need closeness where you can find it."

You and Curtis will decide to fistfight first, just to prove to God that you think that boys who are thinking about cuddling should be beaten up. After one of you wins the fight, curl up together and spoon.

Curtis will say, "This was a good idea."

You'll say, "I never knew myself until I grabbed hold of you."

Curtis will ask what you mean. Tell him you're just singing a rap song.

Before you go to sleep, Curtis will start to cry and ask if you think he'll ever find his dad. Tell him yes, then penetrate him. Just as a joke to cheer him up.

Happy Traveling Boys Who Cuddle Day!

OCTOBER 25   THE CLEANING LADY'S GET WELL CARD DAY!

Your office cleaning lady's appendix burst, and she went into the hospital for about ten days. When the news hit the floor, a "get well" card was passed around for everyone to sign. Unfortunately, you had called in sick that day so you never heard anything about any card.

At 3:00 today you're going to find the cleaning lady standing behind you. She's going to thank you for the card, and you're going to assume she's confusing you with someone on the floor who has a name that is similar to yours. She'll explain that she's referring to the card that everyone signed. Your face will go blank for a moment, than you'll try to save the situation and you'll say, "Don't mention it."

The cleaning lady will have spotted your hesitation and she'll take another look at the card. When she discovers that your signature is not on it, she'll run back to your desk crying and calling you a liar who doesn't care about the little people. Everyone else on the floor will listen in, and word will quickly spread that you did not bother to sign the cleaning lady's get well card, but that you took credit for it anyway.

You'll try to explain to whoever will listen that you would have been happy to sign the card, had you been in the office that day. You'll send around an officewide memo explaining that you only pretended to have signed the card because you didn't want to create an awkward situation by telling her you never signed it. No one will pay heed to your explanations, so you'll have to pay someone to kidnap the cleaning lady's daughter so that you can pretend to rescue her and return to your workplace a hero. You must win their hearts and minds.

Happy the Cleaning Lady's Get Well Card Day!

OCTOBER 26 YOU'RE IN LOVE WITH A CAR THIEF
(BUT WILL HE BELIEVE IT?) DAY!

A white man in his mid-thirties stole your Nissan Stanza eight months ago. For a few days, you didn't know what to do or how to get around. You had many appointments to keep, hair appointments, lunch appointments, appointments with men vying for your hand. Your problems were solved when that white man in his mid-thirties appeared on your doorstep and gasped when he saw your face.

"I found a photo of you in your glove compartment," he said. "I had to come here and risk getting arrested just to see if I could see that face in person."

"You stole my car," you said. You intended to sound angry, but you couldn't. Not when you were looking in his eyes. "Give it back. I need it to get around."

He said, "Then I'll keep it forever. And I'll drive you wherever you need to go."

You invited him in.

The arrangement has worked out swimmingly. He keeps the keys hidden and is ready at a moment's notice to drive you to the shops, to a lake, or to the best restaurant in town. When he's not chauffeuring you in your car, he's making love to you the way you once dreamed someone might, a dream you'd abandoned a few years out of college.

He's the one for you, no question. But are you the one for him?

"I love you," tell him.

"I love you," he'll answer. "Forever."

Say, "I want you to give me back the keys to my car."

He'll object that if you were able to drive yourself, what would you need him for?

"What would someone as wonderful as you need in a car thief?" he'll say. "I have to keep you from being able to drive so you need me for something."

Explain that you need him because of who he is. Because of who you are when you're with him. Because of how happy you are with yourself now that he is near.

"Yeah, but what if all that fades *and* you have keys to the Stanza?" he'll argue. "This is my insurance policy. So if you fall out of love with me you'll still need me to give you a ride."

You can tell him that he doesn't need to worry about that, but it might not work. He's seen love fade before, and he's certain it will happen again. You're going to have to Taser him and grab the car keys out of his pocket. If he won't set you free, you'll have to escape. For the sake of your love.

Happy You're in Love with a Car Thief (But Will He Believe It?) Day!

| OCTOBER 27 | BUYING THE SPECIAL TOY DAY! |

Your kid wants the Mattel Piss Cannon, a toy that has turned into a national phenomenon. It goes on sale this morning at Wal-Mart and will be sold out by 8:00 A.M. Camp out in the parking lot, but do not sleep or you might get your throat slit. When the doors open in the morning, find the biggest toughest mom in the crowd and rip her goddamn throat out her neck to show all the other moms you're not to be fucked with. If you don't acquire a Mattel Piss Cannon this morning, you do not love your son.

Happy Buying the Special Toy Day!

| OCTOBER 28 | WRAPPED UP IN A GIRL DAY! |

When you opened your eyes you were wrapped up in her arms, in her legs, caught up in the gusts of her breath. You were laid flat, rendered defenseless under 110 pounds of a girl you've only had sex with seven times. She wouldn't stop sleeping.

You said, "Wake up, let me go."

Her eyes fluttered and her mouth closed and her lips pursed up into that coy little redheaded smile. Then you wriggled out from underneath her like you just found out she had poison ivy.

She said, "What?"

"I couldn't get away," you said.

She stared, making sure it wasn't a dream. Then she pulled her legs up to her chest and said, so that you could not in a million years think she might need you even the slightest little bit, "Go then." That's when you felt ice cold, like last November, and you stretched back out in bed.

After ten minutes, she wrapped herself up and around you again. After four hours, you said, "I didn't want to leave. It was just . . ." After nine hours she left the bed and came back with an orange cut up into slices.

Happy Wrapped Up in a Girl Day!

| OCTOBER 29 | YOU'RE THEIR COACH! DAY! |

Today you're going to have to do a little more than hand out laps around the field. For the majority of that ragtag bunch of losers (who've got more pluck than you'll find in any rich boy driving to school in a convertible, excluding of course the rich boy who is engaged in a doomed romance with a poor girl) you're the only daddy they've got. You may not have asked for it, but I'm afraid you got the job.

You're their coach! They look up to you. Now one of your players' girlfriends is pregnant and he needs your advice. You tell him to convince her to have that baby and tell him to be a father to his child. Why? I don't know. Just do it!

Tell everyone else to major in auto repair.

Happy You're Their Coach! Day!

OCTOBER 30   WEAR THE SHIRT THAT SAYS "I LOVED HER. I TRIED TO GET HER TO LET ME IN. BUT SHE JUST WANTED TO DIE." DAY!

The guy who administers the driving test will think, "This guy couldn't make a three-point turn if I gave him five points. But somehow I can tell that at one point in his life a woman he cared for got caught in a dangerous downward spiral. He dropped everything to try and help her find her way back, but sometimes people wanna just drop. I can see the tearstains on his collar."

You'll pull the car over and say, "I guess I didn't do that well, did I?"

The guy who administers the driving test will say, "You tried your best, dammit. You're not a god."

Pound on the steering wheel and scream at the sky, "I could have done more!"

The guy who administers the driving test will grab your shoulders and shake you. "You're not gonna find life in your rearview mirror! Life's out there on the road, waiting for you to pull up and give it a ride. Don't! Hitchhiking is illegal."

Say, "Deal."

The guy who administers the driving test will mark you as having passed your driving test. Then he'll cry with you.

Happy Wear the Shirt That Says I LOVED HER. I TRIED TO GET HER TO LET ME IN. BUT SHE JUST WANTED TO DIE. Day!

| OCTOBER 31 | THE RIVER GUIDE DAY!

The river guide is addicted to cocaine. He'll take you to the edge of the earth and introduce you to the horizon of your senses. But first he needs to do some more cocaine, just to give the raft the shove it needs to float on its way.

As he thrusts his giant bamboo rod into the riverbed and drags you along the current at a far enough distance from the banks to avoid blow darts, he starts to imagine his bamboo rod is an enormous rolled-up dollar bill, and he a giant. And the sunny, stretched-out glint of white along the water's surface the most gargantuan and beautiful line of Brazilian cocaine. He gets so excited that he pulls up to the bank of the river to do some more cocaine.

By day three of the search (some guerillas kidnapped your daughter and took her deep into the jungle), the river guide is out of cocaine so he needs some more money from you. You pay, then he starts to drag you back up the river because way back there is the only place he knows that sells cocaine. You realize this is going to bleed a lot of time from the search for your daughter, but you say okay anyway because you need to learn how to assert yourself. You're the kind of person who gives big tips to waitresses even when they're really rude.

Happy the River Guide Day!

NOVEMBER

HE'S JUST A GUY WHO DELIVERS BEDS FOR
SCHEINBERG SEALY SERTA.

NOVEMBER 1 | WAVING A GUN AROUND THE PLACE LIKE A CRAZY PERSON: DO'S AND DON'TS DAY!

Nothing gets people's attention like waving a gun around the place as if you're just going to start shooting everything that queefs. But pick the wrong moment to wave a gun around the place, and you'll totally ruin the mood.

For example, you *should* wave your gun around the place like a crazy person if the place is your son's birthday party and you have something hilarious to say but you can't figure out how to get everyone to keep quiet and listen, because mostly they're all kids. However, you *should not* wave your gun around the place if you're in the middle of a bank robbery. Be a professional. The rest of your crew is counting on you to keep your cool. Wait until you're in the getaway car. Then you can all shoot at the sky in celebration of being good bank robbers.

You *should* wave your gun around the place if you're surrounded by VC. But you most certainly *should not* wave your gun around the place like a crazy person just because you're the best man at a wedding and you can't find the ring. Even if you wave your gun around the place as if you think you're covered in ants, when you stop everyone's just going to ask you to retrace your steps. You can't stop a wedding with a gun. The only thing that can stop a wedding is an uncertain heart.

You *should* wave your gun around the place like a crazy person if you're rescuing your daughter from a crack house. Also, you should fire the gun repeatedly since gunshots can't kill crackheads, but the gunshots will slow them down enough for you to get your daughter the hell out of there. However, you *should not* wave your gun around the place if you're at a dinner party and you suspect someone at the table might have been held up at gunpoint in the past. And you *should definitely not* make anybody open their mouths and suck on the barrel of the gun if you think they might have ever been forced to do that by someone who wasn't making them do it in the spirit of good fun. Get to know your table companions, 'swhat.

Happy Waving a Gun Around the Place Like a Crazy Person: Do's And Don'ts Day!

| NOVEMBER 2 | STOP GIVING YOUR BOYFRIEND
MONEY TO FUND THE DESIGN OF
HIS ROBOT DAY!

It's nice that you believe in your man. You have dreams of one day being revered for having stood by him even when the rest of the scientific community called him "a fraud" and "worse than retarded" and "just a guy who delivers beds for Scheinberg Sealy Serta." But he's determined that he has a grasp on AI, and with enough funding and enough time, he will build the world's first advanced-functioning robot that will finally break down the wall between sophisticated computational programming and artificial intelligence. You don't know what gives him such strong conviction, but by gum you're his lady and you're gonna stand by him.

You really shouldn't. You're a smart, attractive woman with the beginning of a good career in your grasp, and, well, not to sing along with the chorus, but he's just a guy who delivers beds for Scheinberg Sealy Serta. Doesn't it ever occur to you that maybe someone with a background in something like robotics or science or even college might have a shot at beating him to the big breakthrough in AI? There's this place called M.I.T. where they do the kind of thing your boyfriend wants to do, and they do it really well. As far as I know, no one there has a concentration in mattress delivery in their curriculum vitae.

No one's saying break up with him. But last week you gave him $400 for "the little red lightbulbs" he needed to build robot eyes. Today he's going to ask you for $400 more, claiming that he lost the $400 you gave him last week. "I think I dropped it in the park or maybe at the movie theater when I went to see *Doom*. *Doom* ruled."

Just don't give it to him. You don't have to fight about it. Just say that you're out of money right now because your boss is docking your pay for smoking pot on the job. It happens to him all the time, so he'll buy it. And make sure to take all the cash out of your pocketbook and hide it, because in addition to the money he asks you to give him he also sometimes just roots through your pocketbook for twenties.

Happy Stop Giving Your Boyfriend Money to Fund the Design of His Robot Day!

NOVEMBER 3	**PORNOGRAPHY MAKES YOU A BETTER PERSON DAY!**

All twenty-four hours of today are special because today, if you watch pornography, it means you're a better parent. You'll also be able to better accept the fact that good people have to die, even when they're loved by many and do so much good for others. This holiday only comes around once a year, so make the most of it. Rent, purchase, or download as much pornographic material as you can enjoy, and you'll feel yourself grow less likely to suffer from heart disease and more likely to pummel Collins at racquetball this Thursday. Not to mention all those dinner party invitations that

are gonna start pouring in because you're gonna be one hell of a witty sto-
ryteller after watching all that porn!

FAQ

Q: But isn't porn wrong?

A: Who knows?

Happy Pornography Makes You a Better Person Day!

| NOVEMBER 4 | MAKE SOME PROMISES BUT TRY NOT TO BURST OUT LAUGHING DAY! |

You need money to drink for another week, right? I'm betting there's someone who would be thrilled to give you money, a car, even sex if you would
just promise to quit drinking. People go fucking batshit with joy when
someone promises to quit drinking for them. It makes them feel important.
They get way conceited too, acting all, "I matter more than alcohol," as if
that were possible.

It'll come back to haunt them later. Whenever someone is convinced that
her spouse quit drinking for her, she will start blabbing it all over town. She
just can't wait to call up her friends and say, "We're putting the divorce on
hold because Joshua promised to quit drinking for me. That's how fine this
ass is. How's your divorce coming?" Then about ten seconds later, when ol'
Drunkles crashes like seven cars into the living room with a shrug, everyone
in town laughs at the gullible little fool because she got just deserts for being
boastful.

But it's not your fault if someone else brags a lot. All you have to do is
get down on your knees and keep a straight face until you get the cash in
your palm. And once you watch the money unfold in between your fingertips, and you think you might explode with laughter, don't run out the

door without an explanation. Just say something like, "Thanks. Now I gotta go apologize to people for shit I did when I was loaded. I'll be at Flannagan's Tav— Um, *a meeting*." At least you made someone happy for a few minutes, and a few minutes can last a lifetime. Especially if they die a few minutes from now.

Happy Make Some Promises but Try Not to Burst Out Laughing Day!

NOVEMBER 5   DEAD HIPPIES DAY!

More and more dead hippies are pouring out of the sewers into the bay. All of them have dollar signs carved into the back of their heads. As chief of the Coast Guard, it's your responsibility to make sure an investigation gets underway. But no one will listen.

You told the chief of police about it when you, he, and the chief of the fire department met for your Thursday dinner. All he said was, "Hippies. Whoopdie do!" Then he pulled you in real close and told you it's an election year.

The only other two people you told are your wife and the president of the United States. But your wife thinks you're a failure and hasn't listened to a word you've said since 1980. All the president said was, "My hands are tied!" Then he pointed to a chalkboard that had the word "deficit" written on it in big letters.

The going is rough, but you can't give up. Even if you have to spray-paint it onto the face of every child, you must make it known that the hippies are dying. They're almost people too.

Happy Dead Hippies Day!

| NOVEMBER 6 |

SOME GUY'S IN THE BUSHES, AND HE'S GOT A HAMMER IN HIS HAND DAY!

He doesn't look like anyone you've ever dated, but he definitely looks heart-broken. You're only crashing at this house for a few weeks while you wait for all the craziness to die down back in Portland before you go back for the $9,000 you're owed. Your friend Karen lives here with two other girls, Nina and Lisa. You know everyone Karen's ever dated, so this guy must be after Nina or Lisa, you think.

The hammer comes crashing through the glass, and his hand juts through the broken windowpane. The shards of glass slice through his skin like it was all part of the plan.

"Nina and Lisa aren't here," you tell him.

"It's Karen I'm after," he says.

"Really?" you say. "She never told me about you."

"She wouldn't have. She told me I was the one she wanted to keep to herself."

You sit him on the couch and demand to hear everything. His name's Leo and he's a carpenter. Karen had visited his workshop a few times this past spring. One day she said she'd come and never showed, and Leo went out of his mind.

"My business is about to go under. I can't do anything but pursue her. She's breaking me."

"Perhaps you were just a bit of fun for her," you suggest. "If it's not right for both of you, it's not right."

Leo says, "I never thought about it that way."

He apologizes for the window and gets up to leave. Just then you spot Karen outside coming home with her boyfriend. She sees Leo through the broken window and stops in her tracks. To keep Leo from go-ing outside, you grab him and put your tongue down his throat. And thus ends the meet-cute story that you and Leo will one day tell your grand-children.

Happy Some Guy's in the Bushes, and He's Got a Hammer in His Hand Day!

NOVEMBER 7   **SET THE STRAYS FREE DAY!**

Today, you're going to be the last to find out that the city animal shelter puts the animals it rescues to sleep if they aren't adopted within a few weeks. Because you are stupid and you have weapons, you're going to hold the shelter at gunpoint and open up all the cages, trying to get the animals to run out into the street, where they will be cold and underfed and will probably mate, creating more strays. Unfortunately, most of the strays will just run and hide under furniture and in dark crawl spaces throughout the hallways of the building. You'll try to corral them, but it will be hard to gather stray animals while holding the entire staff of the shelter at gun-point. They won't cooperate for very long when you try to lead them as a group through the halls as you look for the animals. Eventually the police will come and you'll turn the gun on yourself. It won't be loaded, but you will point it at yourself and think about what it would be like to die. You'll crap your pants. You'll get arrested and go to jail, where you'll take corre-spondence courses to become a veterinarian. You'll fail them all and turn to white supremacy.

Happy Set the Strays Free Day!

NOVEMBER 8   THIRTEENTH BIRTHDAY!

All across the globe, little boys and girls are taking the big step into adolescence today. They are frightened about what is going to happen to them.

"I'm thirteen now," they'll say. "I'm going to be pregnant soon."

"Only if you're bad," tell them.

"And what's to become of my genitals?" they'll say.

Show them photographs of your and your wife's genitals.

"Oh," they'll say. "And what about smoking?"

Tell them they're not allowed to smoke until they're eighteen, but they should try soon. "To find out whether you like it or not," say. "Pot's a gateway drug," add. "If you smoke a joint, you'll get addicted to crack. You won't be able to control yourself. You'll finish smoking pot and you'll immediately go running out the window to buy as much crack as you can."

When the kids start to talk about the long-term psychological effects of knowing that their fathers are cheating on their mothers, pull them all into a group hug and shout at the sun, "Why?!"

Happy Thirteenth Birthday!

NOVEMBER 9   AFTER THE WAR DAY!

You'll go back to your husband and he'll go back to his wife. Right? That was the plan this whole time. Right? You and he clung to each other only to find some comfort amid all of this bloodshed and insanity. But your hearts were always back home. Right?

"I mean, can you imagine? Us back home?" you'll say with a little too ambitious a laugh from the crook of his arm. (You're on a chopper to Seoul tomorrow, where you'll meet a boat to the States. He's sticking around to pull the tents out of the ground.)

"I can," he'll say. "I'm a five-hour drive from Baltimore."

Your blood will come screeching to a halt in your veins when he says that. "So's your wife," you'll say.

His arm, underneath your head, it's so strong. It's bulletproof. He won't move an inch when he says the following: "I'll be with you in America. If you need me to get a divorce, I will. If you need me to stay married, I will. I'll do whatever you ask, as long as you promise that I'll see you in America. This fucking war brought us together. I'm not gonna let it tear us apart."

You've got some thinking to do, you pretty young black-haired war nurse you.

Happy After the War Day!

| NOVEMBER 10 | COONSKIN CAP DAY! |

The worst part about your wife cheating on you is the way you're going to find out about it. The guy she's having the affair with will leave his hat underneath your bed for you to discover when you're looking for your shoes.

It won't be your everyday kind of hat.

Happy Coonskin Cap Day!

| NOVEMBER 11 | MAGIC PICNIC DAY! |

Plant the bottle of white into the bed of the creek and let it chill. When you get back to the blanket, your companion (Marie, third date) will be sitting there talking to an adorable little six-year-old boy with a bowl haircut.

"Well, who do we have here?" you'll say as you kneel down to the boy.

"You're not gonna believe this," Marie will say. "Tell him."

"I'm Ernest," says the boy.

"Ernest," you'll smile. "Unusual name."

Marie will say, "That was my brother's name. He died when he was sixteen. I was seventeen."

"You never told me . . ."

Marie will shush you with a wave of her hand. "Tell him who you are. Really."

Ernest will smile like he's trying to hold in a giggle. "I'm going to be your son."

Before you get a chance to think twice you'll look at Ernest's nose and think, *That's Marie's nose.*

"Those are your eyes," Marie will say to you.

You'll drop on your ass onto the blanket, staring into the boy's face. Ask how old he is.

"Six."

"And when will you be born?" Marie will ask.

Ernest will giggle and give a shrug that makes your heart melt. Place your hand on Marie's shoulder and she'll grab it like you're pulling her out of a stormy sea.

"I'm your daddy?"

Ernest will nod his head real big.

"And I'm your mommy?"

Ernest will nod again. "You're my mommy," he'll say, proud to know the right answer.

You and Marie will start to laugh with Ernest, occasionally putting your hands to your mouths to stifle a gasp.

"Can I have a grape?" Ernest will ask.

You'll let him pick five grapes from the stalk and he'll stuff all five in his mouth at once, making his cheeks bulge out until he sucks in air and squishes it all down and starts to chew.

"Well," Ernest will say. "Bye-bye."

You'll hold out your hand to shake. "It was nice meeting you, Ernest."

Marie will lean over to kiss his forehead. "I can't wait until we meet again."

Ernest will run across the grass to disappear into the woods.

You and Marie will watch the woods be still for a while, smiling. You won't be able to look at each other without filling up with a blush. You'll kiss a couple times, but you won't say anything. Not even when you get up to get the wine.

When you get to the creek, the bottle of wine will be nowhere to be found. You'll spend maybe ten minutes searching up and down the bank, but it will be gone. You won't help but think that Ernest had something to do with it. And after he's born into your home with Marie three years from now, every time he giggles and shrugs you'll be dying to shake him by the shoulders and accuse him of running off with your booze that day three years before he was born when he came to you as a specter.

Happy Magic Picnic Day!

| NOVEMBER 12 | THE WORLD'S SO BAD TO THE
TEENAGE GIRLS DAY!

It's deep autumn and you don't have a boyfriend anymore. He broke up with you after the Halloween bonfire, saying, "Let's be honest with each other. Before Christmastime, ya know? I mean, what if we bought each other gifts and all?"

The deck chair is wet through your jeans. The sky is steel gray. It's cold enough out that it hurts to cry, but you came out here to the leaf-covered pool so you could be alone and let it all out. You didn't count on your dad finally getting around to summoning the pool guy to gather up the leaves and seal up for the winter.

"Why your daddy bring me out so late?" he asks you from the foot of your chair. Your face was in between your bent knees and you didn't see him coming. His name's Clarke and he's got a dark gray-white pallor, like his whole body is covered in five o'clock shadow.

"He couldn't afford it until now," you say. You sniffle. You don't hide from Clarke that you've been crying. He got to interrupt you several times last summer when you were straddling and kissing your boyfriend in that deck chair, the two of you dripping in your bathing suits. Now he can suffer the repercussions. The tears when the boy's all gone.

"I better get started before I end up shoveling snow outta there," Clarke says. "You go turn on the pump."

You furrow your brow. "That's your job, right, Clarke?"

He didn't hear you. "I'll get my net outta the van."

Clarke leaves, and you shrug and do as he said, turning on the pump before returning to your chair by the pool. Clarke comes back and tosses three metal rods at you, one with a net on the end. "Put that together for me?" he says. Then he goes to the rolled-up pool cover and starts untying the rope holding it tight.

You get his far-reaching net into one piece and hand it to him. Then you stand by his side as he fishes bunches of leaves from the water. When he steps along the edge, you follow.

"My daughter's two years older than you," he says from silence. "Can I ask you something?"

You nod, but his eyes are on the pool. He takes your silence as assent.

"Why are you all so miserable?"

You laugh in spite of yourself. "It's not our fault," you say.

"The world's so bad to the teenage girls?" Clarke says.

"Maybe the teenage girls were just hoping for something better," you say.

Clarke hands you the net. "Grab those leaves into that pile by the side over there. I'm gonna use your bathroom."

Clarke goes into your house and leaves you floating the net just under the water's chilly surface, grabbing up leaves like schools of fish. You like what you said to Clarke. None of this is your fault. You've just been let down again.

Happy the World's So Bad to the Teenage Girls Day!

| NOVEMBER 13 | MAKE HIM TAKE THE COMMUTER TRAIN ALONE DAY!

He was so excited that you agreed to come home with him for Thanksgiving. Not because he wanted you to meet his family, but because in you, he would finally have someone to ride the discount commuter train home with. He didn't want a girlfriend so much as he wanted someone to help him endure the stench of elderly flesh billowing up from the seats, the mothers beating their children half to death, the businessmen screaming jovial obscenities back and forth across the car in between sips from their twenty-four-ounce cans of Miller Lite. It's going to be hard to crush his hopes, but breaking up with somebody is never easy.

"I'm sorry," tell him. "I don't like you enough to meet your mother."

Look at his face, for God's sake. That's the face of a man who is about to have a family of nine crushing in around him. He can already feel the gum on his shoes, the spilled soda seeping through the seat of his pants, the punch to his eyes he'll receive from an unattended toddler.

"I just don't feel like we talk enough," say.

But what about the ticket-takers? He's scared of the ticket-takers. They slap at his feet when he puts them on the seats. One of them even called him "Mary" once.

"There's no real spark is all," you say. "I don't know if there ever was."

But sometimes people on the train bring their Roy Rogers chicken meals with them and the processed stench fills up the car like a fog rolling in.

"Have a nice Thanksgiving," tell him. You'll notice how the blood drains away from his face, and you'll feel like you've really broken a heart. Don't beat yourself up over it. He'll just be remembering what it's like to share a three-seater with a dry-humping teenaged couple. It makes him feel a little tender in the stomach.

Happy Make Him Take the Commuter Train Alone Day!

NOVEMBER 14 — GIVE YOUR GIRLFRIEND A BOX OF BULLETS DAY!

Tell her, "These are for your handgun."

She'll say, "Baby, you know I don't have a handgun."

Say, "That's where you're wrong." Then give her the handgun you bought for her from that guy. She'll be so happy.

"Oh my God, where on earth did you get the money for this?"

Tell her that you got the gun at a discount because it was used for something pretty bad. But that it's clean. No traceable serial numbers.

"The owner just wanted to get rid of it because he knew the police would trace his crimes back to him one day and he would be made to pay. When that day comes, he doesn't want the weapon in his house. He wants there to be no physical evidence. He wants to be convicted based only on the accusation and his confession."

Your girlfriend will already have started shooting stuff.

Be encouraging. Say to her, "Wow, that was a nice one," when she hits her intended targets.

This is going to be what makes her realize you are the greatest person on the face of the planet. This is going to be what makes her kiss you all over your face, even on your open eyes.

Happy Give Your Girlfriend a Box of Bullets Day!

| NOVEMBER 15 | YOUR CHAUFFEUR KNOWS WHERE THERE ARE HOOKERS DAY! |

"You are very lucky to have me as your limousine chauffeur for the evening," Hector told you when you began your ride from the airport. "I know where there are hookers."

You told him that you just wanted to get to your hotel so that you could get some sleep and then wake up bright and early to reconcile with your daughter after all these years. He seemed hurt.

"But . . . don't you want to know where there are hookers?" he pouted.

You said, "Okay, Hector. Show me where there are hookers."

The first place he took you was an underpass.

"See?" he said. There were indeed hookers for as far as the eye could see.

"That's great," you said. "But you know, it is an underpass. Everyone knows that the hookers live underneath the underpass."

Hector said, "You are very brilliant. I will take you someplace where you never would have guessed you would find a hooker."

Hector took you to 378 Oak Tree Lane. He knocked on the door and an old woman answered. Hector told her, "He wants to see the hooker."

She led the two of you quietly up the stairs to a bedroom where a twenty-year-old woman was napping. She looked quite pretty.

"My daughter," the old woman whispered.

"Your daughter is a hooker, yes?" Hector asked excitedly.

The old woman nodded. Then closed the door softly.

Back in the car, Hector said, "Impressed?"

"Yes, Hector, I never would have guessed there was a hooker in there. Can I go to my hotel now?"

Hector said he wanted to take you to one more place where there are hookers. The place he took you to was a Stop and Shop.

"There," he said, pointing at the supermarket.

"Hookers are here?" you asked. "Which aisle?"

Hector didn't like your joke. He peeled out of the parking lot and started speeding down the highway.

"I'm sorry, Hector. It was just . . ."

"The hookers are in the back of the store inside the loading dock! But you do not deserve to know where there are hookers!" Hector said. "You deserve to be tied to a wall and carved open while you are still alive."

That's what Hector's doing to you right now. It's awful, and you'll die soon. Just a day before you were finally going to pull your daughter back into your life.

Happy Your Chauffeur Knows Where There Are Hookers Day!

NOVEMBER 16 | MAKE YOUR BUILDING'S DOORMAN JEALOUS DAY!

Tell him about the five-course dinner you just ate. And the big expensive play you just saw. And the operation you elected to have. And the big expensive things you constantly buy. When you bring hookers home, have them stop in front of the doorman, and say to them, "Ladies, tell Jerry how much each of you cost."

Then go down the line as each of your evening's hookers sounds off with her price tag (don't do this if any of your evening's hookers costs less than $500).

Additionally, sometimes your doorman brings his son in to work with him. Usually on Saturdays. That's when you should have your son play with his most expensive toys in the lobby. And hire a clown to come to the lobby and play with your son.

If your doorman doesn't get jealous at all that, he must be pretty happy with his life. He's probably in love. Or he's a Taoist. You can't piss those dudes off.

Happy Make Your Building's Doorman Jealous Day!

| NOVEMBER 17 | YOUR WIFE'S TEETH ARE DISGUSTING DAY! |

Getting your wife to brush her teeth is no small feat. She hates the feeling of having something plastic inside her mouth, and she thinks her teeth are indestructible little weapons more powerful than solid steel. And when you tell her that her breath smells, all she says is, "Fuck you royally."

You're going to have to combine brushing her teeth with a race for some chicken. Tonight, come home from the store with a full rotisserie chicken in a see-through container. Your wife will see the chicken and throw herself from her chair, swinging her arms out in front of her to grab at the bird and stuff it into her mouth. Just hold the tray up above her head and make her jump for it and kick at your shins. Once she's settled down a bit, tell her you want to play a game.

Put the chicken up atop the kitchen cabinets and take her into the bathroom with you. Tell her that on the count of three, the two of you will start to brush. And the first person who manages to scrub every accessible surface of every tooth three times gets the entire chicken.

"And the loser?" she'll ask.

"The loser doesn't eat until morning."

Your wife will smile that same beautiful smile she wore when she looked up and said I do.

"Hope you had a big fuckin' lunch, dickhead, 'cause you're going down!" she'll say.

Your wife will snap her fingers in front of your eyeballs, then wheel around and grab for a toothbrush. Before you start the count, she'll strip down to her waist (she has to do that before brushing). When she's ready, apply toothpaste to each of your toothbrushes.

"One . . . two . . . three . . . and BRUSH!"

And simple as that, your wife will brush her teeth with such a fury her naked breasts will ripple like a lake in the rain. Those grunts coming out of her mouth will be the sound of months and months of plaque and grime being ripped away from her teeth. You'll look into the mirror at the steady cascade of foam pouring from her lower lip and you'll want to cry. You'll have done it. Your wife's teeth will finally be clean.

"YEAH!" she'll scream through her mouth full of foamy paste, her toothbrush held in the air. "Go get me my chicken, bitch, and I want your skinny ass to watch me eat every bite! Go on!"

You'll rinse your mouth clean and then go and set the chicken down in front of your wife's seat at the table. You'll sit across from her and watch her as she makes exaggerated groans of ecstasy after every bite. You'll have to eat a quick dinner before you come home every night from now on. But it's worth it. Her teeth are worth it.

Happy Your Wife's Teeth Are Disgusting Day!

NOVEMBER 18   HOMOEROTICA DAY!

Today, all homoerotica is half off. This includes homoerotic literature, homoerotic pornography, and the homoeroticism of the dirty conversations you have with your roommate. The kind where your roommate, purportedly straight, asks you if you've "banged" a particular woman you've been seeing, and you respond that, yes, you and she are pretty serious now. Which elicits a frothing response from your roommate, something along the lines of "Aww yeah! Yeah! You banged that pussy! Yeah! Make that pussy SCREEEAM! Yeah! I really like pussy. Really. I really do." Your roommate then presses you for details, which you refuse to provide. Your roommate asks questions about the woman's anatomy, such as, "Does she have big tits?" and "Does she have a nice ass? You know the kind." You just shake your head. At which point, without explanation yet without fail, your roommate launches himself across the living room to tackle you on the couch and bounce his weight upon you, occasionally crawling up to grind his ass into your face,* all the while screaming in a high-pitched voice as if he were the woman you were having sex with. That conversation, for today only, is half off.

Happy Homoerotica Day!

NOVEMBER 19   ON TO THE BARS DAY!

Hit the bars tonight. Bring Dave and Joey and tell them to bring some girls. Bring Brad, Johnny, and Frank, and tell them to bring some girls. They know girls. Bring Kevin, Lewis, Jeff, Amrit, and Jacques, and tell each of them:

"Don't forget. Six girls each."

Six girls each that you don't know. Six girls each who don't know your nickname (the Heater). Six girls each from Kevin, Lewis, Jeff, Amrit, and Jacques equals thirty girls right then and there.

"How can I lose?"

You'll find a way, baby. So stack the odds. Invite Theodore. He always has girls. Tell him it would be a good idea if he brought some of them with him.

"The hot ones, Theodore. Not Deborah!"

"Ah," Theodore will say. "But Deborah is the most beautiful of all. You just haven't spoken to her long enough to see what depths she possesses. For instance—"

"Shut it, Theodore! Her teeth are too big."

"Her teeth," Theodore will say. "Such stark white totems of . . ."

Hang up on Theodore and hit the online personals. Create a profile so witty and weighted down with obscure pop culture references that no HoneyBaby will be able to resist. Check back an hour after the profile posts and scroll through the replies, reading only the ones that have the phrase, "LOVE Your Profile! ROTFL!" in the subject lines.

---

*He once bloodied your nose.

Still a couple hours before you have to hit the first bar. Call everyone in forty-five minutes to see how they're doing with the whole "corralling women" project. The two guys who are showing the least incentive should be disinvited. Then, hit the chin-up bar. Get those arms into "feel this muscle" shape. Tonight's your night.

Make.

It.

Count.

Happy On to the Bars Day!

| NOVEMBER 20 | THAT KID'S NOT GONNA DIE DAY! |

He's the one we all look to for hope. We always knew there had to be someone out there who would just by some weird accident or chance of circumstances never ever die. He's Bobby, and he's immortal. Apparently.

Bobby has cancer, but he's hanging in there. He's really weak and vomits constantly the way everyone with cancer is real into doing. When you see him, you'll think, "That kid is definitely going to die. And actually, I wanna get outta here because I think it's gonna happen right now." But medical doctors think otherwise.

"That kid is not going to die!" said Dr. Davis, a medical doctor, right after he examined Bobby. And though he found all the telltale signs of a dying boy, nonetheless he came to the conclusion that "this kid's got the stuff. He's going to outlive us all. Even our energies that linger in rooms and lead people to believe in ghosts. He'll outlive our energies," Dr. Davis went on to say.

"I concur with Dr. Davis," said Dr. Daniels, also a medical doctor. Dr. Daniels gave Bobby the thoroughest of look-sees, and though Bobby had no pulse and his lungs were drowned in bile, Dr. Daniels countered all objections with, "Look, who's the doctor here? Are you a doctor? You? How about you? No? Well then, I guess I'm the only one up in this shit that can say what up. And I say this kid's in it to win it. He was clearly born from a power dark and unholy."

Later, Dr. Dougherty, an additional medical doctor, joined Doctors Davis and Daniels in their optimistic prognosis. "They're right," he said.

What no one realizes is that, though Bobby slips in and out of a feverish coma-like vegetative state only to vomit or shriek in anguish, he can hear what everyone is saying. And he is very excited that he's the kid who's not gonna die.

Happy That Kid's Not Gonna Die Day!

NOVEMBER 21   POWDERED CREAM DONUTS DAY!

Your boyfriend is gonna break up with you tonight, and he's gonna bring a dozen donuts with him when he does it. He called earlier to say he's coming over to your apartment, and his tone let you know it would be happening tonight. But when you open the door you'll see him with a resolute look in his eye and a pink cardboard box in his hand. You'll let him in without saying anything.

All the way upstairs you'll think, "Did he bring a cake? Cupcakes? Maybe I was wrong. Maybe he just wants to . . . is it my roommate's birthday?"

You'll get him all the way to the couch and then you'll go to the bathroom to ponder what the fuck could be in that box.

A hat? A kitten? Um . . . a hat?

You were determined not to primp in the slightest for this, but when you suspect that, instead of breaking up with you, he might be about to give you a hat or a kitten, you'll put your hair in a clip.

A deep breath will take you back out to the living room, where you'll sit down next to him on the couch. You'll let your left arm spread across the back of the couch so your hand will be near his hair.

You'll ask, "What's in the box?"

"Donuts. Look, this just isn't working out. I think you're great but you're stuck in a part of my life I left behind a long time ago. I think I've just grown past you is all."

Nothing will happen for a long time. Then you'll say, "Donuts?"

"I'm sorry but I've made my decision," he'll say. "I'm going to be causing you pain no matter how I do this, so I'm just going to get out of here now to avoid drawing this all out. This way you won't say anything you might regret saying later. Good-bye."

He'll get up and leave. You'll stay on the couch, staring at the pink box in the middle of the kitchen table.

You'll take a walk. Meet a friend at a bar and get a little drunk. When you come back it will be nighttime. Your roommate will be sitting at the kitchen table. The donut box will be open.

"Did you eat some of those donuts?" you'll ask.

"Yeah," she'll say. "They were great."

"Jeff brought them," you'll say. "We broke up."

The lid of the box will be open. There will probably be nine donuts left. You'll wonder if any of them might be jelly.

Happy Powdered Cream Donuts Day!

| NOVEMBER 22 | **RUNNING FOR PRESIDENT DAY!**

Instead of running for president, you're gonna get drunk with your boyfriend, have sex with him one last time, then break up with him.

"I just think we don't really have a shot at anything awesome," say to him. You'll sit Indian-style on the edge of the bed, giving your naked stomach a crease. He'll lie along the length of the bed with his back up on the pillows.

"You're just trying to kill it before you have to put any effort in. It's what you always do," he'll say.

"What do you mean, what I always do? What else have I given up on?"

His eyes go wide with disbelief. "How's that presidential run coming?"

"2008. You'll see."

"And the massage therapy license?"

"Carpal tunnel. I told you."

"Right," he'll say. "And how's the drug dealing coming along?"

"Oh, for God's sake. There's too much competition."

"You never even tried to get a supplier!"

"Maybe I would've been dealing drugs by now if you'd offered some words of support instead of throwing all my failures up in my face all the time."

He won't say anything at first. Then, "You're right. I'll try harder to be supportive if you'll stay."

Say, "No."

Happy Running for President Day!

| NOVEMBER 23 | BREAK SOME WINDOWS DAY!

You've had a hard day at work. Lots of yelling and unrequited lusting. And you got fired. You deserve a little "I Deserve a Little Something" time. So go over to the house that's been up for sale for two years and join the latchkey kids who show up every day in the house's backyard to idly toss rocks through the house's windows. After each of you sends a stone through a window, you can look over at the kids' dissatisfied faces and say, "Honestly, this is as good as it's gonna get, so don't give up on it too soon. Let's throw a few more and see if we light any fires in our bellies, huh?"

You and the latchkey kids will break a bunch more windows, then the latchkey kids will ask you to buy them some ice cream. Say, "No. I gotta save my money. I got fired today." One of the latchkey kids will say, "My dad used to get fired a lot. Then he left us."

Happy Break Some Windows Day!

| NOVEMBER 24 | **LOOK AT THE PRETTY BIRD, DADDY DAY!** |

Your daughter just saw a pretty bird in the sky. She said, "Look at the pretty bird, Daddy!" You looked at it, then you looked down at her and said, "You're right, it's a very pretty bird."

No shit it's pretty. She wasn't asking your fucking opinion. She was trying to alert you to a little fleck of natural beauty soaring through your day. But you had to use it to get all DAD on her and turn it into a fucking lesson. If only she were old enough to say, "Thanks, genius. I really needed your input here. By the way, Mom's thinking twice."

Get off your high fucking horse and just love the shit out of your daughter for a little while. If you were here, standing in front of me right now, I'd get up out of my desk chair and punch you in the goddamn mouth. Christ almighty. I'm gonna go take a bath.

Happy Look at the Pretty Bird, Daddy Day!

| NOVEMBER 25 | **YOUR FATHER'S GOING TO COME INTO YOUR BAR TONIGHT, AND HE'LL HAVE BLOOD ON HIS SHIRT DAY!** |

You'll come in to close the place up early. You've been doing that a lot lately. It's not even that there is any new competition in town pulling your customers away. The place is just in a slump.

If you stuck around for a year or two, you would probably see things pick back up. Towns like this one don't let their bars shutter. But you don't think in terms of years. You never intended to die in Texas.

"A guy finished the Heart of the Lone Star State tonight," your bar-back will tell you.

The Heart of the Lone Star State is a five-pound slab of shitty steak. You got a bunch of them with the last meat order that came in right before you switched suppliers. You instituted that half-assed promotion to try and get rid of it. Anyone who finishes the Heart of the Lone Star State drinks for free.

"How much booze did he hit me for?" you'll ask.

"Nothing," he'll say. "He didn't even seem to enjoy eating the steak. Just finished it like he had a job to do, then waited for me to take his Polaroid. Then he was gone."

The bar-back will point to the Polaroid on the bulletin board behind the bar. "Check out the steak sauce all over his shirt," he'll say.

When he points to the Polaroid, you'll be all the way across the bar sitting in a booth counting out that night's bank from the drawer. Something will pull you out of your seat and send you over to take a look at that Polaroid.

"What in the hell are you doing still alive?" you'll ask your father's frozen smile. Just then the window will shatter and the bar-back will take a bullet in the shoulder.

"Out back!" you'll shout when he falls into your arms. You'll drag him through the office out the back door and into your car. You'll peel away, watching in the rearview mirror as the flames quickly engulf your bar.

The bar-back will be bleeding and howling in the backseat. "Who was that? Was that the guy in the Polaroid?" he'll shout.

"Yeah," you'll say. "That was my dad. He's been pretty pissed at me ever since me and my mom left him to drown in a lake. Fucker's supposed to be dead." Then you'll explain to him that you're going to have to roll him out of the moving car at the Emergency Room's entrance because your dad probably has you in his rifle sight as you speak and you can't risk slowing down.

Happy Your Father's Going to Come into Your Bar Tonight, and He'll Have Blood on His Shirt Day!

NOVEMBER 26   SHE WISHES MORRISSEY AND
MARR COULD'VE TRIED TO WORK
IT OUT DAY!

"Girlfriend in a Coma" just began on the stereo. It's late and it's autumn. You're driving and you're drunker than Dave and Mary, both asleep in the backseat. Karen's awake and dreamy-dumb like she always is. Karen thinks there could've been more records.

"They were just so good" is the extent of her argument.

Karen can't get what is obvious to the rest of us. Even you, the reader, can hear the sleep-deprived petulance that makes *Strangeways* such an exceptional album, yet such an unpleasant listen. It was over, in a big angry way. Karen thinks her favorite rock bands should go on making her favorite records forever and ever.

"Wouldn't it be great if there were like ten more albums that we never heard before?"

Yeah, great, Karen. Just fucking awesome. "Girlfriend in a Coma" ended two minutes ago and no one got to hear it because she couldn't just settle into a car ride that everyone else can enjoy just fine without running their fucking mouths off about shit that's just wrong.

"And what have they done since then? Nothing nearly as good."

You can't take it anymore. If she says one more thing, you're going to have to say something and the tone in your voice will send her to bed as soon as you get back into the house and you'll just end up drinking on the couch in front of HBO. Which doesn't sound so bad, honestly. But wait until she says something else. Maybe she won't say anything at all.

"They broke up too soon."

"No they fucking didn't. They broke up just in time. 'Death of a Disco Dancer,' for God's sake. Or 'Paint a Vulgar Picture,' if it's not obvious enough. Come the fuck on. They were over and done with, and 'Viva Hate' was one of the most logical progressions from great band into adequate solo effort in music ever. Come on, Karen."

Karen's quiet now. And Dave and Mary are awake in the backseat. You're the big dick of the autumn car ride.

"Bands can't go on forever is all I mean."

Nice save, dickhead.

Happy She Wishes Morrissey and Marr Could've Tried to Work It Out Day!

| NOVEMBER 27 | **SOME GIRLS ARE MORE AMENABLE TO COMMITTING SUICIDE THAN OTHERS DAY!** |

You really, really, really want your girlfriend to kill herself. You've had the big day for your own suicide circled on your calendar for six months now. All that time, all you had to do was look up at that circle and think, "Few more weeks and good-bye to my heartache and my misery and my always having to pee at movies."

But then you went and fell in love and grew conflicted. You still want to die, no question. But this girl, she's really pretty. And when she speaks it's like she's reading the story written on your soul and shit. When it comes down to it, you don't want to be without her. If you kill yourself and she keeps on living, she'll probably start seeing someone else and you can't handle that.

But suicide is your lifelong dream. You can't stay alive just because someone else wants to. Follow. Your. Bliss.

What has to happen is you just have to come right out and ask her if she wants to kill herself with you. A lot of girls are into things you never would have guessed they'd be into. Approach the question with some caution, and if she says yes, don't act like she's some kind of slut all of a sudden.

But if she says no, take the circle off the calendar. No one who's in love ever kills himself unless he's in love with someone who doesn't love him back, or his parents are dicks about it. If she says no, you're just going to have to wait until you don't love her anymore eleven months from now.

Happy Some Girls Are More Amenable to Committing Suicide Than Others Day!

| NOVEMBER 28 | WALK OUT ON THE HUMAN PINCUSHION DAY! |

You're gonna walk out on the Human Pincushion today. Right before you drop your keys on the kitchen counter and leave, you'll say the same thing as the previous four girls who've walked out on the Human Pincushion.

"I'm really . . . Oh Jesus Christ, I'm just so, so sorry."

They all say this, because toward the end of a relationship the Human Pincushion diverts his attention from the impending doom by focusing all of his energy on his craft. In other words, he sits around all day sticking pins in himself.

Can't we address this?

Sideshow auditions are in May. I need to rehearse.

And then he sits in the middle of the Persian carpet on the living room floor and stabs himself with small metals. Every prick a distraction from the seething glare piercing the back of his head.

By the time they split, he's where he is right now. On the carpet, in a pair of white boxers, covered in needles from head to toe. When he looks up at you today, it'll be the first time in a month that he's looked you in the eye. And the pins sticking out of his temples and cheeks will bob just a bit with the movement of his head. The bobbing of the needles and the pathetic plea in his eyes are what's gonna make you say, "I'm really . . . Oh Jesus Christ, I'm just so, so sorry."

Then you'll run out the door, taking the stairs instead of the elevator, trying to shake off the memory of that pitiful sight by slamming your weight down on every step.

Happy Walk Out on the Human Pincushion Day!

| NOVEMBER 29 | MELVIN IS A MAGICIAN NOW DAY!

With the flowers in your left hand, you use your right to push the doorbell for the first time in thirteen years. His mother will answer.

"Yes?"

She'll be in a bathrobe. It's new. Or at least, it's not the flowered one she used to wear when you were in high school.

"Mrs. Ames?" you'll say.

She'll put her reading glasses on and squint into your face. She'll say, "Alicia?"

"It's me, Mrs. Ames," you'll say. "I've come back for Melvin."

Go on. Do it just like you rehearsed on the drive down.

"Mrs. Ames, when Melvin and I broke up after prom, it seemed like a good idea. I didn't know who I was then. I had a lot of growing up to do, as I'm sure you can understand."

Mrs. Ames can understand. This will be evident by the nod of her head.

"I've been with a lot of men since Melvin, Mrs. Ames. A lot more than I ever thought I'd be with. I don't know statistics, but I'm pretty sure I've been with a lot more than might be considered average. In fact, considering only my immediate circle of friends and acquaintances, way more than average."

You'll start to drift with some rather delicious memories. Mrs. Ames will grow uncomfortable. Stay on target.

"These men, Mrs. Ames, they taught me many things. Things that would be unseemly to go into right here and now. But the most important thing I learned from them was that not a single one of them could ever measure up to your son, Melvin. I'm in love with your son, Mrs. Ames. And I want him to be mine. I drove three hundred miles today to give him these flowers and ask if he'd like to have dinner and perhaps a life with me. Could you go get him?"

Mrs. Ames will look so thrown you'd think you just proposed to *her*. She'll remove her reading glasses and drop them back into the pocket of her robe. Then she'll wring her hands and say, "Melvin is a magician now. He moved out of the house about ten years ago."

The hand holding your flowers will drop slowly to your side. "Oh," you'll say.

"He's doing two shows tonight at Lem's Lobster and Dinner Theater off of Route 80."

You'll look up at her with a question in your eyes. Mrs. Ames will grab your shoulders in her hands and say, "Go."

Happy Melvin Is a Magician Now Day!

NOVEMBER 30   STEVE BROKE UP WITH JANET
VIA AN OVERPASS DAY!

Tonight at 5:00 P.M., everyone's going to see it. Everyone with a nine to five and a bitch of a commute is going to know. Janet's heart is going to break two miles deep into the heavy logjam leading up to the Jackson Street turnabout.

Spray-painted in valentine red across the expanse of the Turner Boulevard overpass: "It's over, Janet. I can't stay on the turnpike with you anymore. I'm hitting the expressway. Also, the sex has been pretty blech lately, am I right? Steve."

Janet won't call the house or his cell. She won't whip out her Black-Berry to see if there's an addendum there telling her what she can expect to find when she gets home. She'll know what is waiting for her. She'll sit in the dead-still traffic jam, staring up at her good-bye, and cataloging everything that's his, creating the vision in her head of all those negatives. In her vision, there will be blank white spots where his things used to be. Where he pulled a book off a shelf or a shirt off a hanger, white nothing so glaring the color of it hums. Her whole house will be humming when she gets there.

The easy smile on her face will be unshakable. He won't do this to her. These people are her fellow commuters. They've shared this traffic jam with her every evening for seven years now. They've stared across the lanes at her behind her wheel, wondering where she's coming from and where she's headed, what she's wearing underneath that skirt and what she's going to watch on TV tonight. She will not let them see her crying into her hands, proving that she is the one whose relationship just ended on the side of an overpass.

She'll feel their eyes search her and her car's interior for any signs of disturbance. Like soldiers hunting down holdouts. She'll feel like they can see it, but that's silly. They know the make and model of her car and that sometimes she sings without being aware of it. They couldn't pull a Steve from so little, could they?

After some panicky breaths, she'll feel strong enough to turn her head and meet their gaze dead-on. She'll find their eyes are not on her, but are in their own laps. Their heads will shake sorrowfully from side to side. Occasionally her fellow commuters will look up at the overpass and then slap their steering wheels in anger.

They'll be with their Janet. Though they won't know which car is hers, they'll see this scrawl on the overpass as an assault on the commute and all those who take part in it day after day. "Steve," they'll say to no one in their cars. "Steve probably works from home," they'll say. "Probably trying to get an online business off the ground," they'll say. "Probably has more than enough time to come out in the middle of the afternoon and hang off the side of an overpass and spray-paint some filth that'll break the heart of his Janet.

"Janet," they'll say. "She's on her way home. She's looking forward to her home," they'll say. "She's been working where she doesn't want to be, just like me," they'll say. "And when she intended to do nothing but push ahead into whatever space she can find to just inch a little closer to home, she had to look up and find that nothing is waiting for her anymore."

All at once, every single one of them, alone in their cars and unbeknownst to each other, they will all say in unison, "Janet is me."

Happy Steve Broke Up with Janet via an Overpass Day!

DECEMBER

THIS ISN'T HOW YOU WANTED HER TO SEE YOU.

| DECEMBER 1 | GAS PUMP DAY! |

Make a friend.

"$2.89 a gallon. You believe that?"

"You said it."

Stare at the meters on your pumps.

"You wanna get together later?"

"You said it."

Order another pitcher.

"Sixteen bucks for a pitcher of beer. Where do they get off?"

"You said it."

Sip from your beers.

"Wanna help me kill my wife? I'll split the insurance."

"You said it."

Sprinkle lime into the shallow grave.

"Seventy bucks for a twenty-pound bag of this stuff. Highway robbery."

"You said it."

Lean on your shovels.

"I'm moving to Tahiti when the money comes through. Wanna come along?"

"You said it."

Sip daiquiris inside your rented cabana.

"Twelve bucks an hour for a goddamn linen tent. Nice racket, huh?"

"I feel like I could tell you anything."

Sip your daiquiris.

"Let's just live. Huh?"

"You said it."

Happy Gas Pump Day!

DECEMBER 2 | *THE PASSION OF THE PEOPLE WHO ARE HAVING SEX* DAY!

That's what you would call the porno version of that Easter movie. Another good one would be *The Passion of the People with Each Other's Genitals in Their Mouths at the Same Time.* That'd be awesome.

Satisfied that you've adequately channeled the morning's inspiration, you rise from your composing desk and go upstairs to check on your mother. She'll be on the floor and her nightgown will be up over her belly. You heard the thump and the shouting earlier, but you couldn't pull yourself away from your work.

"Mother," you'll say, "how many times do I have to tell you? If you want me to change the channel, ring the bell."

"I fucking did!" she'll say.

Hoist her up and back into bed. "Well, keep ringing until I answer."

"I fucking rang the bell for forty minutes," she'll say. She'll be crying now.

Say, "You're just going to break your hip again."

"You'd like that, wouldn't you? Keep me in this fucking attic until I'm dead. You'd fucking love that."

She's right. Since you agreed to provide her with in-home care, the writing has been flowing like water. As evidenced by this morning's list of pornographic variations on the title of that Easter movie. You have to plead dedication to your craft, but you know that you wouldn't hesitate to take a crowbar to her bones if it would mean your muse might stay by your side.

Happy *The Passion of the People Who Are Having Sex* Day!

| DECEMBER 3 | PUT HER SON ON YOUR KNEE DAY!

You're thirty-four now and you're working as a shopping mall Santa Claus, the steadiest work you've had all year. You don't mind kids, and sometimes you get tips from the parents who are used to just handing out tips to everybody they see. It's been a pretty okay gig, until today. Today's the day you're gonna see Marie get in line with her son.

Marie left town after high school, just like everyone else who had a head on his or her shoulders. But you didn't care about everyone else. Marie was your girl for junior and senior year. She was a smart girl, and she made you feel good about yourself. No matter how many times your daddy told you that you weren't worth nothing, one kiss from Marie would drown him out. Even though you never left town or went off to college, Marie made you feel like you were supposed to.

As soon as you see her, you'll be so glad you're wearing a big white beard and furry hat. What's she doing here? The last you heard of her was six years ago, when you got word that she was living outside of Chicago with a banker. Maybe it didn't work out. Maybe she decided back home is where she belongs. Maybe she kept thinking that she never had it better than when she dated that nice boy in her junior and senior year of high school, so she came back home to see if he still has some room in his heart for her.

"Go and say hello to Santa, Robby," Marie will say to her son.

The boy will climb up onto your knee and wait patiently for you to say, "Ho ho ho."

"Ho! Ho! Ho!" say, making your voice a little deeper and hoarser than usual. "What's your name, little boy?"

Marie's son will tell you his name is Robby.

"Do you live nearby here, Sonny?" ask Robby.

Robby will say, "I'm not supposed to tell strangers where I live."

Marie will say, "It's okay, Robby." The she'll say to you, "We're just visiting. He lives in Chicago."

Robby will say, "I'm visiting my grandpa."

She's just having Christmas with her parents. Just a visit. Why would she ever come back? Who would ever come back to your town after they were lucky enough to get out? Who would ever come back for you?

"What do you want for Christmas, Robby?"

Robby will enumerate a list of the same video games and electronics accessories that you hear all day, day in and day out until it all sounds like the gibberish you might hear on a science fiction TV show you've never watched before. When he's done, pat him on the back and slide him off of your knee.

"Back to mommy now, Robby," say. "Such a pretty mommy."

Marie will begin to walk down the path to the exit, but she'll stop and turn back to you and say your name. "Is that you?" she'll ask. Her smile will be excited.

Say, "Ho! Ho! Ho!"

Marie will look closer at your eyes. "Is that you? Do you remember me?"

Say, "Ho! Ho! Ho!"

Marie will take a step closer. Still looking at your eyes. "Um, it's me, Marie. Is that you?"

Say, "Ho! Ho! Ho!"

Marie's smile will turn polite. "I'm sorry. I thought I recognized you."

Don't say anything.

Marie will say, "Merry Christmas, Santa."

Don't say anything. Just wait for her to go.

Happy Put Her Son on Your Knee Day!

| DECEMBER 4 | BORE SOMEONE WITH TALK ABOUT YOUR SMOKING HABITS DAY! |

How many years? How many packs a day? Cutting down? Picking up the pace? Does your wife want you to quit? These are the questions to which your friend does not want answers. But guess what, today you're gonna tell him anyway!

Happy Bore Someone with Talk About Your Smoking Habits Day!

| DECEMBER 5 | BOOTH BY THE WINDOW DAY! |

It's Tuesday again so you're drinking alone. You took the booth by the window because you want to look at faces. Tomorrow you'll remember it more as if you were waiting for a face.

Down the block, crossing the street toward you will be Jonathan. He had a small part in an awful one-night play you got roped into eight months prior. You shared twenty-seven words with him that night, and you remember liking him and hoping he might come out to the bar after the show. He did not and you decided he probably did not drink and therefore had nothing in common with you. You forgot about him.

He'll get close enough for you to see that his is not the face of a man who wants to come in and catch up over a Tuesday evening drink. He'll be close enough for you to see that he's broken. You won't put on your coat before you run out after him.

You'll have to run half the block before you're within arm's length of him. You'll grab his left hand. He'll wheel around like he would if he were getting arrested.

You'll watch him take in your face and go from puzzlement to recognition, then back to puzzlement. He'll say, "Oh, hey. How've you . . ."

You'll squeeze his hand tight in both your hands, then you'll look up and let him know without saying so that he can keep on looking terrible in front of you.

His face will fall and he'll take a deep breath. Eight months ago, you shared twenty-seven words. Tonight he'll take two steps into your embrace and you'll stop thinking about how cold it is outside. He'll kiss the side of your head, your cheek, then your lips. Then you'll walk back to the bar with your arms around each other and you'll take a seat in that booth by the window. He'll have a whiskey, thank goodness.

Happy Booth by the Window Day!

| DECEMBER 6 | END IT VIA A FINGER PAINTING OF A DRAGON DAY! |

You met on parents' night. He came alone, one of the only dads who was there alone. He lingered behind after you'd finished your presentation because you're one of the only teachers in the school who isn't shaped like a medicine ball.

"Does Mike have talent?" he asked, examining his son's construction-paper rendering of a tree in a field on a sunny day.

"He doesn't eat the paste," you said. He walked you to your car.

You've spent a total of eleven hours together, split up over four individual nights, but that first night was the best night of all. When he sat in the passenger seat of your parked car and the two of you watched the parents walk to their parking spaces.

"That's the Lamberts," you said when Kevin Lambert's parents came walking out of the main entrance. "Their son Kevin got beat up in the rain after school last Thursday."

The Lamberts were laughing as they approached their Hyundai.

"The Morrisseys," you said when the very tall and shaven-headed Mr. Morrissey walked past your car with his tiny wife. "I bet when their girl Jessica hits middle school she'll be the most popular kid in the place."

"I'll tell Mike to start laying the groundwork, get in early," he said.

You said, "Jessica would never go steady with Mike."

He looked shocked, and you laughed, then you leaned in and kissed him for four minutes.

"Keep a close eye on Mike's artwork," you told him that night. "If I give him three gold stars, you're to meet me at the Super 8 the following evening at 7:00 P.M."

"And what if I want to see you?" he asked.

"We'll see each other only when I wanna see you," you said. "And when I never wanna see you again, poor little Mike won't get any stars that day."

"Why does Mike have to be involved?"

"I'm Mike's art teacher," you said. "Don't try to forget that."

→ ←

Mike cried on his way home today, his finger painting of a dragon crumpling at the edges where his fists held it close to his chest. He didn't ask you why you skipped him when you were giving out the stars. But he waited at his desk long after the rest of the class had left. You walked out with your eyes to the floor, unable to look at him.

It's bad enough that you are expected to assign grades to the first creative endeavors of children. You'd always tried to give out the stars so arbitrarily you thought it might even be fun to use that grading system for your lascivious communiqués.

There'd been so many days when you wanted so badly to see Mike's dad. But those were days when Mike had turned in work that was decidedly less than three-star quality. You found you just couldn't do it, and so you'd give him the stars he deserved and spend the following night at home alone. And whenever Mike turned in a three-star project, it was always in a week when a rendezvous would have been impossible.

You've managed four nights together, and each night required you to give Mike an inappropriate star grade. But today was the last straw.

Today, Mike made a finger painting of a dragon. It was the best work Mike had ever done. The best finger painting of the entire class since school began last autumn. A decidedly five-star piece. But you wanted to see his daddy tomorrow night.

You couldn't give this piece a three-star grade. When you looked at that painting, you knew the affair had to end today. And to punish yourself for falling into such a state of compromise, you broke a student's heart on the day he'd done his best. You condemned yourself to the lowest point in your teaching career.

Mike cried on his way home. And so did you.

Happy End It via a Finger Painting of a Dragon Day!

DECEMBER 7   JUMPER (LONG LUNCH BREAK) DAY!

Coming back from Subway today, you're going to find the street surrounding your building barricaded and a crowd of heads tilted back and eyes up high. Someone's on the ledge of your building, maybe nineteen floors up. She's got her hand on one of the abutments just behind her. She looks like she's afraid if she lets go she'll fall.

Your department pays you for the time you're kept out of the building due to bomb threats and fire drills, and you're certain you'll get no argument when you submit your hours for this afternoon. So you're perfectly fine with this lady (you might have ridden the elevator with her once or twice, you can't tell) staying up there as long as she wants. Perhaps she has an ex-husband in Connecticut who's being driven in to talk her down. You might get to stay outside for the rest of the—

Oops, there she goes.

Happy Jumper (Long Lunch Break) Day! Back to work, baby.

DECEMBER 8	EIGHTEEN HOURS DAY!

Your husband flew out last night. You're tying up the loose ends and fly-ing out tonight. It's 6:00 A.M. You have to be at the airport by midnight. The speed limits don't go above 35 mph in your little suburb. You're doing 57 so that you can get inside a house across town with as little of the re-maining eighteen hours wasted on travel time as you can manage.

He lives almost dead smack en route to the airport. All those times in the past, when you said never again, when you panicked, thinking your hus-band knew, you never imagined your very last visit would be a pit stop on the way to leaving town forever. You never noticed that he would be right there on the way. You haven't been back for months. You only just contacted him to tell him good-bye, and he said once more please let me kiss you. When you looked at the map, the convenience of stopping by washed away all guilt. So convenient it belongs on your to-do list. You're delirious, yes, made evident by the fact that you feel you could tell your husband about the stop when you see him tomorrow and begin a laundry list of everything you got done.

Canceled the paper. Turned off the electric. Dropped off the spare sets of keys to the realtor. Grabbed Kevin by the naked clavicle and didn't let him go for eighteen hours straight. Took Rex to the vet . . .

You have nine more minutes of drive time. You've driven there enough to know it. It's 6:08. You'll find him smoking on his step at 6:17. By no later than 6:18, he'll hold you. That leaves you only seventeen hours and forty-two minutes. Strange to know for certain that such a brief window of time opens out on the rest of your life.

Happy Eighteen Hours Day!

DECEMBER 9   KILL IT!!! DAY!

I think he ran up the door frame! Get it! No, wait. Oh Christ, I just had this place sprayed for— Fuck, it's got fucking wings!!! Kill it! Kill it!

Because today's Kill It!!! Day!

DECEMBER 10   HAVE AN AFFAIR WITH SOMEONE YOU MET DURING AN AIR TRAFFIC CONTROLLERS' STRIKE DAY!

There's going to be another air traffic controllers' strike tonight at midnight. You will have boarded your red-eye to Denver in the hopes that at the last minute talks would be extended. The plane will sit on the runway for forty minutes after your appointed departure time. Just long enough for you to get acquainted with your very attractive seatmate.

"How old are you?" she'll ask right before the announcement comes from the cockpit that everyone is to return to the terminal. When you give your age, she'll say, "I'm two whole years older than you."

You'll return to the terminal together and you'll learn that there is no chance of any planes departing tonight, but tomorrow is a possibility. The airline will try to secure hotel rooms for everybody, but due to the demand, passengers traveling alone will have to pair up.

You and your seatmate will both look down at the rings on each other's fingers. Your seatmate will say, "If there are any flights tomorrow, I have to be on one."

You'll say, "We got no choice but to get a room, I guess."

At the Radisson, the first hour will be spent trying to appease each other's consciences.

"I love my husband," she'll say.

"I love my wife," you'll reply.

She'll say, "I am also very pro-union. And if it took the entire airline industry being brought to its knees for us to be together, I have to respect that."

Say, "I don't cross picket lines."

Undress each other. Having sex will be lots and lots of fun because you don't know each other that well. Things will get a little bit awkward after, though. And tomorrow, when it's announced that a contract has not been reached, but passengers are welcome to stay in their hotels and wait for the possibility that controllers will return to work in another eighteen hours, you'll both opt to return to your homes and your families.

Happy Have an Affair with Someone You Met During an Air Traffic Controllers' Strike Day!

DECEMBER 11 || THE AMERICAN FLAG DAY!

Normally, when a building hangs an American flag outside, it's saying to everyone who walks into the building, "This building takes place in America." But for today only, if a building has the American flag waving out front of it, it means, "Here inside this building, someone just farted." This is all day long, every time you see a building with an American flag raised, you are to take it to mean, "That building stinks of farts. I bet everyone inside is giggling and going, 'Oh man, who farted?'"

Happy the American Flag Day!

DECEMBER 12 | **A FLAVOR OF INCENSE THAT MAKES PEOPLE IMAGINE WHAT YOU'D LOOK LIKE GIVING A BABY A BATH WHEN THEY BREATHE IT IN DAY!**

Whether you have a big date tonight or you've invited your boss over for dinner, light up some of those special incense sticks you bought from the back of that white van over the weekend. No, not the flavor that makes people believe their eyeballs have been replaced with live waterbugs. Light the flavor that makes anyone who breathes it in imagine what you'd look like giving a baby a bath.

It'll really lighten the mood. Once the air is good and cloudy with the aroma, you'll find your guests just staring at you with big grins on their faces, tilting their heads to the side as if they want to say, "Awww," but are trying to refrain since you're using your quiet voice to tell the story about the ambulance visit the other night responding to your elderly neighbor's latest coronary. They'll start saying things like, "You keep such a warm, wholesome household," and, "It's just impossible not to like you right now," and, "Here comes the tugboat!" but they won't really know why. Or at least they won't know that you know why.

Happy a Flavor of Incense That Makes People Imagine What You'd Look Like Giving a Baby a Bath When They Breathe It In Day!

DECEMBER 13 | TURN A HOSE ON THE PEOPLE WHO ARE PROTESTING YOU DAY!

Today you'll be trying to sleep in but the protesters out on your lawn will be chanting, "Up and at 'em! Rise and shine! You're a terrible person! Hey!" Let them know that they can't push you around. Turn a hose on them. If you don't have access to a fire hose, just use the garden hose. It won't force them to disperse, but if it's chilly out they might catch cold and every time they sneeze, they'll know it's because they thought they could mess with you, and they were wrong.

If they come back later in the evening while you're trying to eat dinner and they start chanting, "Stop eating! You're a pile of shit! Hey!" apparently the hose wasn't enough to scare them away. So go get your rifle and shoot into the thickest part of the crowd. Just a few rounds.

Happy Turn a Hose on the People Who Are Protesting You Day!

DECEMBER 14 | DON'T DO AS YOU'RE TOLD DAY!

For example, let's say your mother says, "Take the sheets off of the couch and get out of the house before your brothers get here. If your brothers find out I let you stay here with me they'll cut me off and I'll end up out on the street. You want that?"

Of course you don't want that, but you have no choice but to leave the couch covered in bedding and stay put in the house because today is Don't Do as You're Told Day. So you have to do the exact opposite of what you're told (sort of like Opposite Day, except today necessarily involves other people and what they command, whereas Opposite Day can be observed simply by telling a big fat kid that he's skinny).

It's a shame your mother didn't know what today is. Now you have to just sit tight and wait to see what happens when your brothers' bluff is called. Will the two fuckers go so far as to cut your mother off just for giving you some shelter for a week? Or will they finally sit down and let you tell your side of the story? Either way, you're not moving until somebody tells you where your daughter is.

Happy Don't Do as You're Told Day!

DECEMBER 15   FADED BEAUTY DAY!

He's only nine, but your son is already past his prime. Danny foolishly thought he could trade on his looks forever. But his stark blond hair started to darken, and he broke his nose in kickball.

He felt dizzy when the "Outstandings" that once littered his report cards without any effort on his part suddenly vanished to make room for so many "Satisfactories." Girls stopped giggling when he threw rocks at them and instead registered complaints with teachers. Boys stopped calling him a homo. It was a harsh lesson to learn, but Danny had no choice but to slide into a life of being merely passably attractive.

"I'm through," Danny will tell you today in the car.

Keep quiet for a minute, then say, "Look, people do just fine with average looks. You're just gonna have to put your nose to the grindstone. Learn a trade."

"Like what?"

"I bet there's good money in computers," tell him. "Or . . . you know . . . computer repair."

Danny will sob, "But I wanted to pass as gentry!"

Pat Danny on the knee. You had hoped that when Danny's looks went, you'd get along a little better, have some real conversations. Before, whenever you looked your son in the face, it was such a beautiful vision you'd just start to sing. With a better control over yourself, you're looking forward to teaching your son things and giving him advice.

But Danny has no desire to listen. He hates the thought of being of the same ilk as his most decidedly average-looking father.

"Even if I were to have my skin melted from my skull with acid, I'd still frown down at you," Danny will mutter to himself.

"What was that?" you'll ask.

"Buy me ice cream," Danny will plead. With some trouble he'll add, "Daddy."

Happy Faded Beauty Day!

DECEMBER 16   PLAN SURPRISE PARTIES FOR
EVERYONE YOU KNOW AND YOU'LL
NEVER HAVE TO QUIT DRINKING
DAY!

You drink lots and lots of liquor. Many people want you to quit because, according to them, they "care about you." Don't take it too personally. People who care about people always try to get them to give up the only thing that helps them to keep living, especially if that "only thing" happens to be either alcohol, illegal narcotics, gambling, or a teen.

The way to put off quitting drinking is to put the gears in motion on some surprise parties for whichever of your friends have birthdays coming up. Whenever someone quits drinking, everyone takes a closer look at him to try and figure out what was wrong with his life so they can say, "Thank God I'm a far more grounded and successful human being than that ticking time bomb."

But if you were to quit drinking while you're planning surprise parties for people, the birthday boy or girl might take a closer look at your life looking for signs of wreckage and discover some streamers instead. In order to keep the party a secret from the birthday boy/girl, you're just going to have to tough it out and go further and further down the spiral of addiction. "I'd like to quit," you can tell your spouse/relatives/pets. "But I can't ruin the big four-oh for Sharon. I'm just not that selfish." Then pass out fast before anyone can offer alternatives.

Happy Plan Surprise Parties for Everyone You Know and You'll Never Have to Quit Drinking Day!

DECEMBER 17   YOUR FAVORITE YOGA POSITION DAY!

Today, your favorite yoga position is the "Airplane Crashing into Kittens." This is where you stretch out your arms and legs wide and lie on your belly making propeller noises with your lips. There must be several kittens roaming freely about the "Dojo" or "Yoga House." Whenever a kitten wanders near you to poke its nose up at your chin, you have to slam your head into it trying to crush it with one butt of your skull. Kittens are quicker than you think so you'll miss a lot and your forehead will open up into a gaping concussion, which is where the inner peace can enter your head, provided it has exact change for the "Inner Peace Paytoll." This position is rarely used because it does nothing for the bowels. And 99 percent of the time, when you ask someone why they do yoga, they say, "Because I was told it will make my bowels stop aching when I am all alone in the night."

Happy Your Favorite Yoga Position Day!

DECEMBER 18 NEARLY CHOKE TO DEATH THREE TIMES DAY!

Best if it's in a Chinese restaurant. Usually, the only wall decoration in a Chinese restaurant is the Heimlich maneuver diagram.

You should order a dish with great hunks of meat, nothing shredded and no noodles. And you should be sure to really choke, especially on the first and second go-rounds. If it looks at all like you might not have been entirely in danger the first or second time, then your fellow patrons might not rush to your aid on the third round and you really could die.

That's what makes today fun.

When the food arrives, start gorging on the pile of meat, shoveling in hunk after hunk of flesh along with shards of green pepper and a forest of bamboo shoots. When the food slides down your windpipe, let it rest there gently for a moment to make sure it's really in before you start to gag and retch. Remember, your fellow patrons have to really believe that they're saving you. The best way for that to happen is to choke so bad you come within seconds of death.

Once you start to make your horrible sounds, they'll come running. Two of them will scuffle over who gets to give you the Heimlich. It will take four or five lifts from your sternum before the wad of food is released and lands on your tablecloth.

Thank your hero very much. He'll laugh and say, "Don't eat so fast." Nod, then sit down and as soon as your blood resumes its flow, start gorging again.

Your hero won't come nearly as fast this time. When everyone turns to see you choking, the one who just saved you will look to the one who also got up to save you and they'll both share a look as if to say, "The hell?"

No one will move for a few seconds, even though you're turning red and pointing at your neck. Once your color starts to move toward purple, the other one who got up to save you the first time will get up unchallenged this time and he'll dislodge the food with three heaves. He'll gloat inwardly that he got the food out faster than the previous hero.

Now as you catch your breath, an older woman at a neighboring table will shout at you, "You really should eat much more slowly!"

Nod at her, then start the shoveling again. Shovel fast and loud with lots of scrapes of your fork against your plate. The entire restaurant will be watching you. They won't take their eyes off of you for the entire three minutes of gluttony leading up to you suddenly freezing in your seat, bugging your eyes out a bit, and then releasing one terrible sound.

Everyone will let out a groan and some of them will throw their hands in the air in frustration. You'll make lots more terrible noises and you really will turn purple. Your two heroes will shake their heads at each other in disgust. You'll start to panic.

Get up from your seat and bounce your midsection on the back of the chair. The food won't come out. Jump up and down on the wood until your vision starts to go gray. Then just stand there, waiting to fall down. Finally, the cook will grab you from behind in his big white arms and he'll send the food flying with one strong hoist of your body against his chest.

You'll have to sit on the floor for a few minutes afterward, but no one will pay attention to you. Pay your check and head for the door. Just before stepping out to the sidewalk, turn around to the dining room and shout, "You saved my life. I'll never forget that." Then go outside and walk home. It's a nice night.

Happy Nearly Choke to Death Three Times Day!

| DECEMBER 19 | FALL IN LOVE WITH SOMEBODY DAY!

What are you waiting for? Love feels good. It makes you smile and slack off at work and you eat at very nice restaurants much more often. The sex is really good because you care about it or something and you really want it. You walk around with this stupid face on your head that tells criminals that you're easy to rob, and even when you do get robbed it's no big deal because you found that special someone whose nudity is somehow much more important than the nudity of others. And when you're in love with someone and you see them, you feel happy just for having eyes to see with.

Happy Fall in Love with Somebody Day!

| DECEMBER 20 | HOT DATE WITH A CONSPIRACY THEORIST DAY!

"Simply put, I believe my father was assassinated," he'll say. His eyes will suddenly bore into your own. "I am alone in my conviction," he'll continue. "And my refusal to concede to the conclusions reached by others regarding his death has sentenced me to a lonely life."

Nod here.

"There have been other women," he'll say. Now his look will turn accusatory. "Women who appeared to ally themselves to my cause. Some proved weak, unwilling to do what was necessary to help me bring the truth to light. Others were lonely. They were liars willing to humor me to secure a warm body in their beds at night."

That's you. Keep going.

"I live only to learn how and why my father was killed, and to bring his assassins to justice. My allies are as dear to me as the blood in my veins. My enemies are those who doubt me."

Now you speak. And it's okay to ask the question. It won't scare him off. He would suspect you if you didn't ask it.

Say, "Do you have any evidence that he was assassinated?"

He'll say, "Not yet. The evidence is out there. But I haven't gotten around to looking for it yet. But tomorrow I plan to find out where the library is and use their microfiche machines to look up old newspaper articles. See if there are any clues."

When the check comes, pay it. Tell him, "Save your money. You'll need it for bribes." Then take him back to your apartment and have sex with him. I know it seems like the whole thing is going to be interminable, but it really won't be that hard to pull off. Once you do you'll be having sex with somebody. And the best part is, if you like having sex with him and you want to keep on doing it, all you have to do is pretend to believe, or rather, pretend you give a shit about this assassination crap and he'll keep having sex with you. And as soon as you don't dig his plow no more, all you have to do is tell him you think he's full of shit, and he'll declare you "blind for the light" or whatever and he'll never talk to you again.

He will ask you for money, though. "For the investigation." But it won't be all that much since he really does believe everything he's spewing and he won't be able to justify spending money on items unrelated to the search. But since he doesn't know what he should do to begin the search and he's really lazy about getting started, you're really only going to be buying him sandwich makings for the bag lunches he'll take to the library. Now put on your party dress and bag yourself a man!

Happy Hot Date with a Conspiracy Theorist Day!

| DECEMBER 21 |

GOD IS SO INTO YOU RIGHT NOW DAY!

God hasn't been able to take his eyes off of you all night long. Did you see how when that guy shot that arrow straight at your face God really clumsily intervened to make sure it killed the guy you've been sleeping with? And I swear, as soon as you complained of having forgotten to bring a sweater with you on such a chilly night, God made it like ten degrees warmer out. And how about when your mom called to say your grandmom just got up and started walking around her hospital bed, cleaning things? All because you got a little drunk and started crying about how you're scared your grandma might die soon. And you told me yesterday you just wish she would finally die so that you don't have to go visit her no more. You just wanted to cry about something in front of everybody again, didn't you? But God must not have known that because as soon as he saw a tear glint in your eye he made your grandma all better. He's a really chivalrous lover, God. He can't stand to see the girl he loves in the slightest distress.

Anyway, you're lucky, and I think you should give God some. I'd go crazy to have a boyfriend so into me that he'd, like, alter destiny and shit. I mean, people talk about considering the grand scheme of things. But as long as you have God pining after you, the grand scheme of things is gonna change every time you scrunch your brow.

Just don't play games. If you and God make it work, you're gonna be rich.

Happy God Is So into You Right Now Day!

| DECEMBER 22 | "NEED TO GET OUT OF CITY ASAP. PLEASE HELP!" DAY! |

She can't be more than seventeen and she's covered in piercings. She's sitting with her back up against the wall of a bank, her face is in her knees, and the sign is propped up against her boots. Just in front of the sign is a coffee cup containing maybe three dollars in change. Go to her.

"Are you in danger?"

"No," she'll say.

"Do you have a funeral to get to?"

"No," she'll say.

"A wedding?"

"No," she'll say.

"The pollution getting to you?"

"No," she'll say. "Well, kind of," she'll say. "But that's not it," she'll say.

"Then what is it? Why do you have to get out of the city so bad?"

"Because I just can't take it anymore," she'll say. "Please help me," she'll say.

Hold her. Tell her not to cry, that things are going to get better, and explain that you don't give money to panhandlers. You prefer to help the needy via legitimate charitable organizations. Then go to dinner.

Happy "Need to Get Out of City ASAP. Please Help!" Day!

| DECEMBER 23 | IMMERSE YOURSELF AND YOUR GIRLFRIEND IN THE CHRISTIAN FAITH DAY! |

Things have pretty much cooled down between you and your girlfriend, and now you're certain that it's only a matter of time and circumstance before she starts cheating on you. But what can you do about it? Girlfriends cheat on boyfriends, they've done it ever since 1996.

But there is a special kind of girlfriend who won't cheat on her boyfriend. She's a Christian! And she's been taught that if her skirt ever hits the floorboards of an unknown apartment, she's going to rot in hell when she dies. That'd keep me from handing out my pussy to any pair of khakis with enough spare change to pay for my Michelob Ultra. Jesus saves.

Christianity will also cut down on your girlfriend's stealing. And I'm not just talking about shoplifting. She'll even believe that taking twenties out of your pants while you're asleep will sentence her to an eternity trying to get a good night's sleep on a bed of the hottest hellfire.

But if you really want this to work, you're going to have to pretend that you're way into Christ yourself. A lot of lazy boyfriends have tried to avoid the whole going to church and studying for confirmation quizzes thing by just saying to their girlfriends, "I sure wish I could, honey. But Christianity is a *women's* religion." Eventually your girlfriend will remember her grandfather saying grace at Thanksgiving and she'll know she's been punk'd.

Happy Immerse Yourself and Your Girlfriend in the Christian Faith Day!

| DECEMBER 24 | THE PAINTING PARTY DAY!

Turn your painting party into a super fun time by inviting everyone to paint a deep dark secret on the wall and allow everybody to read it before they all silently paint over the secret and let it disappear into the walls forever.

Say, "I'll start." Then paint on the wall, "When I was six, I killed my best friend. I held a plastic bag over her head. Our parents thought it was an accident, but she struggled, and I fought her to keep the plastic bag wrapped around her neck."

Paint over the secret, and then hand the brush to whoever's nearest. It will be Deborah, your friend Mark's wife. Deborah will paint, "When I wear earrings, I feel like a whore."

And then Deborah's secret will be wiped away, and the brush will be passed around the room as everyone gets excited to spill their beans all over your wall. Kevin, your former neighbor, will paint, "I have genital warts. Bad." Linda, your coworker, will paint, "I often hope that my elderly grandmother will pass away. I know that's not an uncommon wish, since the burden can be too much. But there you go. I only came here to paint some walls and meet a guy." Everyone will laugh as they paint over Linda's secret. And Brad, your old boyfriend, will sidle up a little closer to her.

The secrets that are shared will come from all sorts of places.

"I've sabotaged the work of several of my colleagues to rise to where I am in my career."

"I was still doing heroin when I was pregnant with Alicia."

"I am a contracted killer, hired to murder someone you all know but who never seems to show up at any of these parties."

"My dick stinks. Everyone says so."

By the time the last secret is being painted, the only wall space left will be a little corner of the coat closet. Joe, your husband, will paint, "I hate party games. I hate secrets. From the very beginning I've felt that we weren't right for each other but something keeps me by your side. Something I can't live without."

Your guests will all read it and they'll break the rule of silence and start guessing at what your husband can't live without. *Your laugh! Your pussy! Your cooking! Your knees! I really think it's your pussy! I mean think about it! Could be her breasts! Come on, breasts can't hold a marriage together! I'm with Sarah, it's your cooking! Will you people shut up! It's got to be her pussy! Have you ever seen the thing? It's awesome! Your tender and caring demeanor! Your pussy! Did someone say that already?*

They'll all just keep on shouting while you kiss your husband with all you've got, his left hand on your back and his right brushing away his secret with a heavy coat of periwinkle.

Happy the Painting Party Day!

| DECEMBER 25 | STUFF YOUR UNDERWEAR INTO MY MOUTH AND PUNCH ME IN THE NOSE UNTIL I CAN'T BREATHE THROUGH IT DAY! |

You're seventy-eight years old, and a blood disease has reduced you to not very much more than an embodiment of pain. You had a discussion some time ago with Manny, your home health aide who has been with you for over a decade.

"If you think it's time for you to go," he told you, "I can take you out. However you want it to happen, as long as it won't pin a murder rap on me. I'll do what you ask."

Today you're going to tell him the way that you've always dreamed you could go out. Manny is a man of his word. After considering it for a moment, he'll tell you, "It will have to look like someone broke in here. Tomorrow morning when I'm supposed to be at the supermarket. You didn't leave me anything in your will, did you?"

Shake your head no.

"Good," Manny will say. "I've been bilking your bank account for years anyway."

Laugh with Manny. That's the last time you'll laugh before the end.

Manny will say, "Do you want the underwear to be soiled?"

Nod yes. Tell him if you don't get to watch him remove his underwear first, he might as well just hold a pillow over your face.

Say, "I need the poetry."

Happy Stuff Your Underwear into My Mouth and Punch Me in the Nose Until I Can't Breathe Through It Day!

| DECEMBER 26 | "SHOW ME YOUR BREATH" DAY! |

Today's the day to let your eyes shuffle through the giant streetside window of a bar and just get kind of blanked out by all the same-old, same-old outside. Cars pass, folks bend their shoulders against the cold and pull their hats down tighter. Homeless people pee without knowing it. Seen it all before, yeah, but it's all so much more beautiful than anything in that novel soaking up the circle of condensation from your pint.

And just then, a couple will walk out of the restaurant next door and stop in front of your window to adjust their hats and gloves. They'll be smiling, radiating the glow of a romantic meal and much wine. They'll look at each other just to smile at each other. They're in love. And one of them is an ex of yours from a brief relationship not four months dead.

If someone were to look from the street, it would look like they're flanking you. Each on either side of you, equidistant from that bewildered look on your face. You'll look from one to the other, wondering if they planned this out: "Oh my God, my ex is in that window. Let's just go stand right out front and moon at each other for a second!" You would of course be overjoyed to know that someone who has long since forgotten about you would so much as break stride on the sidewalk to make sure she has your attention.

Your ex will say something you can't make out. The companion will start to pant in your ex's face. Your ex will pant in turn so that they both send gusts of hot breath, the steam visible in the cold, into each other's faces. That's what your ex said. "Show me your breath," said the one you just never clicked with. Then they'll stop the panting to check each other's eyes for glimmering before a quick kiss. And then they'll be gone.

Sure, you were glad it ended between you two. All the same, watching them through the window of the bar just then, you won't help but feel a little pang of regret. But relax, everything looks better through the street-side window of a bar. Go belly up and buy yourself one too many.

Happy "Show Me Your Breath" Day!

| DECEMBER 27 | YOUR COMMEMORATIVE 9/11 BONG IS IN BAD TASTE AND YOU SHOULD BE ASHAMED OF YOURSELF DAY! |

No one wants to suck smoke out of a miniature plastic replica of the Twin Towers. I know you think it's because they don't know how to hold the bong without banging their noses on the antenna atop Tower Two, but the real problem is that each time someone takes a hit, everyone has to sit and watch as leftover smoke billows up from Tower One. Consider the mellow harshed.

It was cool at first, true. But that was only because of the inscription at the bong's base: 9/11: WE REMEMBER.

Considering that the "we" in that inscription refers only to you and your pothead friends, it's not likely that all that much is being remembered. More important, everyone's been complaining of bad dreams lately (especially Clyde). Just throw the thing away and break out the R2D2 bong again. Everyone loved that one. Even though you refused to smoke out of it ever again "in protest against the crimes George Lucas has committed against my childhood with the release of episodes one through three," it's safe to say that Lucasfilm Ltd. never got the press release.

Break out R2. Clyde's gonna be by any minute now.

Happy Your Commemorative 9/11 Bong Is in Bad Taste and You Should Be Ashamed of Yourself Day!

| DECEMBER 28 | **MUD FIGHT DAY!** |

Today your supervisor is going to tell you that you used up too much vacation time and you're going to have to wait for more time to accrue in your bank. Tell him that you're tired of him walking all over you and you want to settle this in the mud out back.

Due to poor landscaping, the lawn flanking the rear of your corporate plaza turns into an expansive mud field with every rainfall. The company is in trouble so no funds can be allocated to better seed and maintain the lawn. So it was decided eighteen months ago that lemonade would have to be made from lemons.

"We'll use it to settle stuff," your CEO announced. "Like this budget measure. Ms. Loehmann, meet me in the mud."

Your CEO and CFO had the first of many mud fights out there, and it was way hot. Ms. Loehmann even lost her white blouse and the blue bra underneath. But she beat the crap out of Mr. Grisham. The budget measure was voted in.

Mud fights seemed to take place at least once a week out there for a while, and it was suggested that a league be organized to rank the employees. That suggestion was scuttled as soon as a mail clerk was killed in a bout with a VP who was always calling down to the mailroom to see if his packages had arrived yet. The VP strangled the mail clerk with his tie. No charges were pressed (Code of the Mud) but it was decided that no league should be instituted since the league would then have to regulate the fights and be responsible for deaths, whether accidental or intentional. The mud would only be used to resolve disputes.

The mud field is free at the moment, and you and your supervisor certainly have an issue in dispute.

"Let's go, bean counter. I wanna bury your face in some brown," tell him.

"Think I'm scared?" he'll say.

Take a step closer and look directly in his eyes when you say, "You'd better be."

He really should be scared. You're so good in that mud that people have a nickname for you around the office. It's "Swamp Thing." Whenever you win they all sing the song "Wild Thing" as you walk back to the office, but they replace the word "Wild" with the word "Swamp." It's funny.

Happy Mud Fight Day!

DECEMBER 29   CANDLELIT BREAKFAST DAY!

Strange men you bring home at 3:00 A.M. never want to wake up at 6:00 A.M. like you do. You stopped asking when you were twenty-five.

You slip out from underneath whatever limb he left on top of you when he passed out. You put on some underwear and a shirt. You go to the kitchen and you start coffee.

Your thick white bowl always has yesterday's oatmeal stuccoed to the sides. The kitchen is cold in the morning, and it takes hot water and a butter knife to get the bowl clean. You pour in today's oatmeal, close the door on the microwave, push a button. The coffee is done and your cigarette is lit and in your fingertips.

You must have sleepwalked for a bit because the next thing you remember you're sitting at your table, the cigarette in your hand in the air by your head, your face taking in the steam over the full black of the coffee cup. The oatmeal is hot in front of you. You need to do something to make sure you're awake. You get up and get a spoon.

A few spoons of oatmeal. A cup and a half of coffee. In the middle of your second cigarette, he wanders in. This happens sometimes.

"Coffee?"

You smile the way you smiled at 3:00 A.M. He finds his own cup, finds his own spoon, looks for milk but finds none. The sugar is already out. He stirs, sips, sits. Across from you.

"How you feeling?" He asks the way one asks after the recently bereaved. You smile the way you smile at 6:00 A.M.

You haven't taken any more spoons of oatmeal and you don't plan to. He's making his way to the white of his coffee cup. There's nothing to say. No newspaper to read. No cat to watch do stuff. But there's half a candle on a candlestick holder sitting right between the two of you. You pick up your cigarette lighter and you light the wick.

Of course he's confused. You smile the way you smile when you want to allow something you did to be funny. He laughs one short hmph.

"Romantic," he says. You smile the way you never do.

He gets up with lots of grunts and goes into the bathroom. You sip your coffee. He flushes and shuffles into the bedroom. You put your finger to the surface of your oatmeal. He returns to the kitchen in his overcoat and tells you he has work to go and get to.

You walk him to the door. Someone says "again." You kiss him and shut the door behind him and listen against the door to his footsteps on the stairs. Then you go back to the kitchen to sit and watch a candle burn at 6:23 A.M.

Happy Candlelit Breakfast Day!

| DECEMBER 30 | THE BOY ON THE BRIDGE MIGHT HAVE BEEN FUN TO DATE DAY! |

Sometimes, you wish your boyfriend were someone else. Someone you haven't known for two years already. Someone who doesn't gargle with mouthwash before sex, perhaps. Maybe even someone who doesn't announce to you at the end of every month just how much of his credit card debt he's managed to pay off.

Someone like that boy on the bridge you're going to pass on the way home tonight. He'll stand out because he'll be the only one on the bridge who is neither in a couple nor on a bike. He'll just be standing by the railing at the very middle of the bridge, sobbing out into the expanse of the river below while he scribbles what is most likely a good-bye note onto the back of a Lost Dog flyer.

You'll look to your boyfriend. You'll listen to the song he'll have been whistling for the majority of the past three weeks. Then you'll look back at the boy on the bridge, who will be loading up the pockets of his jacket with heavy stones. "Why couldn't you have been my boyfriend for the past two years?" you'll wonder. "You would have been exciting. I'm young and I need exciting right now. Anyone who finds himself sobbing off the side of the bridge in the middle of the night has to be fun in the sack too, right?"

You'll keep walking, and it will be all you can do to keep from turning around to take one last look at the boy on the bridge. "Maybe if he sees me looking at him he'll find in my eyes some reason to keep on living. Then I'll have to break it off with my boyfriend and go with the boy on the bridge because a life will be at stake."

"MAAAARTHA!!!" you'll hear him shout out at the cityscape. Good God, what you wouldn't give for your name to be Martha. To have a boy so wrapped up in you that he's got nothing else to do but head to the middle of a bridge and scream your name as loud as he can.

"Think you'll ever scream my name like that?" you'll ask your boyfriend.

"Maybe if you're in danger. Like if you're standing in the bus lane while waiting for the crossing light to change. You should never do that, you know."

You know. You know that even if you were to break it off with your boyfriend right then, you still wouldn't be able to run and make something happen with the boy on the bridge. You would have to have met him two years ago, right before Martha met him. Then you'd be the reason he's standing on the bridge summing things up on the back of a Lost Dog flyer. Then it would be your name he's screaming into the wind. And then he'd jump, and you'd run out and recover with someone safe. Someone like your current boyfriend of two years.

"Oh gosh," your boyfriend will say. "*Seinfeld* reruns start in ten minutes. We have to book it. It's the 'Master of Your Domain' episode."

You and your boyfriend will trot the rest of the length of the bridge to make it home in time for him to watch *Seinfeld* reruns in bed. Only once will you look back at the boy on the bridge, when you're pretty far away. He'll be gone. Whether he jumped or just had a change of heart and walked home, you won't know. You'll only know that he's gone.

Happy the Boy on the Bridge Might Have Been Fun to Date Day!

DECEMBER 31 | NOT-YET-RIPENED PEACHES DAY!

In the morning you will find that the peaches in the refrigerator are not ripened to an ideal degree of deliciousness. You will squeeze each one twice and maybe three times before you tell the toaster, "I guess I can't eat my peaches yet." That's when everything will go black.

You'll say to the toaster, "Looks like someone cut off the electricity. Must be trying to bust into the building." You'll try the phone, but it will be dead. Then you will see a man in black rappel past your window. And he will see you. He will pause just long enough to put his finger to his lips in a gesture of "shush" before he continues down the side of the building.

You will say to the toaster, "Guess I'd better be quiet for a little while. At least until that guy's gone. Talk to you later, toaster." You will go into your room, lie in bed, and listen to the smashing of glass and the screaming.

There shall be gunfire.

Happy Not-Yet-Ripened Peaches Day!

ACKNOWLEDGMENTS

I owe a great deal of thanks and love to my parents, Helen and Richard, to my sisters, Mary, Helen, and Pat, and to my brother, Ted. To Todd Levin, for his invaluable friendship and encouragement, without which I might not have bothered. To my editor, John Parsley, for keeping a genial demeanor while sifting through endless piles of filth. Thanks also to Thomas Dunne and everyone at Thomas Dunne Books. To Byrd Leavell, for working tirelessly to make it all happen and for being Southern. To Kara Baker and Sara Self for getting it all going. To Chris Regan for all his help. To Andres DuBouchet for the lunch. To the Lindsay Milligan Society for all the nice e-mails. Thank you to Andrew Pogany at *Flaunt* magazine for giving me work to do, Rosecrans Baldwin and *TheMorningNews*.org for printing some of the stuff in this book. To Leslie Harpold for giving me a place to put everything, and Chloe Weil for the decoration. For their advice and assistance, thank you Mike Albo, Fred Armisen, Allison Castillo, Adam Felber, John Hodgman, Susannah Keagle, Dan Kennedy, Sam Lipsyte, and Lisa Whiteman. To everyone who has ever read GirlsArePretty.com and everyone who has ever come out to "How to Kick People," thanks so much. And, of course, to Amanda Melson, the greatest of all time. Thank you.